Jose Toro Hardy

OIL
VENEZUELA
AND THE PERSIAN
GULF

editorial
PANAPO

"From Luzon for the world
Forever Venezuela reads
to the memory of Pedro Flaquer"

Editorial Panapo, c.a.

OIL: VENEZUELA AND THE PERSIAN GULF
José Toro Hardy

©1994, José Toro Hardy
©November 1994, Editorial Panapo c.a. , Caracas
All rights reserved.

ISBN: **980-230-662-2**

Production: **Editorial Panapo , c.a.**
Cover jacket design: **Valentina Blasini**
Electronic Diagrams: **Alfredo Sánchez**

Translated by Paulette Pagani

Printed in Venezuela by
EDITORIAL TEXTO - CARACAS

Free distribution by
Editorial Panapo, c.a.
Av. José Angel Lamas
Centro Industrial Palo Grande
Edif. 1 Piso 1
Caracas- Venezuela
Phones: 462.3631 - 462.9847 - 462.9457 - 462.1341
461.9062 - 461.3948 - 461.3956 - 461.5866
Fax: 461.4423

Dedicated
to my mother.

This book analyzes the Suez Canal crisis (1956), the Six Day War and the closure of the Suez Canal from 1967 to 1975, Qadaffi´s revolution (1970), the Yom Kippur War and the arab oil embargo (1973), the fall of the Shah of Iran (1979), the Iran-Iraq war (1980-1988) and Iraq´s invasion of Kuwait (1990). Each of these situations sowed the seed for future crises. The Persian Gulf and the Middle East are perceived by many analysts as a powder keg, although important efforts are being carried out to bring peace to the region. This book also sheds light on problems such as the origin of the permanent struggle between shiites and sunnites, Islamic fundamentalism, the Arab-Israeli antagonism, the Palestinian problem, the war in Lebanon, the artificial countries and frontiers in the region, the Kurds (the forgotten people), etc.

All these conflicts and factors have periodically disrupted the stability of world oil markets. In each crisis, Venezuela came to the rescue of a world troubled by energy shortages. At present, this country has admitted the need to foster new partnership formulas in its oil industry with participation by private foreign and national capital.

As a contribution to this new perception, EDITORIAL PANAPO, the ZUMA GROUP and Jose Toro-Hardy are pleased to present this book as a gift to those interested in becoming acquainted with the brilliant perspectives currently opening up in the Venezuelan oil sector.

ZUMA

editorial
PANAPO

INDEX

Foreword _ 9
INTRODUCTION _ _ _ _ _ _ _ _ _ _ _ _ _ _ _ _ 13
Notes _ 41

Chapter I
THE SECOND WORLD WAR _ _ _ _ _ _ _ _ _ _ 43
The Axis vs. the Allied Forces _ _ _ _ _ _ _ _ _ 45
The 'Blitzkrieg' needs fuel _ _ _ _ _ _ _ _ _ _ _ 48
The Synthetic Fuel _ _ _ _ _ _ _ _ _ _ _ _ _ _ 52
Hitler pays no heed to Rommel _ _ _ _ _ _ _ _ 53
The Axis is left without Fuel _ _ _ _ _ _ _ _ _ _ 57
The U.S.: Arsenal to the Democratic Nations _ _ _ _ 60
Venezuela: The Fuel of the Democratic Nations _ _ _ 63
Oil in the Post-War Era _ _ _ _ _ _ _ _ _ _ _ _ 75
Germany and Japan: Winners in the long term _ _ _ 77
Notes _ 74

Chapter II
THE SUEZ CANAL CRISIS _ _ _ _ _ _ _ _ _ _ 81
The Nationalization of the Suez Canal _ _ _ _ _ _ 83
The Invasion of Egypt _ _ _ _ _ _ _ _ _ _ _ _ 85
Nasser Defeated/Nasser the Hero _ _ _ _ _ _ _ _ 90
The Six Day War _ _ _ _ _ _ _ _ _ _ _ _ _ _ 96
Petroleum: "The Sword of Islam" _ _ _ _ _ _ _ _ 100
The Closure of the Suez Canal _ _ _ _ _ _ _ _ _ 109
Notes _ _ _ _ _ _ _ _ _ _ _ _ _ _ _ _ _ _ _ 112

Chapter III
THE LIBYAN CRISIS _ _ _ _ _ _ _ _ _ _ _ _ _ _ _113
The Libyan Alternative _ _ _ _ _ _ _ _ _ _ _ _ _115
Historical Background _ _ _ _ _ _ _ _ _ _ _ _117
A Bloodless Coup _ _ _ _ _ _ _ _ _ _ _ _ _ _ _117
The Price Revolution _ _ _ _ _ _ _ _ _ _ _ _ _120
The Confrontation with the U.S. _ _ _ _ _ _ _ _129
Notes _135

Chapter IV
THE FIRST OIL SHOCK _ _ _ _ _ _ _ _ _ _ _137
The Yom Kippur (or Ramadan) War _ _ _ _ _ _139
The Arab Oil Embargo _ _ _ _ _ _ _ _ _ _ _ _151
The Price Hike _ _ _ _ _ _ _ _ _ _ _ _ _ _ _159
Background of an Economic Crisis _ _ _ _ _ _162
Notes _170

Chapter V
THE FALL OF THE SHAH OF IRAN _ _ _ _ _171
The Islamic Revolution of Ayatollah Khomeini _ _ _173
The Hostage Crisis _ _ _ _ _ _ _ _ _ _ _ _ _177
The Second Oil Shock _ _ _ _ _ _ _ _ _ _ _ _182
Recycling the "Petrodollars" _ _ _ _ _ _ _ _ _186
The Financial System Crisis _ _ _ _ _ _ _ _ _188
Debt and the Third World Crisis _ _ _ _ _ _ _190
Crisis in the Industrialized Economies _ _ _ _ _192
Steps for Saving Energy _ _ _ _ _ _ _ _ _ _ _194
Production Surpluses _ _ _ _ _ _ _ _ _ _ _ _195
Notes _ _ _ _ _ _ _ _ _ _ _ _ _ _ _ _ _ _ _198

Chapter VI
THE IRAN-IRAQ WAR _ _ _ _ _ _ _ _ _ _ _ _ _ _ 199
Saddam Hussein vs. Ruholla Khomeini _ _ _ _ _ 201
Centuries of Antagonism: Endemic Violence _ _ _ 202
The Basis for the Conflict is Set _ _ _ _ _ _ _ _ 205
The Gulf War _ _ _ _ _ _ _ _ _ _ _ _ _ _ _ 213
Chemical Warfare against the Holy War _ _ _ _ 226
The Geopolitical Problem _ _ _ _ _ _ _ _ _ _ 228
The Oil Problem _ _ _ _ _ _ _ _ _ _ _ _ _ _ 231
Notes _ _ _ _ _ _ _ _ _ _ _ _ _ _ _ _ _ _ 234

Chapter VII
IRAQ'S INVASION OF KUWAIT _ _ _ _ _ _ _ _ 235
The Third Oil Shock ? _ _ _ _ _ _ _ _ _ _ _ _ 237
Historical Background _ _ _ _ _ _ _ _ _ _ _ 239
The Basis for the Conflict is Set _ _ _ _ _ _ _ 247
Saddam's Assumptions _ _ _ _ _ _ _ _ _ _ 252
Operation "Desert Shield" _ _ _ _ _ _ _ _ _ _ 258
Operation "Desert Storm" _ _ _ _ _ _ _ _ _ _ 262
October 1994: Saddam´s attempted brag_ _ _ _ 270
Notes _ _ _ _ _ _ _ _ _ _ _ _ _ _ _ _ _ _ 274

Chapter VIII
THE MIDDLE EAST:
A REGION CONDEMNED TO VIOLENCE _ _ _ 275
The Birthplace of Civilization _ _ _ _ _ _ _ _ 277
Islam_ _ _ _ _ _ _ _ _ _ _ _ _ _ _ _ _ _ 278
The Arab-Israeli Conflict _ _ _ _ _ _ _ _ _ _ 286
The Palestinian Problem _ _ _ _ _ _ _ _ _ _ 295
September 1993: Begin and Arafat_ _ _ _ _ _ 311
The Israeli-Jordanian Peace Agreement_ _ _ _ 318
Artificial Countries and Frontiers _ _ _ _ _ _ 320
The Kurds: The Forgotten People _ _ _ _ _ _ 324
Notes _ _ _ _ _ _ _ _ _ _ _ _ _ _ _ _ _ _ 327

Chapter IX
OIL MARKET PROSPECTS _ _ _ _ _ _ _ _ _ _ 329
Perspectives for the World Oil Marktes _ _ _ _ _ 331
Production Cost per Country _ _ _ _ _ _ _ _ _ 334
The Case for Venezuela _ _ _ _ _ _ _ _ _ _ _ 336
Opening up the Venezuelan Oil Industry _ _ _ _ 346
Notes _ _ _ _ _ _ _ _ _ _ _ _ _ _ _ _ _ _ _ 350

CONCLUSIONS _ _ _ _ _ _ _ _ _ _ _ _ _ _ 351

BIBLIOGRAPHY _ _ _ _ _ _ _ _ _ _ _ _ _ _ 359

Foreword

Oil has undoubtedly been the most relevant economic agent of the 20th century.

The organization of the oil industry around the Achnacarry agreement in year 1922, was the crucial factor and the starting point, for the sustained growth experienced by industrialized nations during four decades of relative stability, only barely perturbed in 1938 by the nationalization of the Mexican oil operations, in 1954 by the initiatives of Iran which led to the foundation of the National Iranian Oil Company (NIOC) and by the permanent pressures exerted by OPEC after its foundation in 1960. Later on, beginning with the unilateral actions of Lybia, the decade of the 1970's shifted the world around, exposing the vulnerability of the oil supply and consumption network. The several oil shocks that followed, radically altered market conditions, changed the way of doing business in oil and generated profound sociological changes, all around the world, specially in the major consuming societies. Political considerations have always been present in each and every process experienced by the oil world; this comes only naturally, when dealing with such a strategic product as oil, which certainly can not be inscribed in the same picture with normal commodities, no matter how important they might be. Political radicalization surrounding the most important oil region in the world, the Persian Gulf, has for many years become a point of special concern for everybody. The persistent belligerence and the recurrence of war actions, have imposed a permanent question mark for anyone seeking a stable and organized supply. It must be the hope of the whole mankind, that soon, an everlasting peace comes to this region, that for such a long time has been plagued by adversity and suffering.

However, it must unfortunately be admitted, that the diversity and complexity of the forces acting in the region, make it a difficult achievement in the foreseeable future. This, no doubt, will continue to have an important bearing on the present and future situation of the energy world, and in the correlation of the Middle East with other oil countries and regions around the globe.

It is in a rich way, but at the same time simple and of easy and pleasant reading, that this brilliant and distinguished economist, Jose Toro-Hardy, leads us along the history of oil in the modern era, combining a concise narration of the facts with an excellent interpretation of economic incidence world-wide, as well as in the different incumbent countries and economic blocs.

Many have written about the paramount role of oil in the 20th century; not many, though, have found such a precise synchronism and correlation between facts and implications, to produce such a useful platform for the design of adequate strategies and policies for the future participation in the oil and gas world.

Along his story, Toro-Hardy repeatedly refers to the importance of Venezuela as an oil country along this century, and when looking ahead to the incoming one. Certainly, Venezuela deserves the attention that he is calling for. His assessment about the Middle East as a powder keg is accurate and shared by many other analysts and writers. Surely, the oil possibilities of other countries and regions such as Venezuela, Russia, Colombia and the North Sea, constitute a natural counterbalance in the permanent search for stability. I believe, however, that even if peace were achieved in the Middle East once and for all, his arguments and conclusions about the importance of Venezuela as a secure and stable supplier for the industrialized nations, would still hold. In a world that will continue to demand growing amounts of oil as a source of energy for many more decades, the reserve base, the maturity of the oil industry, the global policies already in place, represented by a strong upstream-downstream integration, the excellent geographic position and the democratic tradition, place Venezuela in a privileged and very strong stance.

As it has been the case in many occasions, Toro-Hardy presents us with a scientific work but also a pleasant story, where he sheds light on the intricate political and religious realities imbedded in the Middle East, and the special attractive of Venezuela as an oil country. I am certain, that not only analysts, students and scholars will benefit from the reading of this book, but everyone will enjoy this great piece of work, by a man that has become a prolific symbol of excellence as an economist, teacher and writer.

Luis E. Giusti Lopez

12

INTRODUCTION

Oil as a source of energy is more than a fundamental factor for progress. Rather, it is currently an indispensable condition thereof. Developed and developing nations alike are in need of this fuel.

The technology that enables nations to develop, is closely related to energy sources. If, for any reason whatsoever, supply of the various energy sources were to be interrupted, very soon the conditions for human life would suffer a setback of several centuries.

Comprehension of this phenomenon has helped in making oil the most important current source of energy worldwide, with a market that, due to its high degree of complexity, cannot be compared to any other international trade commodity market.

Having this in mind, we can understand the serious effects the occurrence of alterations - which shall be studied in this book - has had on world economic order in the past fifty years, that have somehow affected contemporary man's voracious appetite for energy.

During the past half century, we have witnessed seven major crises:

1) The Second World War
2) The Suez Canal crisis
3) The Libyan crisis
4) The Arab Oil Embargo
5) The fall of the Shah of Iran
6) The Iran-Iraq War
7) Iraq's invasion of Kuwait.

These crises shall be examined in detail in the course of this book. Undoubtedly, they have not been the only crises to have affected the oil markets. However, they have been the most important due to their international repercussions. Venezuela has played a very important part in all these situations, helping to alleviate the energy demands of a distressed world, by increasing its oil production.

Let us however stop here and present a brief summary of the above-mentioned situations, since this will enable us to better understand the context of the facts that shall be referred to in the following chapters.

Let us begin with the Second World War, a period during which, for the first time, Venezuela's extraordinary strategic importance as a reliable supplier of energy was made evident. Whereas the Axis lacked sufficient fuel or had to synthetically produce gasoline fuel by means of complex coal-generated hydrogenation methods, the Allied armies, a gigantic crushing machine, marched forward, thanks largely to an abundant supply of oil from Venezuela. It is worthwhile mentioning that during World War Two, Venezuela was the second largest supplier of oil, after the U.S., to the Allied forces. Furthermore, during the final attack that started with the landing in Normandy and which led to the final defeat of Hitler's armies, close to 60% of the fuel used by the victor's military machinery came from Venezuelan soil.

Although the Suez Canal crisis did not cause any long-term crude oil price increases, the result thereof was a series of conflicts that originated in the Middle East, the effects of which would be periodically felt in the international oil markets. The crisis in reference, fostered by Nasser's policies, led twice to the closure for navigation of the Suez Canal. In the last of these blockades, the canal remained closed from 1967 to 1975, thereby bringing about deep changes in international trade due to the interruption of communications between the Mediterranean Sea and the Red Sea. Nasser was the first leader to realize that petroleum could be waged as a powerful political weapon in the pursuit of Pan-Arabian intentions.

The crisis unleashed by Nasser was not yet over, when a disciple of this leader emerged, with a similar messianic vocation who believed he could prevail where the prophet had failed. His name: Moa'amar al-Qaddafi. Thus, the Libyan crisis opened a new chapter in the endless series of episodes in which the Arab world has placed its oil-based resources at the service of the Islam cause.

At other times, alterations produced by the Middle East crisis gave rise to sharp increases in crude prices as were the cases of the two oil shocks of the 1973 Arab oil embargo and the fall of the Shah of Iran in 1979, increase from which no-one benefitted in the long run.

Suffice it to say that between 1969 and 1979, oil prices in the spot market increased from 1.20 dollars per barrel to $41.00 (1). The result was that by 1983, developed nations had an accumulated total figure of 33 million unemployed and, in many cases, a negative growth rate in the production of goods and services. The U.S. fell into a deep recession, only surpassed by the Great Depression of the '30s. In other industrialized nations, the situation was just as bad or worse. For the first time, by 1982, international trade had seriously contracted, a phenomenon that had not occurred since the end of the Second World War.

Non-oil producing developing nations fell into an even deeper depression, from which many of them have not recovered yet. To avoid total economic bankruptcy, they were left with no other choice than to resort to international indebtedness. Offers abounded for this type of financing, inasmuch as at that time, the banking system urgently needed to 'recycle' the surplus of petrodollars garnered from deposits by OPEC nations.

Thus, by 1983, the debt of underdeveloped nations was in excess of $500 billion, five times the amount of 1973. In interest alone, this figure represented annual payments of around $51 billion. The situation continued to worsen and by 1986, the Third World public debt had reached the astounding figure of $1,040 billion (2). In some Latin American countries, inflation would pass the four-digit figures. Enrique Iglesias, President of the InterAmerican Development Bank (IDB) declared the '80s to be 'the lost decade'. During those years Latin America's global debt increased by 75%. Each dollar increase in price per barrel of oil represented for those nations additional payments of $400 million a year. While oil prices dramatically increased, the price of raw materials exported by Third-World nations plummetted to unprecedented levels.

In truth, statistics and figures are far too cold to reflect the widespread misery and suffering in developed and underdeveloped nations alike, though undoubtedly some countries felt it more than others. In terms of human suffering, there is no way to put into words the consequences brought about by the sudden hike in hydrocarbon prices.

Certainly, oil price increases were not the only factors responsible for the catastrophe that was under way. In effect, from 1958 onwards, the upwardly spiraling U.S. fiscal deficits had been covered by issuing money which, in practice, did not have the backing they had in theory. If said deficits did not force the American economy into an inflationary pandemonium, it was because money surpluses did not remain in the U.S.

Since dollars were welcome everywhere, these surpluses were drained towards other economies and were fed into a control-free, unsupervised stateless monetary system, known by the name of 'Eurodollars'. General Charles De Gaulle declared that "The U.S. is exporting its own inflation". In fact, recognizing its inability to exert any form of supervision over this new system which had acquired monstruous proportions, Nixon's government was forced to break the link between gold and the dollar in March 1973.

As we shall see in the following pages, by autumn 1973, the time of the first Arab oil embargo, the international economic situation was in such a serious state that Paul Johnson was led to declare that "the financial basis for world economy was disintegrating"(3). However, there is no doubt that the sudden increase in hydorcarbon prices was the spark that finally unleashed the crisis.

Other authors, economists Paul Hallwood and Stuart Sinclair among them, maintained that the combined effects of inflation, world economic growth deceleration and the protectionary measures adopted by the industrialized nations provoked far-reaching negative effects for the developing nations, far greater than the 1973 oil price increases (4).

On the other hand, it is very probable that if the industrialized nations had understood the need for accepting a progressive crude price increase, and had connected it, for instance, to a manufactured goods price growth index, as the Shah of Iran had once proposed, then mankind could have been saved much suffering and many serious traumas would have been avoided for world economy. As it were, the dramatic rises in hydrocarbon prices in the '70s could only have occurred as a consequence of a continuous price decrease between 1951 and 1972, when compared to the price of manufactured goods. This decrease, which in relative terms was acute up to 1963, also became acute in absolute terms from then onwards up to 1969.

Unfortunately, the industrialized nations did not understand this phenomenon until it was too late. Henry Kissinger, upon analyzing the problem, affirmed that "world supply and demand conditions for the consumer changed relentlessly for the worst" ... "market conditions would have brought about an explosion in prices, although perhaps during a longer period of time." (5).

It would be worthwhile to analyze, at least superficially, the impact of the two first oil shocks on world economy from three different perspectives: energy supply, energy demands and their results in OPEC countries.

As to energy supply, one can safely say that, faced with the fear of an ongoing and indefinite price increase, the world at large undertook extensive programs to save energy, to seek new oil-producing fields, and to develop alternate sources of energy such as atomic, coal, solar, eolic, etc.

As was to be expected, the global impact of these programs from the energy supply viewpoint was considerable. To begin with, increased oil prices helped to develop new and prolific fields, the exploitation of which would have had doubtful income-generating capacity in the past. This was the case in the North Sea and Alaska, where, in both cases, production was quickly developed, yielding substantial contributions in energy supply for Europe and the United States.

In effect, although the existence of potential oil reserves in the North Sea was already known, its exploitation had always remained utopian. This was the case of off-shore oil fields, so much the costlier to exploit since they were located in northern waters, with such inhospitable climate conditions that the platforms had to be designed to withstand 125 miles-per-hour winds and 90 foot-high waves, as high as a 10-story building, not to mention Alaska, where extreme climate conditions were coupled with the even more extreme reactions of the ecologists. Time would take care in both places of showing the tremendous cost of these operations. In the North Sea, giant platforms, unable to withstand the rigors of nature, would collapse, with the subsequent tragic loss of human lives and multimillion investments. Meanwhile, in Alaska, the ecologic tragedy of accidents such as the Exxon Valdez oil spill would also reach dramatic proportions.

Nevertheless, even at these elevated costs, oil companies showed that they were capable of sorting out all manner of obstacles to compensate for the situation in the Middle East. After all, in areas such as the North Sea and Alaska, natural conditions and the fury of the elements contrasted with the peaceful political climate.

New crude oil-producing countries came into the fore while other countries greatly increased their participation in the international markets. Examples of these two latter groups are Mexico, Colombia, Angola, Egypt, Cameroon, Malaysia, Ecuador, etc. In conclusion, dozens of nations have had successful exploratory programs, thereby contributing to increase their internal supplies and decrease the pressure on the international demand for hydrocarbons.

In general, the hike in oil prices was translated into a stimulus for production of this commodity. We therefore notice that the oil produced by non-OPEC nations (excluding centralized economy countries) went up from 17 million barrels per day in 1977 to 24 million in 1985. At the same time, OPEC's production went down from 31 million barrels per day in 1977 to 15 million in 1985.

During this time, many nations undertook important atomic energy development programs. A considerable amount of atomic plants were built in the U.S., some of which were destined to become inoperable due to the subsequent fall in oil prices. However, this type of facilities have become undesirable for ecologic rather than for economic reasons, especially after some of the mishaps which have occurred such as the Three Mile Island nuclear reactor accident or the terrible tragedy of the Chernobyl atomic plant in Russia.

The most relevant example of the contribution of atomic energy to world energy requirements is the case of France. By 1982, 40 per cent of French electricity requirements was supplied by nuclear plants. By 1990 this percentage was well over 70%.

But if the rapid increase in oil prices between 1973 and 1980 had an important effect on the supply of energy, even more impressive was the impact it had on oil demand.

Spurred on by the increased cost of energy, consumer nations implemented large-scale energy saving programs. In the entire world, a sort of mass hysteria took over - not without reason - in favour of the idea of saving energy. The success of these conservation programs far surpassed the most optimistic governmental expectations in the big consumer nations.

For instance, the automobile industry reacted by manufacturing smaller, more efficient vehicles which consequently burned less gasoline. New buildings were equipped with thermal isolation systems that left out the cold during the wintertime. At the same time, people started lowering their thermostats. All in all, industry and large consumers sought new and more efficient energy-saving equipment.

Let us now provide some representative examples of the previous statements. Between March 1979 and April 1981, free world oil consumption decreased by 14%. Although economic recession became more serious, demand for the product also decreased. In 1982 alone, the use of oil in the United States went down by 11% and the consumption of residual fuel in the American industry - of special importance to Venezuelan exports - went down by 41%.

However, more important than quantitative reductions are the effects in the lifestyle of people. In effect, the more efficient use of energy is evidenced in confirming that in 1973 the world at large (excluding centralized economy nations) required 3.31 barrels of petroleum to generate 1,000 dollars of GDP (6). By 1985, oil requirements to arrive at the same results had decreased to 1.48 barrels (7).

In sum, the scenario based on the two oil shocks was expressed in a decrease in the demand for hydrocarbons in non-communist countries, from 52.4 million barrels per day in 1979 to 45.5 million in 1982. In the meantime, OPEC's participation in the world oil market went down from 74% in 1974 to 44% in 1988.

By 1980 some experts predicted that the price of oil would soon pass the 80 dollars-per-barrel mark. Nevertheless, the results of the efforts carried out to increase oil production were so successful and the decreased demand for the product so marked that Newsweek magazine, in its edition of May 25th, 1981 (less than two years after the fall of the Shah of Iran) reported that: "OPEC's immediate problems arise from a surplus of oil, due to the global decrease in the economy which has curbed energy demands... Oil production now exceeds demand in approximately 2 million barrels per day and, according to some estimates, the surplus could increase to 4 million barrels a day by the end of the year." "Nobody is buying oil nowadays because everyone is certain that it will be cheaper tomorrow" declared at the time Wanda Jablonsky, editor of the Petroleum Intelligence Weekly.

Perhaps the most surprising effect of the drastic hikes in oil prices from 1974 onwards was felt in OPEC nations themselves. In terms of income, petroleum had contributed 7 billion dollars to OPEC nations in 1970, whereas in 1980 this figure exceeded 300 billion.

The question to pose is the following: What has happened with the enormous volume of resources that those nations had at their disposal ? What effect did this wealth have on these societies?

The answer is simple. None of these countries was in any condition to efficiently absorb the volume of income in such a short period of time. In fact, the quality and quantity of human resources was not enough to achieve the ambitious development goals that had been set out. Therefore, in most of the member countries of OPEC, the bonanza brought more harm than good.

Let us for instance examine the case of Iran. By 1979 destabilization due to the surplus of wealth had reached such proportions that the Shah's political position had become untenable and he was forced to leave the country. Control was passed to a theocratical government headed by the Ayatollah Khomeini. From that time on, Iran, led by fundamentalist Muslims, became for a long period of time - and perhaps still is - a destabilizing element in the entire Middle East region.

A short time later, in 1980, the Iran-Iraq war broke out, bringing about the sacrifice of hundreds of thousands of young people's lives and a notable success in causing each other the worst harm possible. At present both countries suffer from the ominous consequences of a war which ended eight years later, having yielded no special advantages for any side and having left both contenders exhausted.

As a result of that war, Iraq's economy was left in a serious predicament and the country's rate of indebtedness was astronomically high. To solve the problem, Iraq decided a few years later to invade Kuwait, a small but immensely rich neighbour state, formerly one of its main benefactors - close to $16 billion had been lent to Iraq by that nation during the conflict with Iran. This invasion gave rise to a serious trauma worldwide at a time when it was thought that the end of the cold war would usher in an extended era of peace that would benefit all mankind.

Even Saudi Arabia, the richest member of OPEC, has had to face serious economic problems that have led this nation to successive currency devaluations and the postponement of its ambitious development programs. At present, many analysts consider that the ruling house in Saudi Arabia could find it hard in the long run to survive unhurt the trauma caused by Iraq's invasion of Kuwait.

Also in a compromising situation is Nigeria, a country submerged in tremendous social problems, the consequence of a large population of close to 95 million inhabitants. Since 1979 there have been several coup d'etat attempts.

As far as Libya is concerned, the problems of this nation are also of dramatic proportions. This country has become a destabilizing factor, the tentacles of which have extended throughout the entire world, sponsoring the most varied terrorist activities. The consequent tragic and countless loss of human lives thereof is too difficult to count. According to American authorities, there is evidence that Libya is capable of manufacturing chemical warfare weapons, including lethal gas. This nation's attempts to procure missiles that can reach Israeli territory are well-known. On several occasions Libya has had aborted aggressive confrontations with the United States, including the American navy's bombing of several strategic enclaves in Libyan territory.

In the case of Venezuela, after the bonanza of the '70s, the acute and prolonged crisis the country has suffered is known by all. In 1990, the level and standard of living of Venezuelans was lower than in 1973. The most deplorable consequence of the sudden wealth that encompassed this nation during those years was the deep moral crisis and the tremendous disarray of values which that society has suffered.

As a result of the extraordinary revenues reaped from the two oil shocks, the country became accustomed to a level of public expenditure that became untenable once the oil prices went down. Successive governments were however unable to reduce the expenses. This brought about massive foreign indebtedness, the progressive devaluation of the currency and inflationary levels unheard of in that nation up to that time. A reduction in the real salary of the workers and the perception of widespread corruption led to the impeachment by Congress in 1993 of president Carlos Andrés Pérez . Venezuela never abandoned nevertheless the constitutional route and continues to be Latin America's oldest democratic nation.

In short, the examples provided are enough to present a general panorama of the delicate situation in OPEC countries. All, without exception, have lived through serious economic, political and social situations.

On the other hand, in 1980, international trade surplus of the member countries of OPEC had reached the amazing figure of $109 billion. Not less surprising is the fact that only two years later, in 1982, the international trade deficit of these same nations was well over $18 billion.

Apart from this, in an effort to maintain price levels, OPEC was forced to impose production quotas on its members. We thus observe that production in these countries fell from around 31 million barrels per day in 1979 to an amount in the order of 15.5 million barrels daily by 1985. Setting the quota corresponding to each member has become a source of continuous friction and disagreement among the members of OPEC, most of which openly violate the production shares assigned to them.

Additionally, OPEC's sacrifice in restricting production has served in good measure for other exporting countries not affiliated to the organization to increase their participation in the international oil markets.

On August 2nd, 1990, the date of Iraq's invasion of Kuwait, once more there appeared the threat of a third oil shock. Crude oil prices, which had plummetted in 1986 - having reached a low of around 7 dollars per barrel in the summer of that year - started to escalate violently during the second half of 1990. A few weeks prior to the date of invasion, OPEC was unsuccessfully striving to maintain an official price of 18 dollars per barrel, imposing stringent production quotas on its members. However, by October 10th, 1990, the price of light crude in the futures market reached a price of 41.15 dollars per barrel in the New York Stock Exchange (NYSE), the highest price ever quoted for a contract of that type in that market. In subsequent weeks oil prices oscillated according to the statements, intentions and even the dreams ascribed to Saddam Hussein.

As was to be expected, once the conflict ended, oil prices once again fell to levels even lower than those prevailing prior to the invasion, in spite of the fact that Iraq's production had been kept out of the international oil markets for a long period of time.

Sooner or later, this depression in prices is bound to be reverted. In fact, by mid-1994 the prices of hydrocarbons had started to experience an upward trend. This increase was partly due to the civil war which broke out in Yemen, another Persian Gulf country, as well as a strike affecting oil production in Nigeria and repair works being carried out in the oil fields located in the North Sea.

It is expected that the hard lessons learnt by producer and consumer countries during the past 20 years will be of help for the mistakes of the past not to be repeated. We trust that common sense shall prevail this time round and that the international oil markets shall recover their reasonably stable positions, thereby enabling changes that would benefit mankind.

In effect, it would be particularly interesting to analyze the energy prospects for the next few years and Venezuela's possible role in a foreseeable scenario.

Based on these premises, petroleum shall continue to be for several decades the most strategic, versatile and abundant source of energy at the disposal of mankind. According to Dr. S. E. Subroto, former Secretary General of OPEC, "world (oil) demand shall increase at a rate of 1 to 2 percent per year in the coming years". These statements highlight the need for more oil reservoirs in order to cover this growing demand. To this effect, Dr. Subroto stated that:

"It is well known that the reserves of OPEC member countries are - in broad terms - the most extensive in the world, close to 84% of total proved reserves of approximately 910 billion barrels (excluding centralized economy countries). At the current rates of production, reserves in non-OPEC nations shall last about 19 years, whereas those of OPEC shall last over 100 years". (8)

According to the most recent estimates, world oil consumption shall increase by only 1.2 percent per year until the end of this century. This however implies an increase of approximately 800.000 barrels per day per year. On the other hand, the World Energy Council has predicted that the world oil demand shall double before the year 2020.

In the next few years, a strong decline in oil production is expected in many nations and in the United States in particular. This reduction shall barely be balanced out by expected increases in production in countries such as Colombia and China. The main responsibility in meeting growing world oil demands shall fall on OPEC countries

Of the thirteen countries members of OPEC, only six are in condition to substantially increase their oil production levels to cover the growing requirements of the international marketplace. These six countries, by reason of their volume of proved hydrocarbon reserves - representing over 91% of OPEC's total proved reserves - are the following:

Saudi Arabia
Iran
Iraq
Kuwait
United Arab Emirates
Venezuela

Evidently Venezuela stands out among the aforementioned six nations since it is the only country not located in the conflictive Persian Gulf region and also because it has traditionally been the most reliable supplier of oil to industrialized nations.

In fact, it would be safe to say that Venezuela has kept up an ongoing struggle to increase its petroleum-generated resources. However, the country's aspirations have always revolved around economic conditions and in this sense, its achievements have always been reached through negotiations with international oil companies. Venezuela has never placed oil at the service of any political cause, except in the case of World War Two, when all its oil production efforts were put forth to contribute to the efforts of the Allied Forces to win the war. In evident contrast, the remaining five nations on the list have at one time or another, used their oil as a political weapon.

Let us stop once more and review the possibilities open to Venezuela, as long as the country adopts coherent policies that would enable it to take the fullest advantage of its hydrocarbon wealth.

Let us begin by referring to our oil reserves. In this regard, it would be convenient to state that there are usually various types of reserves: in the first place there are the "proved" reserves which are those that have been most precisely quantified by means of drilling and production testing. Then there are the "probable" reserves, which are those found in little-explored fields or those which could be extracted from the known fields if extraction procedures were improved. Lastly, there are the "possible" reserves, the estimation of which is based on the extrapolation of discoveries that have already been made or by analogy with the geologic conditions in favorable areas.

The Ministry of Energy and Mines of Venezuela has conservatively estimated the amount of the country´s "proved" reserves in around 65 billion barrels. This figure represents roughly 7% of the entire world's proved reserves and approximately 9% of those of OPEC. These proved reserves would theoretically last around 75 years.

However, the Ministry in its official statistics does not refer to the "probable" reserves. To this effect, it would be worthwhile mentioning that the domestic oil industry has been aiming its exploration efforts towards increasing the higher-grade oil reserves, i.e., light, medium and condensate crudes. Said efforts are primarily focused on the demarcation of the large hydrocarbon fields to the north of the State of Monagas, a region considered to be one of the most important oil areas in the world. In fact, many technicians in the industry affirm that these fields harbour reserves of around 12 billion barrels, that is, an amount exceeding that found in the North Sea and Alaska.

The same optimism is reflected in the new discoveries found in the north Andean flank towards the southeast of the Maracaibo Lake basin and in the geographical area of Guarumen, located between the states of Portuguesa, Cojedes and Guárico. To sum up, throughout our country's oil history, beginning with Zumaque Well No. 1 in 1914, Venezuela has exploited relatively shallow hydrocarbon reserves composed mainly of heavy crudes. Modern technology is enabling better and deeper seismic evaluation, as well as drilling of much deeper wells. All the operations carried out up to the present indicate that there is an enormous potential that is practically untouched. Perhaps the major advantage of these discoveries is the quality of the crudes being found.

If the "probable" and "possible" reserves being found in the above-mentioned regions were to be included, as well as others with promising prospects, we would be placing the amount of light and medium crude oil, without being overly optimistic, in a figure of around 50 billion barrels, aside from the proved reserves that have already been mentioned.

We have not however yet mentioned the reserves of a hydrocarbon which, due to its low-polluting characteristics is considered one of mankind's greatest future sources of energy. We are referring to natural gas. In this regard, Venezuela also has abundant quantities of this element and the volume of proved reserves is about 20 billion equivalent barrels of petroleum.

Lastly, let us mention the greatest oil deposits known in the entire world: the Orinoco Belt. To give an idea of its magnitude, suffice it to say that the world's proved oil reserves are estimated at around 999 billion barrels. The Orinoco Belt in itself is estimated to contain over $1.3 (10^{12})$ trillion barrels of oil "in situ". Most of it is extra-heavy crude oil, the exploitation of which up to now had been economically non-attractive. However, at present, thanks mostly to Venezuelan technology developments, oil in this belt has become economically exploitable.

Proved reserves in the Orinoco Belt exceed 270 billion barrels(9). This estimate of the reserves, which include only those economically exploitable by current procedures, is highly conservative. As development techniques are improved, the figures for proved reserves shall increase.

The oil in the Belt, besides its conventional uses when subjet to deep conversion refining processes, is the raw material for manufacturing Orimulsion ^{tm}, a fuel that can replace coal as base load for power plants.

Therefore its international commercialization has begun very successfully. It as been launched in the market under the label "liquid carbon". Worth mentioning is that, because it is a product that competes with coal, its price is necessarilly lower than that of other hydrocarbons, therefore the margin of revenues is much lower. That is why it is catalogued as a different branch in the hydrocarbon industry. Income for the country will depend on arriving at high production volumes.

The hydrocarbons found in the Orinoco Belt can also be used to produce upgraded crudes, although heavy investments have to be carried out for this purpose. Despite its high cost, this type of crude is in great demand in industrialized nations, particularly since it does not yield residue when refined.

In sum, Venezuela's energy potential consists of the following:

65 billion barrels of proved oil reserves.
50 billion barrels of probable and possible reserves of light.
20 billion equivalent barrels of oil in proved natural gas reserves.
270 billion barrels of proved extra-heavy hydrocarbons in the Orinoco Belt.

If we were to add our very abundant coal reserves to these figures, as well as the enormous hydroelectric-generating capacity of the Caroní river and the Andes, the conclusion is that Venezuela probably is one of the countries with greatest energy potential in the entire world.

From the analysis of the above-mentioned data, an initial conclusion can be derived. There is nothing more absurd than to talk about the "post-oil" Venezuela. The truth is that our country is barely beginning its oil history.

On the other hand, it is evident that there are two major geographical areas on the planet with a volume of reserves that could cover the continuously increasing demand in a world ever-thirsty for energy, as long as proper investments are made to develop the production potential thereof. These two areas are Venezuela and the Persian Gulf.

The following pages shall provide an analysis of the deep religious implications unleashed by the seed of Islamic fundamentalism in the Middle East region. Muslim religious leaders almost unanimously consider that there has already been an intolerable contamination with western ideas and this constitutes a serious threat for Islamism. For these leaders, the current reigning degeneration had not existed since before Mohammed's appearance on earth. Sunnite and shiite scholars, historically enemies, now agree that pro-Western government rulers have carried the Muslim world to a state of apostasy and barbarism (jahiliyya). The only cure according to pious Muslims would be that Islamic followers return to the political arena they have abandoned.

To sum up: religion, nationalism, politics and petroleum constitute the most explosive mix in the world. To create a conflict of terrifying proportions, suffice it to combine these ingredients and shake slightly.

INTRODUCTION

Faced with the chaotic mosaic of uncertainties that marks the situation in the gulf, Venezuela's position stands out as the most evident alternative capable of eminently contributing to meet the growing energy demands of the Western world. In this regard, the following is a transcription of a testimony by General R. Knowles, President of the South West Energy Council presented on November 8, 1989 before the U.S. Senate Banking and Finance Sub Committee, evidently before the crisis generated by Iraq's invasion of Kuwait. In our opinion, General Knowles' address constitutes the best summary of the energy situation in the U.S. and the corresponding perspectives open to Venezuela:

"The U.S. consume approximately 4.5 billion barrels of petroleum per year. In 1985 we imported 31% of our needs. This figure increased to 40% in 1987 and reached 50% by February 1989."

"International trade deficit, attributable to imported petroleum, was in excess of 35 billion dollars in 1988. Estimates for the year 2000 surpasses the 200 billion-dollar figure."

"If we must increase our oil imports, it would seem prudent, insofar as possible, to do so from our neighbours of the Western hemisphere, who would more probably return the money we spend on imports with a greater trade exchange with the U.S."

"During the 1973 oil embargo only 8% of our oil supply was imported. We all know how that affected our economy and lifestyle. It was during that period that Canada, Mexico and Venezuela came to our aid to sit out the storm. Currently, over 17% of our imported oil comes from Saudi Arabia. If this flow were to be interrupted for any reason whatsoever, we would be under a lot of pressure to keep up our standard of life and, more importantly, our safety."

"According to the former Marine Secretary, John Lehman, our military commitments last year for defending the Persian Gulf flow lines cost 40 billion dollars. This placed the real cost of Persian Gulf oil at an approximate figure of 140 dollars per barrel."

"Obviously, state legislators cannot affect the conditions of the world oil market; however, we can induce and back the Executive Chamber and Congress in sponsoring policies that could be translated into more reliable sources of energy and more stable conditions for the development of energy. The South/West Energy Council proposes the formation of a PanAmerican energy treaty that would become the basis for this stability."

"Agreement among Western hemisphere nations with the greatest producing capacity shall significantly contribute to our defence by ensuring oil supplies in our sphere of influence. This union would encourage trade among the democratic nations of the hemisphere, would improve panAmerican relations and would help to solve the debt crisis incurred by Latin America."

"Besides, we have a long-standing friendship and reciprocal exchange history with Venezuela. It would be worthwhile to mention that during World War Two Venezuela was the second largest nation, after the U.S., to supply oil to the Allied Forces."(11)

It seems therefore evident that Venezuela is in a condition to begin a new and fruitful era as an oil nation. It is up to us to take advantage of this "last opportunity" as stated by Dr. Arturo Uslar Pietri, an eminent intellectual personality in our country who has delved deeply into this problem.

Alfredo Toro Hardy, in his book "The Venezuelan Challenge: How to have influence over American political decisions" has fully analyzed the need to make the best of the "favourable opportunity". The author quotes John W. Kingdon, which we think is timely to repeat: "'Windows' is a term used in space launches when an opportunity for launching arises. Objects in space are in the proper alignment at a given time, but this situation does not last for long. Consequently, launching must be carried out while the window is still open". Further on, Mr. Toro Hardy states the following: "What factors, however, determine the appearance of a favourable opportunity? Basically a 'political window' is open when a new set of factors appears ..." (12)

Now therefore, Iraq's invasion of Kuwait has opened a 'political window' for Venezuela. This is the most favourable moment and we should take advantage of it. However, there are two conditions: the first, that the industrialized nations, and particularly the U.S. must understand that they cannot tie their future to the planet's most unstable region alone.

In this regard, in order to meet growing energy requirements, there is a much safer alternative. This is the case of Venezuela, a country strategically located in the Western hemisphere, historically qualified as a reliable and trustworthy supplier, geographically situated in an optimum point, politically incorporated to the group of democratic nations and culturally part of a Western christian civilization.

The second condition to be able to take advantage of the opportunity that lies ahead of us does not depend on other nations but on ourselves. We must leave behind this so-called 'nationalism' based on sometimes well-grounded historical complexes, but that nevertheless do not mirror our true national interests. In the world today, borders have come to have a different meaning, otherwise they would become obstacles for the efficient usage of the resources in an increasingly inter-connected world where relations among nations are defined by technologies that advance at an overwhelming pace. These circumstances have led nations to become structured in economic blocks or common markets.

Competition among these blocks would promote greater changes in international economic relations. These changes would tend to weaken even more the old barriers based on nationalism and would give rise to a new economic order, offering tremendous opportunities to the nations or blocs of nations entering into this new historic trend.

For Venezuela to take the path of sustained economic growth, gain quick access to the group of developed nations - and consequently achieve a higher standard of living for its inhabitants - its energy resources must be negotiated in a coherent and mature fashion.

Venezuela has a good starting point: its extraordinary experience in hydrocarbons, very capably managed by PDVSA, a company that has transformed itself into a first class worldwide corporation.

It is only natural and logic, that using the huge hydrocarbon reserves as cornerstone, Venezuela should take advantage of PDVSA as the instrument for an effective integration into the global economy. This integration implies sustained growth and investment, for which an opening policy is crucial. This opening is a natural bilateral complement of the downstream integration that PDVSA has achieved during the past 10 years.

On the other hand, if the goal of our governments has been and should be the diversification of our economy, it would be a contradiction to continue concentrating large sums of public investment on the oil sector, a sector characterized by continuous oscillations. The logical step would be to accept contributions by private local or foreign investment, in a manner such that the profits received by the nation could be allocated to contributing to an even more accelerated development in other sectors of the economy. Oil production, though a good business, is marked by swings brought about by situations alien to Venezuelan life. This movement drags the country's economy along with it, from a frenetic abundance to an abyss of uncertainties, depending on events in the Middle East. This means that when things are tough over there, here they are going well. Thus, ordinary problems start to accummulate as a result of poor public administration, that sooner or later are resolved through some extraordinary event originated in the Islamic world.

In our opinion, the complete development of our energy potential requires the "depolitization" of the oil subject. This proposal seems utopian at present. However, faithful believers in the "Theory of Historic Cycles" set forth by the eminent historian Arnold Toynbee are convinced that Venezuela is now nearing the end of a 30-year historic cycle that began in 1960. The political discourse will necessarily have to change, since the audience no longer pays attention to what has been repeated for more than thirty years. The political arena is evidently disintegrating and this is one of the requirements for transition into a new cycle. The nation is tired of slogans that have almost become dogmas, despite the evident failure of its axioms. The time has come to place before the country the best possibilities for the future of our oil and not what have been its worst disgraces. This last subject was in vogue in the past but does not respond anymore to our current or future needs as a nation. Our country's new leaders must have a shrewd and deeply penetrating vision of the opportunities open to us in the Twenty-first century.

Since 1958, Venezuela had announced that no new oil concessions would be granted. The objective pursued at the time was to nationalize the country's oil industry, a goal that was achieved before it was expected due to the impeccable negotiation process carried out in 1975 with the foreign oil companies. From that time onwards, PDVSA, the state oil company, has been responsible for developing our hydrocarbon industry. This company has achieved an extraordinary performance in this field. In a matter of years it has become one of the world's leading oil companies and its scope is far-reaching.

However, within the process of glogal integration, the next natural step for Venezuela is to open the upstream to the participation of foreign capitals, which certainly will multiply the strength of its oil cooperation.

For the first time since 1958 (except for some service contracts that were granted towards the year 1970) but which were never fulfilled), Venezuela is opening up to foreign investment in the hydrocarbon sector.

In this regard, 1993 came to represent a decisive year. National congress adopted the first three "Strategic Partnership Contracts", the first referring to the Cristobal Colón Project for the development of natural gas reserves in the northeastern part of Venezuela´s continental shelf. participation by Lagoven, Shell, Exxon and Mitsubishi. The other two partnerships are between Maraven and Conoco on the one hand and Maraven, Total, Itochu and Marubeni on the other, for the exploitation and upgrading of the gigantic extra-heavy crude reservoirs in the Orinoco Belt. These three projects will have a combined investment of 10 billion dollars.

Also, in 1993, PDVSA awarded service operational to several national and international companies to reactivate marginal fields throughout the country. This program has brought about an additional production of 30,000 barrels of oil per day in 1994 and implies an investment of 1 billion dollars in the first three years.

Venezuela is preparing to enter a new stage of openness to foreign investment in its oil sector with exploration and production partnerships in new areas. The partnership model to be used is known as "Profit-sharing" Agreements.

According to estimates by PDVSA geologists, new reservoirs with up to 40 billion barrels of light and medium crudes could be discovered. In view of their high margin of profitability, these crudes could represent an enormously attractive option for Venezuela.

The Venezuelan oil company is at present purchasing close to 700,000 barrels between crude oil and refined products per day of crude oil per day in the international markets in order to complete the volume required by its own markets which have gradually been expanded through sound acquisitions of refineries and distribution systems in USA and Europe (CITGO, Ruhr Öel, Nynäs, etc.). This added production from the exploitation of its own fields thanks to the new program promoting foreign capital investment shall open up the possibility of substituting with Venezuelan oil the volumes of light and medium crude being currently purchased in the international markets.

In the more promising areas to be opened for bidding in 1995 to private national and foreign investors, some 23 billion barrels of light and medium crudes could be found, as well as some 10 trillion cubic feet of natural gas. The investment required to prove the existence of these reserves is estimated at around $6 to $8 billion, whereas the total investment to develop the new areas is calculated at approximately $8 to $10 billion during the next decade. Through these investments in addition to some 20 billion which the own affiliates will invest in traditional areas, it is expected that Venezuela's oil production potential could increase from some 2.9 million barrels per day in 1994 to 4 million b/d towards the year 2002.

PDVSA has announced an investment program plan in excess of $50 billion to be completed between 1994 and the year 2002, encompassing the sectors of exploration, production, refining processes, orimulsion processes and transportation. Close to 65 percent of that amount shall be covered by resources from the company and the remainder by third parties, engaged in associations with PDVSA.

* * * * * * * *

It is important to state, however, that we would gain nothing by having a brilliant oil future if the wealth of resources provided by nature continues to be squandered as has been the case up to now, or if this wealth is only used to accentuate the deformities in our economy and the aberrations of our society. In this regard, we feel optimistic about the possibilities open to the nation. Once again, we quote Dr. Arturo Uslar Pietri:

"It is a great challenge to attempt to correct deep-rooted evils, set in place during endless years of lack of controls and complacency... For a long time, many Venezuelans have been realizing the dangerous artificiality of the country's economic situation. Venezuela now counts on a numerous team of capable people in all areas of social activity, people who have been properly educated and prepared to play the role that corresponds to them in this broad-scale endeavour of economic transformation... Now is the time for Venezuela to bring to the fore its moral reserves and its ability to face difficulties and go forward. Thus will emerge a new Venezuela that shall be healthier, more vital and the product of a joint effort; a better nation than the one we have called our own."(13)

NOTES

1.-Jack Anderson with James Boyd. OIL: THE REAL STORY BEHIND THE WORLD ENERGY CRISIS. Introd. page X.

2.-Marco A. Angeli. INTERNATIONAL ECONOMIC ORDER AND OIL PRICES. Page 19.

3.-Paul Johnson. MODERN TIMES. Page 667.

4.-Paul Hallwood and Stuart Sinclair. "An interpretation of economic relations among OPEC and non-oil producing developing nations during the '70s" OPEC Magazine No. 53. 1981.

5.-Henry Kissinger. YEARS OF UPHEAVAL. Pages 858-859.

6.-Ministry of Energy and Mines. Republic of Venezuela. OIL AND OTHER STATISTICAL DATA 1983. page 20. These data are not strictly comparable to one another, since in the first case the base year was 1975, whereas the figures were revised for the data corresponding to 1985, using 1980 as the base year. However we have taken the liberty to use them, in the knowledge that there is an inaccuracy involved but at least they illustrate a trend.

7.-Ministry of Energy and Mines. Republic of Venezuela. OIL AND OTHER STATISTICAL DATA. 1986, page 20.

8.-Dr. S. E. Subroto. OPEC Secretary General. Speech pronounced on the occasion of the 11th Conference of the International Energy Economy Assocation. Caracas. June 26-28. 1989.

9.-Andres Sosa Pietri. President of Petróleos de Venezuela S.A., "PDVSA - 15 years later". Speech pronounced on the occasion of the company's XV anniversary. August 30th. 1990. Documents 90. No. 2. page 5.

10.-Jack Anderson. THE MIDDLE EAST: OIL DEALERS. Page 184.

11.-General R. Knowles. President of the South West Energy Council (an entity that groups together the legislators from the states of Alabama, Alaska, Arkansas. Colorado. Louisiana, New Mexico, Oklahoma and Texas). Testimony presented before the U.S. Senate Banking and Finance Subcommittee. November 8. 1989.

12.-Alfredo Toro Hardy. THE VENEZUELAN CHALLENGE: HOW TO INFLUENCE American POLITICAL DECISIONS. page 199.

13.-Arturo Uslar Pietri. VENEZUELANS AND OIL. page 21.

CHAPTER I
THE SECOND WORLD WAR

The Axis vs. The Allied Forces

The first crisis to be considered is the Second World War, which brought about a profound change in the international oil markets. This war broke out on September 1st, 1939 with the invasion of Poland by German forces. Mussolini becomes allied with Hitler, thereby structuring the so-called Axis, made up at that time by Germany and Italy. Later on, Japan would become a part of it as well. Other nations such as Hungary, Romania, Finland, Bulgaria, etc. would also enter into the Axis.

The parties at war were thus defined. On the one hand, the Axis and on the other the Allied Forces, which, by 1945, were comprised of a group of nations: the U.S., Great Britain, the former USSR, France, Canada, Australia, etc.

On the side of the allied forces stands a nation who until that time had had little importance in the world geopolitical context of the twentieth century: Venezuela. This country would play a fundamental role in the solution of the conflict, a role which has not been fully acknowledged.

The war arose because some nations, especially those comprised by the Axis, needed to obtain vital land from which to garner raw materials, food and, most of all, sources of energy, for the purpose of sustaining ambitious world dominance and expansion programs. In his book 'Mein Kampf', Hitler had already proclaimed that Germany needed to secure a vast *"Lebensraum"* towards the east.

Japan, plunged in a strong economic crisis, had its eye on the raw materials coming from the Pacific and particularly the oil wealth of the Dutch Indies. Nevertheless, in trying to avoid a confrontation with the U.S., attention was deviated towards

China, knowing full well that American public opinion, mostly isolationist, would be hostile to an intervention in favour of the Chinese. In any event, Roosevelt was becoming increasingly less pleased with Tokyo's policy and decided in the first semester of 1940 to ban exports of a number of goods to Japan. Nevertheless, he made sure that oil, which he knew was a vital commodity for Japan, was not included in the list.

In September 1940 the American government adopted a more rigid stance by limiting oil exports to Japan. This directly affected Japanese economy and that country responded by signing the Tripartite Agreement with Germany and Italy. Japan, hungry for raw materials, invaded Indochina and made it into a "protectorate". However, the Japanese government continued to try to reach an agreement with the United States, inasmuch as they did not want this country to enter the war.

Roosevelt was no longer willing to confront the Japanese expansionistic policy with weak economic retaliations, so on July 26th, 1941, he forbid, among other measures, the exportation of high-grade gasoline, indispensable for Japanese aviation. He also personally advised the Japanese ambassador in Washington that if Japan attempted to seize by force the oil in the Dutch Indies in order to alleviate its shortage of fuel, the British would enter the war. If that happened, the U.S. "would be forced into an extremely serious situation" in view of the mutual assistance pact with England.

Japan was now between the devil and the deep blue sea. That country's economy could not survive the oil blockade imposed by the American government in retaliation for its forays into south Asian soil. Deprived of this most vital source of energy, Japan decides to attack. In effect, on September 6th, 1940, during a supersecret imperial conference held in Tokyo, it was convened that "if by the first days of October there is no hope of having our petitions met, we shall begin to prepare for war against the United States, England and Holland". On October 16 of that same year, general Tojo, a staunch believer in the use of force, was named Prime Minister of Japan. The primary objective had already been foreseen by Roosevelt: to take possession of the oil in the Dutch Indies. For this, the military risks represented by the U.S. naval base in Pearl Harbour and the British fort in Singapore had to be eliminated.

On the 7th December, 1941, the Japanese attacked Pearl Harbour. Three hundred and seventy Japanese warplanes attacked the American facilities by surprise. They flew in from an air-sea squadron under the orders of admirals Yamamoto and Nagumo comprised of six aircraft carriers, 2 battleships, 2 heavy and 1 light cruisers, 11 destroyers, 3 submarines, 9 torpedoe boats, 8 big tankers and numerous war vessels that backed the attack by air.

At the time of the attack, some seventy war vessels of the Pacific fleet and twenty-four aid ships were anchored at Pearl Harbour. During the swift attack, five of the eight American battleships in the base were totally destroyed and one seriously damaged. One hundred and forty American planes were destroyed and eighty damaged. Two destroyers and nine ships were also sunk. Military casualties amounted to 2,330 dead and 1,145 injured.

At the same time, the Japanese launched attacks on other regions in the Pacific. Hong Kong, a British colony, was bombed, as well as Singapore. Japanese troops were mobilized into Siam. The conquest of the entire Malay peninsula had begun.

That same day, December 7th, 1941, saw the death of American isolationist policy. American congress unanimously voted to join Great Britain in declaring war against Japan. Three days later, Hitler declared war on the United States.

January 1942 turned out to be a gloomy month. The Japanese were extending their domain over the entire Malay peninsula, the Phillipines and the South Pacific. The powerful British Prince of Wales and Repulse battleships were lost. Singapore, once thought to be impregnable, fell into the hands of the Japanese. Rangoon fell on the 7th of March. India was being threatened. Java fell and New Guinea, Borneo and the Celebes islands of Indonesia after that. By the summer of 1942 the Japanese had reached the summit of their victories.

The 'Blitzkrieg' needs fuel

In the meantime, in the European scenario, events were happening at a maddening speed. In effect, on May 10th, 1940, German troops penetrated simultaneously into Holland and Belgium. Protected by Stuka planes, the heavy tanks opened the attack, followed by light armored cars and infantry on motorbykes. Parachutists and airborne troops preceded the advance of ground armies, thereby disorganizing any possibility of coordinated defence. On May 15th, Holland had already surrendered. Leopold, king of Belgium, signed the capitulation protocol on May 26. However, on the 28th, the Belgian government does not ratify this and decides to continue the fight. But the Belgian army exists no more. Hitler's daringly audacious plan does not stop there: on June 5th, 1940, Germany invades France. With his overwhelming superiority in tanks, bombers and troops on motorbyke, the Germans crush the French with the same terrifying speed as in all the territories they had occupied in Europe by that time. The government of Marshal Petain requests an armistice to the Führer on June 11th. On June 14, the Germans march through the roads of Paris. In the short space of time from May 10th to June 11th, 1940, Hitler had taken possession of

Holland, Belgium and France. This, therefore, was a new style of war: a 'Blitzkrieg', a mechanized war, whose main characteristic was a fantastic consumption of fuel.

Only England was left. "Decisive victory over England is just a question of time" wrote General Jodl in June 1940. But before undertaking this invasion, the Führer decides to resort once more to his tactics based on a motor-impulsed war. Thus, on August 1st, 1940, Hitler signed supersecret superior order No. 17 in his general headquarters to direct war against England. This order specifically stated that "German air force must crush the British air force using all available means". In effect, the Luftwaffe, using all manner of machines, sent wave after wave of planes to bomb England, with the purpose of forcing the opponent to beg for peace or otherwise to destroy British air defence and prepare the invasion. In general every raid assembled 400 to 500 bomber planes and 200 Stuka planes plus the protection of 500 fighter planes and 200 fighter-bombers. From August 24th to October 2nd, the Germans sent about 1,000 to 2,000 planes every day in consecutive waves to eliminate British air planes, crush out aerodromes, destroy radar stations and fuel deposits. Faced with the British resistance, the Luftwaffe set out against the outskirts of London. On the 11th of September Churchill addressed the British with the following words:

"The bombing of London, a barbarian, ferocious and futile attack that the enemy is blindly carrying out, is naturally a part of Hitler's invasion plan... "He has lit a fire that will shine endlessly until the last traces of Nazi tyranny have been burned in Europe and until the Old World and the New World unite in an effort to reconstruct the temple of freedom for mankind..." (1).

England was therefore preparing for the final attack. However, fate would have it otherwise: Hitler's fury was redirected towards the east.

According to the testimony of General Halder written in his diary, from July 31, 1940 onwards, Hitler had personally informed his generals of his intentions to annihilate the Soviet nation. During a meeting at Berghof he had stated his objectives in the following manner:

"We must annihilate the possibility of existence itself. This is our objective. In order to achieve this, we shall unleash two simultaneous offensive fronts: one to the south, towards Kiev and the Dnieper; another one to the north through the Baltic states, up to Moscow. And there the two armies shall meet. After this... a special operation shall be carried out that will put in our hands the oil reserves at Baku". (2)

Sources of oil supply were foremost among the Führer's plans. "The oil fields at Baku are to become German concerns" he ordered.

Hitler finally decided to violate the Non-Agression Pact he had signed since June 1939 with the USSR. The Führer chose to speed up this option in the light of the negotiations held in Berlin in November 1940 between Ribbentrop and Molotov, during which Russia, unaware of the plans being plotted against it, proposed its own adherence to the Axis. At the time Molotov had expounded that Russia was willing to sign the Pact if the following conditions, among others, were agreed:

-Recognition by Germany, Italy and Japan that the south area of Bakú and Batum (in the direction of the Persian Gulf) belonged to the USSR's 'areas of aspiration'.

-Japan's renunciation to its rights on the coal and oil concessions in the northern region of Sajalin island.

These conditions, affecting Germany's and Japan's plans for oil supply, were unacceptable. Therefore, war against Russia was unavoidable.

CHAPTER I

In effect, on June 22nd, 1941, German troops penetrated into Russia. Thus "Operation Readbeard" began. For Hitler the dice were cast. Since the signing of the German-Soviet pact in 1939, the USSR had been providing 900,000 tons of oil per year, thanks to which the Third Reich obtained an important part of the fuel needed by its powerful war machine. By invading Russia the Führer would now possess by force the sources of that oil.

Also, after having guaranteed that Romania would keep its borders, Hitler sent several military missions with the purpose of "defending the oil-producing area". The Rumanian oil fields at Ploesti were strategically important.

Faced with the evident display of Hitler's forces, Hungary, Romania and Slovakia joined the Tripartite Pact on November 20th, 23rd and 24rd, respectively. In March of the following year, Yugoslavia and Bulgaria would enter into the German orbit.

Operation Redbeard followed the same mechanized plan that had been a feature in Hitler's previous campaigns. The Führer's forces committed to the operation were made up of 152 divisions, 15 of which moved by motorbyke and 19 were 'Panzerdivisionen'. The Luftwaffe contributed 1,160 bombers, 720 pursuit planes and 120 reconaissance planes. The Russian forces counted 138 divisions, 20 of which were battleships and 40 brigades on motorbyke. Russian air force had 1,800 bombers (800 of which were modern), 2,000 fighter planes (300 of which were modern) and 800 very old-fashioned reconaissance planes.

Towards the east, the triumphs of the Wehrmacht were resounding. Throughout 1941, Germany had occupied two-fifths of USSR territory. The population had thus been deprived of its most fertile land, half of its industrial resources and two thirds of its coal and iron deposits. The Soviet situation seemed desperate, when at last in December 1941, the icy cold winter of that year finally halted Hitler's armies at the gates of Moscow. At that time the Führer already had other concerns. Hitler's armies had spread too far and the fuel that they had available to feed its thirsty machines was already starting to run out. His attention thus focuses on the south. The Caucasus region and its oil reserves becomes its most sought-after prey. The wells in that area were producing over 300 million tons of crude oil per year. That was enough to capture his greed.

We are now in the year 1942. The Third Reich reaches its height. Nazi domain weighed on Europe from the Mediterranean to the North Cape and from the Atlantic to Ukrania. The Allies, defeated on all fronts, could contribute nothing to the people subjugated in Europe.

Germany seemed to be all-powerful. In the spring of 1942 the Wehrmacht was made up of 300 divisions and over 25 battleships. With the contributions by its allies in Italy and Romania, it had over 9 million men with weapons. In the sea, the Kriegsmarine had an almighty fleet including 5 battleships, 12 cruise ships, 40 destroyers and over 150 submarines. The Luftwaffe had over 5,000 planes. If the magnitude of this powerful war machine seemed surprising, even more impressive was its requirement of fuel.

The synthetic fuel

Contrary to the Allies, Germany did not have enough sources of oil supply. That is why this country had to resort from the beginning to technically complex and costly alternatives, which undoubtedly represented a monumental effort of ingeniousness and industrial know-how.

In effect, the fuel used by Germany was mostly synthetic. This synthetic gasoline fuel was derived from coal by extremely expensive hydrogenation methods. In order to meet the demands of a gigantic war machine using all manner of engines, German production of synthetic gasoline fuel increased from eight hundred thousand tons per year in 1937 to three million eight hundred thousand tons by 1943.

German chemists had undertaken the problem of obtaining gasoline fuel (benzine or synthetic petroleum) from coal. Carbon had to be combined directly with hydrogen. Two methods were used. The first was named after its inventors, Tropf and Fischer and the second carries the name of the famous chemist Bergius.

The method most widely used was the one of Bergius, the secret of which was closely guarded. Explained in very simplistic terms, it consisted in mixing the finely ground carbon sifted with oily residues. This mix was then placed under the action of hydrogen (thus the name "hydrogenation plants") at a temperature of about 450º centigrade and a pressure of 200 atmospheres. A chemical reaction was thereby produced in revolving steel cylinders, due to the intimate contact between the hydrogen and the carbon. A carbon oil was thus formed that was distilled and produced 10% benzine and 90% residues. These were then submitted once again to a hydrogenation process in the presence of a catalyst at a temperature of 500º centigrade. This last phase yielded approximately 40% of synthetic gasoline fuel. The complexity of this process is evident.

Hitler pays no heed to rommel

One of the most interesting scenarios in World War Two took place in the north of Africa and in the Middle East where Mussolini's fascist armies were fighting against British troops. Hitler paid little attention to these events, occupied as he was with what he deemed much more interesting preys in the European continent. Finally, faced with Italy's continuous defeats, the Führer took a decision on January 20, 1941 that would have serious consequences for the British: the fifth motorized division was sent to Africa under General Erwin Rommel's orders. This general was a brilliant specialist in battleship warfare who had covered himself in glory with his "phantom division" during the French campaign. This military genius soon realized the importance of his new post and the vital strategic possibilities that the wealth of the region could have for the survival of Germany.

Mussolini accepted that all the German and Italian motorized and mechanized forces in the desert would be under the unified command of Rommel. Not only did this German general surprise the British; he also surprised the German high command. Having received the order to submit his plans for study by April 20th, he launched his attack on March 31st, 1941 and by April 12th he had already crossed the Cyrenaica and reached the Egyptian border, thereby reconquering the land that the Italians had lost to the British troops.

The situation had become critical for the Allied Forces. An important part of the Egyptian population was pro-German and enthusiastically celebrated Rommel's advances. In Iraq, power had fallen into the hands of General Rashid Alí, who asked for Hitler's help. Syria, under the authority of the French government of Vichy, offered a convenient base for German forces to advance towards the Middle East. Even in Persia, the Sha was an open supporter of Germany, as well as most of the Arab population and leaders in the Persian Gulf. In fact, one can speculate that if Hitler had directed his efforts to the Persian Gulf, where in all probability his troops would have been received as the "liberators from British domination" instead of stubbornly wanting to conquer the USSR, the result of the war would have been very different indeed.

Despite Rommel's prowess and his "Afrika Korps", the German high command did not grasp what the Western oil companies already knew: that a little more to the southeast, below the sands of the desert, lay vast oil resources.

Only Admiral Raeder, Chief of Staff of the German Navy, agreed with Rommel in the need to take more into account the African theatre of operations. Both were convinced that a violent push was enough for the entire apparatus of the British defence system to topple over in the Middle East. Consequently, Raeder once again on May 30th posed before Hitler his request for a "decisive attack aimed at Egypt and Suez in the autumn of 1941, an attack that" Raeder insisted, "would result even deadlier for the British Empire than the conquest of London".

But Hitler did not want to accept this opinion. On May 25, 1941 he gave the order to give aid to Rashid Alí in Iraq, though this help was to be limited to a military mission, some cooperation by the Luftwaffe and the supply of weapons. The guidelines given by the Führer perfectly clarified the strict limitations that had to be adhered to:

"The Arab pro-freedom movement is our natural ally in the Middle East against England... In consequence, I have decided to foster the development of the events in that region by giving aid to Iraq. The possibility of launching a later offensive against the Suez Canal and of driving out the British once and for all from their position between the Mediterranean and the Persian Gulf - and if affirmative by which means - cannot be decided until Operation Redbeard has been accomplished." (3)

How wrong Hitler was. In vain, Raeder and Rommel tried to divert his attention towards the possibilities that were open in the south. Time has shown that perhaps this was the Führer's biggest mistake in his personal strategy, which few of his generals would dare to contradict. In his diary, Rommel wrote the following:

"The German high command, under whose authority I remain, persisted in not wanting to recognize the importance of the African theatre of operations. They have not understood that with relatively few means we could have attained victories in the Middle East that from the strategic and economic standpoint would have had far greater importance than taking the Don's turn. Spread before us we had territories fabulously rich in raw materials, that among other things, could have rescued us from all our worries regarding fuel supplies. Some supplementary divisions would have been enough to ensure the full defeat of the British troops in the Middle East. But they were not sent to me. Our requests for reinforcements have been rejected, allegedly because of the enormous transportation needs to the eastern front and insufficient production in Germany... The consequences have been serious. With three divisions of little offensive power, we had the British in our power during eighteen long months, placing them at risk several times, until our troops no longer were able to resist in El Alamein." (4)

Two extremely important events, whose military phase was well known but have not been perhaps well studied from the economic point of view, probably sealed Germany's fate: one was the loss of El Alamein in November 1942. This marked the beginning of the end for the Third Reich. After that, the final destiny of Hitler's Reich became hopelessly compromised when it lost the oil fields in Ploesti, Romania on August 20, 1944. Both losses deprived the armies of the Axis from the invaluable fuel without which their powerful war weapons were worth no more than junk.

While all this was happening in Europe and Africa, a surprising transformation was going on in the U.S. This nation did not want to enter the war but was attacked by Japan towards the end of 1941. Three days later, Germany declares war on this country. The Americans could no longer stay out of the conflict. Thus, throughout 1942 a gigantic industrial plant dedicated originally to producing items for the welfare and consumption of the population, was totally transformed in less than a year. Weapons, planes, ships, vehicles are produced in those factories that had formerly produced cars, tractors and refrigerators. In the years of the war, American industry produced countless war equipment as well as some 300,000 planes 100,000 of which were heavy bombers, 90,000 war tanks, 634,000 jeeps, 120 aircraft carriers, 50 cruise ships and about 3,500 vessels, apart from a fleet of 63,000 landing ships. In sum, the levels of production were so impressive that this necessarily had to incline the scale in favour of the Allies. A new stage in the war was now starting. The allied nations now had capabilities far superior to those of Germany to carry out a "mechanized war". They also had a decided advantage over the armies of the Axis: abundant supplies of fuel.

The axis is left without fuel

In effect, few phenomena damaged the German armies so much as the scarcity of fuel. This lack reached dramatic proportions when the Allies started to bomb the factories of gasoline fuel. In fact, the Americans had understood that "it would be better to destroy a truly indispensable field than to destroy many fields in a lesser degree." This affirmation is included in a working report from the Economic Warfare Division presented on December 9, 1942. Thus, bombings carried out by the allied forces caused truly serious damage to the Ruhr hydroelectric dams, the ball bearing-manufacturing industries and the gasoline fuel factories.

Albert Speer repeatedly voiced his concern over the lack of fuel to Hitler. As soon as the Germans repaired the fuel-producing industries, new bombing attacks destroyed them once more. During a meeting of the Führer with a group of industrialists, also attended by Goering, Keitel and Speer, to broach the subject, Hitler himself summed up the result with the following words:

"In my opinion, the factories that produce fuel, buna and nitrogen are an especially sensitive point for the progress of war, since a basic substance that is indispensable for the armaments is produced in a small number of companies." (5)

On May 12th, 1944, the VIIIth American air fleet launched an attack with 935 day bombers against several fuel-producing factories located in central and east Germany. Speer, who was in charge of producing the weapons for the Reich, considered that the destiny of what he called "the technical war" was decided that day. After great efforts and around-the-clock repairs, Germany had been able to restore production to normal levels equivalent to 5,850 tons per day in only seventeen days. However a second wave of bombings was launched from May 28 to 29. This time 400 planes of the VIIIth American air fleet achieved greater destruction than those caused during the first attack. Simultaneously the important refineries in the Romanian oil fields of Ploesti were attacked by planes from the XVth American air fleet. Production of fuel in Germany was thereby reduced to half.

Once again the Germans made great efforts to restablish the production of fuel. Nevertheless the bombers returned once more and thus, on July 21st, 1944, production of fuel for the air force was paralyzed in approximately 98%.

In fact, the refineries at Ploesti and the oil fields in Romania would never again provide fuel for the Germany armies, since, a little while later, on August 20th of that same year, the Red Army would displace the Führer's forces from that very important strategic region. The loss of the oil reserves in Ploesti deprived Germany of the only source of crude oil that was left to it.

As a consequence of these devastating attacks, Speer asked the Führer to destine an important part of the pursuit planes to protect the fuel-producing factories, in order to prevent their continuous destruction:

"I repeatedly begged Hitler if it wouldn't be more adequate to momentarily protect the hydrogenation factories on German soil with pursuit planes so that in August and September a part of the production, at least, would be achieved, instead of continuing as at present, since this procedure would imply that, come September or October, all the machines waging war in the front as well as those stationed on native soil, would not be able to fly due to the lack of fuel." (6)

In the beginning Hitler agreed to his minister's request and solemnly promised that the "Reich's" air force would never be allocated to the front. However, with the invasion of Normandy, Hitler and Goering ordered the planes to be used in France. A few weeks later, these planes had been lost with no advantage for Germany.

In effect, the II World War was won by the Allies not on the battlefields but rather in the supply lines. Thus, when the conflict came to a head, the armies of the Axis simply could not continue fighting because their war machinery lacked fuel.

This statement is dramatically put in evidence when studying Hitler's last desperate maneuver to recover the initiative in the war: the so-called Battle of Ardennes of December 17th, 1944. The Führer had gathered 2,500 tanks and had formed 28 divisions, 9 panzers among them, aimed at an attack that in his opinion would push the allies out of the European continent. He also reserved 6 divisions for a parallel attack in Alsace, aimed at backing the offensive of the main force. Goering made 3,000 combat planes available (7). However the entire plan had a very serious strategic flaw. This formidable force lacked fuel in sufficient quantities.

The German advance was finally stopped when its panzers were barely 5,000 feet from one of its most important objectives: a big American deposit containing 12 million liters of fuel. The capture of this well-prized booty would have enabled the German blinded divisions to solve their acute problem of fuel supply.

To give an idea of the fuel requirements for the Reich, suffice it to say that at the beginning of 1944, the needs of the Luftwaffe alone reached 195,000 tons per month. However, an evident proof that the impotence of the German army at the end of the war was based in good measure on the lack of fuel is that by April 1945, the total inventories of aircraft gasoline in the entire Germany were only 11,000 tons, barely 5% of the Luftwaffe's monthly requirements.

THE U.S.: The Arsenal of the Democratic Nations

Even before the United States entered the war, forced by the Japanese bombing of Pearl Harbour, the American position, though neutral, was openly favourable to those who later on would become allies. Roosevelt approved in September 1939 a law known as the Cash and Carry Law. Thanks to this law, the warring nations were authorized to purchase weapons in the United States, as long as they paid in cash and transport was paid by them. In view of France's and England's naval superiority at the time, the effects of the new law would lean in their favour. But Germany's subsequent triumphs turned this situation around, making the American people deeply concerned, even though they still wanted to continue being neutral according to the polls.

As the conflict continued, however, Great Britain's position was increasingly compromised and France had already collapsed in June 1940. In fact, France's powerful fleet had been sunk by the Allies themselves, who preferred this painful alternative to the risk of said fleet falling into the hands of the Germans. Holland and Belgium had also fallen. Naval superiority in the Atlantic could not be guaranteed by Great Britain alone inasmuch as German submarines sailed freely in these waters.

By December 1940, President Roosevelt, in one of his famous 'chats by the fireplace', addressed his fellow Americans with the following statements:

"If Great Britain falls, the powers of the Axis shall control the European, Asian, African and Australian continents. Therefore, these powers shall be in a position to direct an enormous naval and air force against our hemisphere. It is not exaggerated to say that all of us, in America, would be living in front of the barrel of a gun... We must produce weapons and vessels with all the energy and all the resources of which we are capable... We must become the great arsenal for democratic nations." (8)

In view of the new scenario in Europe, the so-called Cash and Carry Law was no longer sufficient. Therefore Roosevelt, who understood like no one the dramatic situation posed and trying to overcome the isolationist resistance of his fellow countrymen, once again addressed them, stating:

"Let us suppose that my neighbour's house is on fire and I have a watering hose 500 feet away. If I allow my neighbour to pick it up and use it in his own water tap, undoubtedly I will help him to put out the fire. Then what shall I do? I am not going to

tell him, of course, that my hose cost me 15 dollars, so you have to give me back those 15 dollars. No, I don't want his dollars. All I want is to recover my hose when the fire has been put out."(9)

In this simple language full of imagery, Roosevelt explained the so-called Loan and Leasing Law to the American people. This law was enforced on March 11, 1941 and authorized the government of the United States to give the Allies all the aid they may require regarding vessels, weapons, planes and other military equipment, and still remain officially neutral.

Simultaneously from London Churchill, also using brilliantly clear words, told the Americans "give us the tools and we shall finish the work."

But Roosevelt understood that the U.S. could not stay out of the conflict for much longer. The case was not just to supply friendly nations but also to prepare and equip the country's armed forces. For that reason, in November 1941, with the purpose of intensifying the military effort and coordinating production, the President approved the Victory Program, by means of which a budget of 150 billion dollars would be allocated in the following two years for national defence programs.

Now therefore, all this enormous industrial effort consumed huge amounts of petroleum. American production itself increased at an accelerated pace. We thus see that the production of crude oil in the United States increased by 40% from 1936 to 1940 compared to the volume produced in the four preceding years. During the time that the Americans were involved in the war, production increased once again by 24%. This undoubtedly represented a huge effort but it was not enough.

On the other hand, Mexico, the other important oil exporter in the Western hemisphere, decided to nationalize the oil companies operating in its territory in 1938. This brought about the disappearance of Mexico from the international oil panorama.

Venezuela: The Fuel for the Democratic Nations

We can thus surmise that, although World War Two breaks out mostly due to the need to ensure sources of supply for energy and raw materials, in the long run, continuity in the supply of the latter is what determined the final outcome of the conflict.

Within the context of the global events that have been set forth, it would be interesting to analyze Venezuela's increasing participation in the web of events that dragged the entire world towards a tragic situation, the magnitude of which had never before been experienced. For this we have to go back to the years prior to the war.

Oil companies had become interested in Venezuela since production in that country had steadily increased. Proof of this was the Trade Reciprocity Treaty between Washington and Caracas, signed on November 6th, 1939. Through said treaty, Venezuela benefitted from close to 90% of the total oil importation quotas authorized by the United States.

The war that was developing in Europe paralized at first Venezuelan oil shipments to that continent. This was however compensated with an increase in demand from America due to the defence programs backed by President Roosevelt. First the Cash and Carry Law, and then the Loan and Leasing Law, increasingly linked Venezuelan oil production to the North American market.

On the other hand, since late 1940, formal conversations on military and political mutual cooperation between the U.S. and the Venezuelan governments were being carried out. Naval consultancy issues were discussed and in this regard, the United States pledged to cooperate in the organization of a Venezuelan coastal patrol force. Likewise, the U.S. would provide open sea patrolling to help guard the coastline 12 miles out. Codes were established for efficient communication between the naval forces of both countries and the reciprocal usage of ports and landing strips was agreed upon, with the aim of a closer cooperation effort.

Exchange of information on the movement or actions of individuals, organizations or forces threatening peace or the safety of both nations was also agreed upon.

The government was increasingly convinced that sooner or later Venezuela would be affected by the war conflict. In this regard, Mr. Parra Pérez, the Venezuelan Chancellor wrote a confidential note on national defence on June 18, 1941, stating that:

"Aside from the general political, moral and legal reasons that would force us to participate in the defence of the continent, strictly national considerations due to its geographical position and oil wealth would lead the republic to coordinate without delay the means of its own defence with the United States. Our neutrality will certainly not save us from aggressions by the powers called the Axis..." (11)

As a result of Japan's bombing of Pearl Harbour on December 7th, 1941, Venezuela made its position official. In effect, that very day, President Medina transmitted to Roosevelt, through Ambassador Corrigan, Venezuela's full support to the United States(12). The country's stance was now clearly defined: no attack against the U.S. nor any other American nation would be launched from Venezuela. Additionally, President Medina addressed the nation, stating the following:

"Our country has always backed democratic nations and, being Venezuela the third largest oil producer, it is of vital importance for democratic governments as a source of fuel." (13)

A committee for the safety of oil fields was created on December 17. It was evident that sabotages and damages to the facilities were feared. In fact, the American admiralty was seriously concerned about the organization of an efficient defence around the Venezuelan oil fields and the refineries in Aruba and Curazao. The eventuality of an attack to those refineries by submarine or planes from a distance close to the islands was not discarded. This possibility also threatened our oil fields and facilities.

On December 31st, 1941, Venezuela announced the break in relations with Germany, Italy and Japan. President Medina himself telegraphed the decision to President Roosevelt, while Chancellor Parra Pérez communicated it to Secretary of State Cordell Hull.

On that same day, December 31st, Chancellor Parra Pérez sent a letter to the Plenipotentiary Minister of Germany in Caracas, declaring the following:

"The Imperial Japanese attack against the United States of America and subsequent declarations of a state of war from Japan, Germany and Italy against the United States have been deemed by Venezuela as a case of aggression"... "The government of the republic has stated its solidarity with all American states from the beginning and its firm disposition to contribute to the defence of the continent by all means available" ..."The government I represent considers that this attitude of solidarity and cooperation, in fulfillment of its obligations with

the United States of America and other American nations at war with the government represented by His Excellency, is incompatible with the maintenance of friendly relations cultivated by Venezuela towards Germany before the deplorable circumstances that I refer to took place." (14)

Once relations with the powers of the Axis had been broken, Venezuela was confronted with the urgent need to defend its coasts. This was an imperious need since it was evident that Germany would attempt to interrupt the supply lines of fuel to the Allied Forces. In fact, Mr. Berle, Under Secretary for the War Defence Department of the United States, confirmed his country's concern regarding the safety of the region. Thus, on January 30th, 1942, he communicated with the Venezuelan ambassador in Washington, Mr. Diógenes Escalante, stating that his Department:

"... had to proceed forthwith to the defence of the refineries in Curacao and Aruba, insofar as there are over 80 German submarines in American waters in the Atlantic and we are afraid that they might enter the Caribbean to attack the bases of oil supply to the Allies." (15)

Initially the American government, urged on by the Dutch who did not want the participation of Venezuela in the defence of the Netherland Antilles, attempted to proceed alone to protect the area. This attitude on behalf of the Dutch government remained invariable until pressure from President Roosevelt forced Holland to accept the need for a three-party cooperation in the region, whereby a pact between Venezuela and Holland was signed.

By February 1942, events would precipitate a tenacious attitude against Nazi activities in Venezuela. Indeed, at 5 am on February 16, 1942, the Germans attacked the refineries in Aruba and Curazao, just as the governments of the U.S. and

Venezuela had suspected. Two Venezuelan vessels were also attacked on that same day, a few miles out to sea.

In the following months the Venezuelan government intensified its security measures and guaranteed military installations to the U.S. for the purpose of protecting itself from the growing threat posed by the increasing presence of German submarines in nearby waters, which were posing a threat to the refineries in Aruba and Curazao and the tankers transporting Venezuelan oil. Thus, in a confidential note dated February 18, 1942, the Ambassador of the United States in Caracas, Mr. Corrigan, was informed that President Medina had authorized U.S. vessels and airships to enter Venezuelan territorial waters. This decision was extended to British vessels and aircraft commanded by the U.S. government(16). A few days later, on February 24th, the government authorized the billeting in the airport of Maracaibo of American planes that had been providing services and avoiding attacks on Curazao and Aruba at the time.

The authorization granted by the government accepted besides that if the patrols were to discover hostile vessels that could threaten any of the facilities on the Venezuelan coastline, that "any urgent military action" could be taken. The only condition was to be that the Venezuelan government should be informed immediately of the action taken.

In effect, the provisions taken by the government of Venezuela in the defence of its coastline were more than justified. German submarines had transformed the marine thoroughfare between Lake Maracaibo and Curazao and Aruba into a hunting ground. Obviously, the intention was to interrupt the vital supply of oil that passed through the area. The Germans waited for the slow tankers loaded with crude oil to enter deeper waters in order to attack them. During February 1942 alone, seven tankers were torpedoed in that route. The solution was to put into practice a convoy system of groups of five to ten tankers, protected by the darkness of the night and by escort ships. During the day plane patrols stationed at Maracaibo protected the route.

During 1942, Venezuelan foreign policy acquired greater ties of affinity with the Allies. Towards the end of that year, Venezuela broke relations with the Vichy régime which it deemed collaborationist with the German occupants in French territory.

On the other hand, by January 1942, a consultancy meeting of American chancellors was convened at Río de Janeiro with the purpose of attempting to define a joint inter-American position. Four stances were envisaged before the meeting: in the first place, the position of the U.S. and the Dominican Republic, wanting a declaration of war, circumscribed to the Central American and Caribbean countries; the second, defended by Venezuela, Mexico and Colombia, advocated a joint rupture of relations with the Axis powers; the third stance, held by Argentina and Chile, seemed to favour a declaration of neutrality and lastly, the remaining nations wished to declare a "non-belligerent state".

Throughout 1942 Latin American nations varied in their attitudes. However, by the end of that year, their positions could be summed up as follows: the countries that declared war against the Axis: Mexico, Costa Rica, El Salvador, Guatemala, Haiti, Honduras, Nicaragua, Cuba, Panama, the Dominican Republic and Brazil. Nations that broke diplomatic relations: Venezuela, Colombia, Ecuador, Paraguay, Peru, Uruguay and Bolivia. Countries that maintained relations with the Axis: Argentina and Chile.

Brazil was the only country in the region with a direct military participation in the Second World War. In effect, after the Allies disembarked in Italy, a Brazilian brigade fought in that front from 1943 to 1944.

At the same time President Medina's government proposed a series of steps to increase Venezuela's participation in the oil business. Thus, in November 1942, his strategy in this regard was publicly announced in Maracaibo:

"This government... respects the legitimately acquired rights and does not regard as opponents the companies that have brought in their capital to intensify the development of our natural resource, but... considers that Venezuela should have a participation in the income generated from the industry, inasmuch as it owns the oil. Also, the industrial processing (of this raw material) should be located mainly in Venezuela in order to multiply job opportunities for Venezuelan workers." (17)

On February 13th, 1943, Venezuela decided to expressly reiterate its adherence to the Atlantic Charter, signed a year and a half before between the U.S. and Great Britain. To this effect, as had been sustained in several Panamerican Conferences, the Venezuelan government considered that the aforementioned document was one of the most important documents in American diplomatic history since it "includes standards that are fundamental to the international conduct in the New Continent."

Venezuela established diplomatic relations with the Union of Soviet Socialist Republics, on March 14th, 1943. The USSR, having signed a non-aggression pact with Hitler in August 1939, was subsequently attacked by the German armies in June 1941. From that time onwards, Russia would have a predominant role in the war and would join the Allies.

By 1944 Venezuela's position as supplier of petroleum to the Allies had acquired fundamental importance. This was made evident when verifying that in that year, our production rose by 42% compared to the previous year. This circumstance led President Roosevelt to invite the President of Venezuela, General Medina Angarita, to visit the United States. Medina was received by President Roosevelt himself and held interviews with key persons in the political sphere, the armed forces and the American industry. He was also invited to give speeches, among which should be highlighted the one in which he addressed the U.S. Congress and the Board of Directors of the Panamerican League.

Venezuela had thus acquired for the first time in the twentieth century, a fundamental strategic place of importance in the concert of nations and had a particularly key role in the development of the conflict that was devastating the world at large. If, as Roosevelt declared, the U.S. was the "arsenal for democratic nations", Venezuela provided the fuel with which those democracies defended the principles they sustained.

In July 1944, the Allied Forces disembarked in Normandy. A temporary government headed by General Charles De Gaulle was constituted in France. This government was recognized by Venezuela on October 23rd of that same year.

In October 1944, Mussolini's fascist government had fallen and Italy had reached an understanding with the Allies. Under these circumstances, the Venezuelan government decided to resume diplomatic relations with that nation.

Towards the end of 1944, it was evident that the defeat of Germany and Japan was just a matter of time. The Allies decided to set the basis for an organization that could preserve world peace in the future. In this regard a meeting was called at Dubarton Oaks, in the United States for the purpose of studying and approving the draft project of this future organization. The name of this entity would be the UNITED NATIONS.

The adherence or signing of the "Declaration of the United Nations" posed a last-minute problem for Venezuelan diplomacy. Our country had many times shown its affinity with the Allies but had not however declared war on Germany. This declaration was a sine qua non condition to enter into the new organization. President Roosevelt himself had addressed a letter to President Medina recommending him "in friendly and cordial terms, the convenience for Venezuela of adhering to the Declaration of the United Nations". To discuss the matter, the President held an extraordinary meeting with his council of ministers, where it was decided by seven votes against three, that Venezuela would declare war on Germany and Japan.(18)

Thus, on February 16th, 1945, Venezuela officially declared a "state of belligerance" against Germany and Japan. The paragraphs setting the grounds for this decision stated as follows:

"The government of Venezuela has not hesitated in lending its political, economic and military cooperation, insofar as possible, to the United Nations. For this purpose, conditions for the joint defense of the Caribbean Sea and the Dutch Antilles was convened with the United States and Holland; certain points on the coastline were fortified, to cooperate with the actions of the allied bases; precautionary steps were coordinated with the British government to defend the Gulf of Paria; the Island of Patos was fortified and combined efforts were carried out with the American base in Trinidad; ports and airstrips were opened to the vessels and aircraft of friendly nations at war; vessels entering Venezuela belonging to totalitarian regimes were seized; guidelines were set up to regulate and curb the activities

of individuals or foreigners that could endanger the safety of any American nation; the movement of funds pertaining to citizens of countries comprising the Axis were inspected; commercial, industrial and transport companies belonging thereto were liquidated or expropiated; and, in short, all measures included in the country's interamerican agreements were strictly executed, thereby always putting in evidence its intention to aid, by all means available, the success of the United Nations."(19)

The final Allied victory would take place in 1945. After the continuous German triumphs in 1939, 1940, 1941 and 1942, its armies started to step backwards. The troops commanded by the Führer fell back first in the USSR, where they were not able to withstand the winter of 1942, then in Africa, with the loss of El Alamein. In 1943 the German troops were dealt a heavy blow with the surrender of Italy, its oldest ally. On the 6th June, 1944, the assault to the coasts of Normandy, better known as D-Day, marked the beginning of Europe's liberation. Germany could no longer do anything to recover its Third Reich. After a desperate counteroffensive at the Battle of Ardennes, Germany's final lot was cast. The final defeat of the Axis came in two parts: firstly, Hitler's suicide on April 3rd, 1945 and the unconditional surrender of Germany on May 8th of that same year; and secondly, days after the U.S. dropped its atomic bombs over Hiroshima and Nagasaki in August of that year, Japan's immediate and unconditional surrender.

It would be worthwhile to stop here and analyze the magnitude of the effort that both contenders put in motion during the years that the war lasted. The following examples will help to form a picture thereof:

In this regard, it would be worthwhile to mention that during the war's culminating point, the Axis had about 20 million armed men, including Bulgarian, Finnish, Hungarian and Romanian forces alligned in the Russian front, whereas the Allies had mobilized about 40 million men.

From 1939 to 1944 warfare production multiplied 50-fold in the United States and Canada, 10-fold in Great Britain and Japan and 5 times in Germany and the USSR.

Counting the equipment previously existing at the beginning of the warfare plus that produced during the conflict, it is estimated that the Axis had total of 66,000 war tanks, 191,400 planes and some 1,300 submarines. The Allies had 238,000 tanks, 506,000 planes and 400 submarines.(20)

Not included above are other machines such as ocean liners, aircraft carriers, aircraft transporters, battleships, pocket battleships, cruisers, destroyers, swift escorts and an impressive variety of other type of equipment such as trucks, jeeps, amphibian vehicles, other means of transport, etc. in such quantities as to defy all imagination. Just to illustrate this point, suffice it to mention that in the course of the war, the Allies alone lost 5,150 merchant vessels, representing about 21.5 million tons of gross tonnage. The Axis forces lost merchant ships with an estimated gross tonnage of 14 million tons. This was the case of a war whose tragic wheels were bathed in rivers of blood and petroleum.

In effect, translated into its most deplorable consequence, casualties in World War Two amounted to 66 million human lives lost. On the other hand, Venezuela achieved vital importance during the conflagration, insofar as the Axis was using up its fuel supplies whereas the Allied armies advanced uncontainably like a gigantic crushing machine, thanks to the abundant supply of oil largely received from our country. The following data should be enough to ratify Venezuela's invaluable strategic participation in pro of the allies during the war:

Throughout World War Two the two main suppliers of oil to the Allied Forces were the United States and Venezuela. According to some estimates, from D-Day onwards, that is, from July 1944 onwards, close to 60% of the petroleum used by the Allies came from Venezuelan oil fields. This country produced 1,523,126,815 barrels of oil during the war. In other words, the fuel that enabled the allied war machinery to advance decisively and the final defeat of the Führer's armies came mostly from Venezuelan soil.

Thus, between 1938 and 1946, the pre- and post-war years, production in Venezuela rose from 515,000 to 1,064,000 barrels per day of crude. This means that production increased twofold.

Nevertheless, between 1942 and 1943, Venezuelan oil production decreased appreciably. This phenomenon had two explanations: first of all, during those years, many of the American and English employees working in our hydrocarbon industry were called to serve in the armies of their countries. This initially affected the organizational structure of the industry with the consequent results that have already been mentioned. But perhaps more damaging was the action of the German submarines that very effectively sank the tankers transporting our crude oil. These submarines came increasingly closer to the shores of our country. In this regard, Aníbal R. Martínez stated in his book entitled "A Chronology of The Venezuelan Oil" that in February of 1942 alone, seven tankers transporting crude oil from Lake Maracaibo to Curazao and Aruba had been torpedoed and sunked. (21)

However, by mid-1943, the Allies had put into practice the system of convoys, with which the efficacy of the German submarines was diminished. This enabled our production of crudes to increase once again and the following production levels were attained: 491,463 barrels per day in 1943, 702,288 in 1944, 886,040 in 945 and 1,064,326 in 1946.

Oil In The Post-War Era

Many people thought that when the war ended our oil production would once again start to decline. Nevertheless, the truth is that Venezuela was one of the countries indirectly favoured by the Marshall Plan. In effect, reconstruction efforts in Europe during the post-war period required huge quantities of energy; thereby our oil industry entered into an era of intense and burgeoning activity. By 1948, Venezuela already was the major world oil exporter. Now therefore, given the enormous production of crude oil that started to come also from the Middle East at the end of the war, an excess of production flooded the international oil markets which kept the prices of hydrocarbons at extremely low levels.

Going back to the years during the war, we must not forget to mention the events that occurred in the Persian Gulf. Four months before World War Two broke out, oil production started in Saudi Arabia. Some years before in Kuwait, an excellent natural port, at that time inhabited mainly by merchants and fishermen, concessions had likewise been granted for oil exploitation. In 1938, the British Petroleum Company discovered a productive reservoir in that country.

This was a start. Nevertheless, during the initial years, the oil companies were not too willing to put forth great efforts since they considered that their investments in that part of the world could be threatened by several factors: first, they obviously feared the possibility of German troops advancing, headed by the fearful General Rommel, the "Desert Fox". Secondly, many Arab leaders had pronounced themselves in favour of the policies of the Axis. Thus, for instance, since 1936 there had been a confrontation in Iraq among the anglophile and German-supporting factions, that ended in 1941 with the access to power of Rashid Ali al-Gailani, chief of the pro-German faction. This in turn provoked a British intervention and the government was overthrown. On the other hand, the Shah of Iran, Reza Khan Pahlevi had also expressed his sympathy to the German cause. For this reason, British and Soviet armies occupied the country. The Shah was forced to abdicate in favour of his son and heir, Mohammed Reza Pahlevi (subsequently overthrown in 1979).

From 1941 to 1945, accumulated oil production in the Middle East amounted to approximately 629 million barrels, or an average of 345,000 barrels per day. However, once the war was over, the Persian Gulf became an endless source of oil supply, inasmuch as astounding amounts of incredibly low-cost production oil flowed from its prolific fields.

In fact the economic boom felt in the entire world during the post-war era, which was prolonged until the beginning of the '70s, was based precisely on the abundant supply of cheap oil. It is significant that the three main areas of Western economy where the boom was mostly felt, i.e., engines, chemical products and electricity, were closely related to energy and definitely to petroleum.

On the other hand, the reconstruction of the countries devastated by the war generated an unsatiable demand for resources capable of financing these programs. Washington showed itself to be willing to provide the dollars required to accomplish the goals at hand, through the Marshall Plan, other foreign aid programs or soft loans. The result was the fastest and most prolonged economic expansion in history. International trade grew in the next twenty-five years at the astonishing average annual rate of 7.27%. Never before had anything like this been seen. Industrial expansion experienced a similar unaccustomed growth. To this effect, Paul Johnson stated in his book Modern Times:

"During the approximately 260 years, of which reasonable figures can be had, i.e. the period from 1705 to 1971, world mass industrial production increased 1,730 times. During the quarter century beginning from 1948, industrial production growth represented over half of that increase." (22)

Of course, the Venezuelan effort oil production-wise during the war and after, gave the country brilliant opportunities to undertake the path towards a process of sustained economic development. It is evident that due to the market surpluses, oil prices remained or were made to remain at absurdly low levels and this would have dramatic repercussions in later years. However, whether the prices were fair or not, the country received huge revenues and underwent important transformations, even though full and long-term advantage of the possibilities that were placed before it during these exceptional times were not taken.

Germany and Japan: Winners in the long term

We think it is now time to leave this subject, in order to present some considerations that will conclude this chapter. In this regard, we would like to mention that practically half a century after World War Two, in the long term, the two nations most favoured by the conflict have been Germany and Japan. In effect, despite the total destruction of the economies of these two nations, they have been capable of arising from the ashes, transforming themselves into two present-day giant industrial powers. Moral reserves, love of work and discipline constituted the forces that galvanized the spirit of these societies, enabling them to dedicate all their efforts towards reconstructing their homelands. In times of peace they achieved what they had not been able to achieve through war. The leaders of those nations plunged the world into a holocaust of terrifying proportions. If blame can be placed on the people of Germany and Japan it would be the fact that they let themselves be carried away by those leaders.

Perhaps, upon analyzing the aforementioned considerations and turning our gaze towards the infinite opportunities that have been wasted in the last fifty years, we, the Venezuelan people, should stop and declare a mea culpa, faced with the acknowledgment that we have also let ourselves been frequently led by populistic or incompetent demagogues or unscrupulous, corrupt and immoral leaders, who, due to their short-sightedness, have condemned the majority of our fellow countrymen to a life of misery.

CHAPTER I

NOTES

1.Edgar Black. CHURCHILL.page 324.

2.William L. Shirer. RISE AND FALL OF THE THIRD REICH. Volume 2. page 175.

3.Guidelines from the Führer No. 30. May 25th. 1941; FüHRER CONFERENCES ON NAVAL AFFAIRS. 1941. pages 50-52.

4.GREAT CHRONICLE OF THE SECOND WORLD WAR. Volume 2. page 239.

5.Albert Speer. MEMOIRS. page 422.

6.Albert Speer. IBIDEM. page 426.

7.William L. Shirer. OP. CIT.. Volume 2. page 465.

8.GREAT CHRONICLE OF THE SECOND WORLD WAR. Volume 1. page 360.

9.GREAT CHRONICLE OF THE SECOND WORLD WAR. Volume 1. page 361.

10."The result of Staff conversations among the representatives of the Venezuelan and American navies" chaired respectively by Commander Antonio Picardi. Naval Director for the Ministry of Warfare and Navy and Lieutenant Commander William S. Campbell.

11.Ministry of Foreign Affairs. Republic of Venezuela. CARACCIOLO PARRA PEREZ. VENEZUELAN CHANCELLOR 1941-1945. Caracas 1989. page 49.

12.Corrigan the State Secretary. NATIONAL U.S. ARCHIVES. "Foreign Relations: 1939-1944. 71000 Pacific World 7700: Telegram No. 280.

13.EL UNIVERSAL Daily. December 12th. 1941. page 1.

14.Ministry of Foreign Affairs. Republic of Venezuela. CARACCIOLO PARRA PEREZ. VENEZUELAN CHANCELLOR 1941-1945. page 67.

15.Ministry of Foreign Affairs. Republic of Venezuela. CARACCIOLO PARRA PEREZ. VENEZUELAN CHANCELLOR 1941-1945. page 9.

16.MIRAFLORES PALACE ARCHIVES. Caracas. Confidential note No. 443. from Parra Pérez to Corrigan. February 18th. 1942.

17.Edwen Lieuwen. PETROLEUM IN VENEZUELA. A HISTORY. Page 94.

18.MIRAFLORES PALACE ARCHIVES. Caracas. Attachment to the minutes of meeting. February 8th. 1945. folios 244 and 245.

19.OFFICIAL GAZETTE OF THE UNITED STATES OF VENEZUELA. February 16. 1945. Comuniqué: "Acknowledgment on the part of Venezuela to the state of belligerance against Germany and Japan". MINISTRY OF FOREIGN AFFAIRS.

20.GREAT CHRONICLE OF THE SECOND WORLD WAR. Volume 3. page 474.

21.Aníbal R. Martínez. A CHRONOLOGY OF VENEZUELAN PETROLEUM. page 114.

22.Paul Johnson. MODERN TIMES. page 662.

CHAPTER II

THE SUEZ CANAL CRISIS

The Nationalization of the Canal

Let us now analize the second crisis around which this book is centered: the Suez Canal crisis. This crisis opens up an era of conflicts in the Middle East, the effects of which would be frequently felt in the international oil markets.

On April 18th, 1954, a government council headed by Gamal Abdel Nasser took power in Egypt. Mr. Nasser was subsequently elected president during the plebiscite of 1956.

Nasser was a charismatic leader with an almost magical magnetism over the Arab masses. The "Bikbachi", as his admirers called him, knew like no-one how to appeal to the most eloquent phrases capable of inflaming the population, tensing and making the deepest ethnic and cultural fibers in the Arab nation vibrate like the strings of a violin, whose idiosincracy he knew better than anyone. The seduction of his words reached not only the multitudes in Cairo and Alexandria but also Algeria, Damascus, Riyadh, Beirut and other far-reaching corners of the Arab world. He was considered the avenger of the common shames of a people and the promoter of a modern nation, respectful of the traditional principles of a civilization that was centuries-old.

Nasser's political vision was based on a furious Pan-Arabian nationalism, strongly inspired by Nazi Germany, opposed to Western capitalism and evidently totalitarian. In this regard, the Egyptian leader clearly stated his views in his "Philosophy of the Egyptian Revolution" of which we hereby quote several phrases:

"Isolationism is over. Today, all nations must look farther than their frontiers"... "In the first place we must know that we are a group of neighbouring nations united by spiritual and moral

ties, more solid that any other ties that have united any other group of peoples"... "This is the first circle in which we must move. This circle is called the Arab zone. The second is the African continent... I call it the circle of our brothers, of those who, wherever they are, look, like us, towards Mecca (to pray)... I am convinced that the unity of the people of Islam can be achieved." (1)

Nasser's ability was such that he was even able to manipulate the Arab way of thinking in an area which is usually uncompromising: religious faith. Faith for a Muslim is more than a religion; it is a way of life. For the good Muslim, the Koran encompasses politics, laws, social behaviour, family relations. In conclusion, it is a synopsis of the entire human knowledge and wisdom. Nasser was probably the first Arab leader to handle the Koran at his will, in order to get the interpretations that matched his personal objectives.

By 1952, Nasser had, together with Mohammed Naguib, overthrown King Faruk, who had been given authority by the British. Soon after, Nasser arose as the first great native governor in Egypt in 2,500 years. He had contributed to end the military occupation in his country, forcing the British troops of more than 80,000 men to leave the territory. He had been the greatest manipulator of the great powers. He had crushed the communist party in Egypt but had procured Moscow's support in the construction of the Aswan dam. He opposed the Anglo-American plans to align the Middle East against the USSR, but had convinced the U.S. and Great Britain to provide economic aid to his country in order to counteract the influence of the Soviet aid. While he received massive aid in weapons from the Kremlin to prepare an attack against Israel, he organized an alliance among the Arab nations and a de facto alliance with Great Britain to thwart Iraq's intentions in failing to recognize Kuwait as an independent nation, with the blessing of the Kremlin.

The construction of the great Aswan dam, "seventeen times larger than the greatest pyramid", was Nasser's most important economic dream. To achieve it, Englishmen and Americans had offered their financial support. However, the United States Congress was hostile to the project and even forbade that funds allocated to the Mutual Security Act be used for the Egyptian project. Eisenhower had retired his personal support from the moment that Egypt decided to recognize the government of Red China and started to purchase weapons from Checoslovakia. In consequence, the U.S. and England decided not to go ahead with the project. Nasser reacted to this by nationalizing the Universal Suez Canal Company, owner of the canal, that belonged to a large consortium of eighteen nations headed by Great Britain and France.

Initially the U.S., England and France attempted to go ahead through diplomatic channels to avoid a confrontation with Egypt. After multiple failures, the case was taken to the Security Council of the United Nations without any acceptable conclusions for any of the parties.

In the meantime, Eisenhower wished above all else that the United States would not become involved in a war conflict in the Middle East. For this reason, he refused to sell arms to Israel and to the Arabs. He did not see with good eyes the warlike attitudes of France and Great Britain since he considered that said actions would lead the Egyptians to invite the USSR to meddle in the area.

The Invasion of Egypt

The United Kingdom and France lost the diplomatic game. That was when the sound of weapons started to be heard. In effect, the night of October 29th, 1956, Israeli armored divisions under the orders of General Moshe Dayan, swiftly took over the

Gaza strip and invaded the Sinai peninsula in a sudden attack that would take them to the shores of the Canal itself, unstopped by the "death volunteers" and the armored "Bikbachi" units.

On October 30th England and France declared that the safety to navigate the canal was endangeeed and gave the Egyptian government 12 hours to consent to English and French troops entering to protect it. Nasser rejected this ultimatum.

The Egyptian leader understood that his main defense was oil and therefore blocked the Suez Canal for the first time on October 31st by simply sinking a vessel. In answer to Nasser's petition the Syrians blew up on November 3rd several pipeline installations that transported oil from Iraq to the Mediterranean. For the first time this leader proposed that the Arab oil-producing states apply an embargo on its oil supplies to the Western hemisphere. This set of actions deprived the countries of Western Europe of about 2.2 million barrels per day of petroleum, equivalent to two thirds of the consumption of those nations.

On November 1st, 1956, the two abovementioned European nations initiated an aerial attack against Cairo, Port Said, Ismailia and Suez. The brand new "Migs" supplied to Nasser by the Soviets were destroyed and, with them, Egypt's remotest chances of defending itself. On November 5th, English and French troops disembarked in Port Said.

Now that the Israelis dominated one side of the Canal and the anglo-French troops occupied strategic positions in Egyptian territory, it was evident that Egypt had been defeated. Nasser could consider himself wiped out of the political arena. However, when least expected, the "Eisenhower doctrine" came to rescue the Egyptian leader. In effect, the President of the U.S. interceded and paralyzed the attack of the European powers.

Eisenhower had lived through the horrors of World War Two and had become a pacifist. His motto was "my program is for peace and bonanza". Once more, faced with the Suez crisis, the American president exerted all his influence in favour of reducing the risks of a new war.

Trying to attain backing by the U.S. and to convince its president of the risk represented by Nasser, Anthony Eden, the British Prime Minister, addressed a letter in 1956 in which he told the president that:

"We are convinced that the capture of the Canal is the beginning of a move as part of a campaign planned by Nasser to exclude all Western influence or interests from the Arab countries. He believes that if he gets his way by challenging the eighteen nations, his prestige in Arabia shall grow so large that this will enable him to organize revolutions of young officials in Saudi Arabia, Jordan and Iraq... These new governments would in practice be satellites of Egypt, if not of Russia. The joint oil resources of these nations would be placed under the control of a united Arabia led by Egypt and influenced by Russia. When the time came, Nasser could deny petroleum to Western Europe and we shall be at his mercy." (2)

However, Eisenhower was not convinced. The U.S. was enjoying an "affluent decade"(3), according to J.K. Galbraith in his well-known book "The Affluent Society", which sustained that the advanced economies had already solved the problem of the production of goods in sufficient quantities and that now the only problem left was the equal distribution of said goods. Capitol Hill therefore did not want such optimistic perspectives to be thwarted through new war adventures.

The American president also had a very definite stance in this regard. In effect, in 1950, the United States, Great Britain and

France had entered into a so-called Tripartite Declaration, and had committed themselves to maintaining the status quo in the Middle East and to respecting existing frontiers. They had also pledged not to sell weapons to the nations in the region that would break the balance of forces. According to photographs procured through U-2 spy planes, the CIA was able to prove that France had broken this commitment and had sold 60 "Mystère" planes to Israel. In the beginning, the American intelligence agency supposed that these planes were destined to attack Jordan and for this reason Eisenhower sent a message to Ben-Gurion, the Israeli chief of government, stating that he should stop his attacks on the Jordan border because if they continued, the Arabs would finally resort to Russia to purchase weapons and the final effect could be the "Sovietization" of the entire region, including Israel.

Finally, Eisenhower realized his mistake. The weapons sold by France were destined in fact to attacking Egypt. In view of those circumstances, the White House demanded that the two allied European nations accept the Tripartite Agreement and abstain from meddling in Egypt by force. In Eisenhower's biography written by Stephen E. Ambrose, the author states:

"He (Eisenhower) said that the U.S. "must let the British know how gravely we view this matter, what an error we think their decision is, and how this course of action would antagonize the American people... 'As to the British claims that Egypt had committed a crime, Eisenhower could only say that 'Nasser was within his rights' and that 'the power of eminent domain within his own territory could scarcely be doubted'."* (4)

Eisenhower did not want to run the risk of an eventual multiplication of conflicts that would create new confrontations with the USSR. From 1953 when the Korean War had ended, the United States was trying to avoid getting involved in new conflicts. This attitude had been repeated in Indochina in 1954 and in Formosa in 1955. To make matters worse, simultaneous to the events in the Middle East, a popular uprising was taking place in Hungary and the citizens of Budapest were throwing Molotov bombs against the Russian tanks that were trying to restablish peace and order in that country behind the "Iron Curtain".

The risk of a confrontation with Russia was evident. In fact, Moscow had addressed a categorical ultimatum to the three governments that had attacked Egypt. The entire planet trembled, faced with the threat of a new world war.

Under the circumstances, Eisenhower's reaction was twofold. On the one hand, he pronounced himself categorically against the "political adventure" undertaken by his European allies - England and France - without the knowledge of the United Nations. In effect, the U.S. had proposed a ceasefire in Egypt before the General Assembly of the UN, and this had been approved. The White House had even imposed an embargo against the sale of oil to the British. On the other hand, he could not remain indifferent to the Soviet ultimatum and gave orders to the Atlantic fleet to set out for the Mediterranean in case of a contingency.

Washington's pressure forced England and France to renounce their actions. In fact, both countries knew that in order to maintain their military positions in the region and to pay for their energy requirements, they needed the financial support of the United States. The war had already cost London over 500 million dollars, an amount that they were evidently not in a position to cover.

Thus, the British and French unwillingly obeyed the decision approved by the UN to cease fire and by the end of November, the Peace Forces of that organism disembarked in Egypt, meanwhile the French, British and Israeli forces pulled out.

In the White House, Eisenhower was able to breathe in peace once more, since not only did he fear Nasser's capacity to pull the Arab nations towards him but was also increasingly concerned about the possible support he could garner from the Soviet Union, in which case the Russian influence in the Middle East would increase considerably.

The United States government likewise organized a gigantic operation to save Europe from the effects of the oil shortage due to the Suez Canal crisis. Venezuela also played a relevant role in this salvage operation. The logistics of the operation implied the deviation of countless tankers and the relocation of the oil production of many nations:

"The emergency aid plan for Europe... was perhaps the second most important program, surpassed only by the Marshall plan, as to the grandiose scale of its design and magnitude of operations." (5)

Nasser defeated/Nasser the hero

Nasser's military defeat was transformed into a resounding political victory. Without the possibility of being deprived of the crude they required and without resources to pay for the higher oil prices that the crisis had brough about, France and England finally gave up and withdrew from Egypt on November 6th of that same year. Nasser thereafter took possession of the Suez Canal. Navigation was reinstated with Egyptian pilots now guiding the vessels and the absence of the European pilots or technicians that had abandoned their duties was not missed in the least.

On the other hand, knowing that once England and France withdrew, Egypt and Syria would attempt to take revenge of Israel, the United Nations sent peace units to watch over the

Egyptian-Israeli border. These units kept the peace precariously for ten years, during which time Egypt never ceased to prepare its vengeance.

The elimination of the English influence in Cairo brought about between 1957 and 1967 a progressively smaller military and political presence of any power whose influence had been decisively dominant in the Middle East. In spite of this, Great Britain, now with a lessened profile, maintained relative stability in the region. However, the Suez fiasco led the British to adopt a policy of progressive withdrawal from Aden and the Persian Gulf, that was completed in the '60s. After that, no international "police" existed in the area. The Shah of Iran would attempt to cover this void by creating a powerful army backed by the U.S.

The success achieved by Nasser with the nationalization of the Canal and the expulsion of England and France greatly increased his prestige in the entire region and created a vacuum of power in the Middle East. This situation enabled the Egyptian president to thrive in such a manner that he seemed to be involved in practically all the important events in the Arab countries until 1970.

In the meantime, Nasser continued to strengthen his military position thanks to Moscow's support and continued to extend his political influence over the Arab states. 1958 marked a decisive point for the Egyptian leader. For instance:

On February 1st, 1958, Nasser achieved a new and spectacular success by reaching an integration agreement with Syria. Thus, the United Arab Republic (UAR) was proclaimed, its president being none other than Nasser. During the proclamation ceremonies, Syrian president Kuwaiti handed over power to the Egyptian leader, but warned him that:

"You are taking charge of a nation of politicians; fifty percent believe themselves to be national leaders, twenty-five percent think they are prophets and at least ten percent believe they are gods." (6)

This was the medium that best suited Nasser, and where he felt in his element. The citizens of the UAR understood perfectly the language of their new head of government. However, Nasser's achievements did not stop there.

In effect, on March 8th, 1958, a peculiar confederation with the reigning monarchy in Yemen was set up. The confederation constituted between the UAR and Yemen was called United Arab States. It seemed as if Nasser's policies in achieving a great Arab nation with one sole leader at its head were well under way.

In 1958, Nasser opposed the pretensions of Camille Chamoun, the Lebanese president, in trying to renew his presidential term. Chamoun asked Washington for help. This time the White House had already learnt its lesson and knew that somehow Egyptian expansionism had to be stopped. Thus, American infantry marines were sent to Beirut. Nasser, always opposed to intervention in the region by the great powers, except when it suited him, became furious. Manifestations and uprisings in Cairo led to a civil war in March 1958. President Chamoun's government was thereby overthrown and power passed to General Fuad Chehab, who counted with Nasser's blessing.

On February 25th, 1955, the so-called Baghdad Pact, inspired by the British, was created and signed by England and Turkey, Iran, Pakistan and Iraq. Jordan would subsequently enter into this pact. To confront the proselytism of the UAR, King Hussein of Jordan and King Faisal II of Iraq created the Arab Federation in 1958. Jordan, feeling protected by an efficient army organized by the legendary English general Glubb Pachá, broke off relations with the United Arab Republic. This deeply annoyed Nasser, who resorted to all the means in his power, including terrorism, subversion and conspiracies, to overthrow Hussein. By means of inflammatory speeches broadcast through Radio Cairo, he promoted rebellions that greatly endangered the future of the Jordan monarchy. He also trained Palestine commandoes to launch attacks against Israel from Jordan territory. This brought about Tel Aviv's unavoidable retaliations against Jordan. To protect the government of Hussein, England decided to send paratroopers to Jordan.

Not content with this, Nasser's forces plotted against the monarchy in Iraq, which was overthrown in 1958. King Faisal II and the heir prince Abdull Illah were murdered and power passed to the hands of General Abdull Karim Kassem, who proclaimed the country a republic. Soon afterwards, in 1959, Iraq withdrew from the Baghdad Pact and the Arab Federation was dissolved.

In 1959, recognizing his powerlessness in the events promoted by Nasser from Cairo, King Hussein of Jordan was left with no other choice but to submit fully to the intentions of the Egyptian leader. In this manner, Jordan restablished the relations with the UAR that had been broken the previous year.

In 1960 the second congress of the Arab Federation Unions, dominated by followers of Nasser, approved a set of resolutions reflecting the leader's true intentions: that the oil wealth of the Arab nations should be deemed the property of the Arab nation as a whole; that the oil revenues from Saudi Arabia should be distributed to meet the needs of the entire Arab population; and that oil concessions should be reconverted so as to reflect the nationalistic aspirations of the Arab people.

Nasser however had his share of mishaps. A coup d'etat occurred in Syria in 1960. Damask called elections, subsequently won by the conservative party and Syria withdrew from the United Arab Republic and entered the United Nations. This constituted a hard blow for Nasser's Pan-Arabian dreams, though these hindrances did not make him lose faith.

On June 16th, 1961, the United Kingdom recognized the independent state of Kuwait. Six days later Abdull Kassem, Iraq's head of government, opposed this alleging that in times of the disappeared Ottoman empire, Kuwait had been part of the Turkish government of Basora, which in turn was part of the present-day Iraqi territory. Backed by Moscow, Baghdad attempted to annex Kuwait. Gamal Abder Nasser opposed these intentions. In effect, although he always maneuvred between the two superpowers and requested and accepted aid from the USSR, Nasser was not a communist. Kassem, openly pro-Soviet, was a menace for the leadership of the Egyptian ruler. Therefore, in order to thwart the aspirations of the Iraqui ruler, Nasser exerted all his influence for the Arab League to back and give aid to Kuwait. The Arab League prepared to send Egyptian, Sudanese, Saudi Arabian and Jordan troops. The British had already sent their forces to Kuwaiti territory to protect it from Kassem's ambitions.

Kassem was overthrown and executed in 1963 by a coup led by the pro-Egyptian Coronel Abdull Salam Aref. In the conspiracy that led to this outcome, Nasser's influence was undoubtedly present.

On the other hand, by stirring up the traditional hatred among the clan of hashemites that ruled in Jordan and the Saudis in Arabia, Nasser had obtained the support of Saudi Arabia in his plans against Hussein. In fact, never had Riyadh been witness to such a reception as the one afforded Nasser in 1956. However, by 1961, the royal Saudi family looked upon

CHAPTER II

Nasser with mistrust, because of the latter's constant and increasingly evident maneuvers against the monarchies in the region. Besides, by 1964, Nasser was continuously demanding the evacuation of American and British military bases in Aden, the Persian Gulf and Libya.

The Egyptian leader's political skills was once more put in evidence in 1965. In effect, on April 25th of that year, he dissolved the Egyptian communist party but days later signed an agreement by means of which the USSR committed itself to supplying 300,000 tons of wheat.

In 1967 the government of President Johnson entrusted Julius Holmes, the former American ambassador in Iran, to carry out a study on the geopolitical situation in the Middle East. The committee that made that study concluded that, thanks to USSR backing, Nasser constituted a threat for U.S. interests in Arab countries. There was an evident risk that Nasser's policies could spread to countries such as Jordan, Lebanon, Libya, Tunisia, Morrocco, Saudi Arabia and throughout the Persian Gulf in general.

The threat posed by this situation on the oil industry was picked up in the Middle East Economic Survey, a very prestigious oil publication that frequently reflected the positions of the Saudi Arabian government.

While all this was happening, Nasser was able to transform Cairo's cultural supremacy into an ideologic weapon. Great universities were founded in Egypt that would become centers of intellectual attraction in the entire Middle East region. For this purpose, Nasser did not hesitate in obtaining support from the best American universities. He hired professors from Harvard, aware that he had to educate an Arab managerial class to replace the Westerners that he wished to expel.

Likewise, Nasser was the first leader to recognize that oil could and should be waged as a powerful weapon to pursue Pan-Arabian purposes.

"Remember that our enemies are taking possession of the oil that springs from its soil. Remember that oil is your lost wealth. Oil must be for the Arabs" proclaimed Nasser in one of his speeches. (7)

This position showed an incredible ability, since Egypt was no oil-producing country but was nevertheless capitalizing on the leader's own political influence.

To complete the hysterical adoration of the masses towards him and to achieve not only full domain over them but also the forced support of the other Muslim rulers, Nasser resorted to the hatred felt by the Arab people against their biggest common enemy: Israel.

However, Israel was only a political recourse to achieve his true objective: to become the greatest leader in a united Arab world in which oil would come to be the property of the entire Arab nation and not only the property of those who produced it.

"Petroleum must be for the Arabs..." he repeated incessantly. *"Oil is the vital nerve of civilization and without it, civilization can no longer exist..."* (8)

The Six Day War

Nevertheless, the hatred against Israel that he contributed to spread acquired such force that at a given moment it escaped from his hands. The increasing tension between that nation and Syria would force it to take a pro-Arab stance, even though it feared that a war with Israel would not be easy to win. However, to show solidarity with the Pan-Arabian principles so openly proclaimed, he proceeded to close the Gulf of Akaba, an important naval artery for Israeli traffic in the Red Sea. At the same time, he increased the deployment of Egyptian troops in the Sinai peninsula.

Finally, on May 16th, 1967, Egypt requested that the United Nations peace force be withdrawn. Dag Hammarskjold, Secretary General of the UN, aware of the consequences that this could bring about, could not oppose this request without violating the principles of sovereignty that the members of the organization had a right to.

Three days later the forces had been withdrawn and that same night Radio Cairo broadcast the following:

"Arab fellowmen, this is our chance to deal a mortal blow to Israel and annihilate that nation". Nasser stated the following: "Our fundamental objective shall be the destruction of Israel." President Aref of Iraq expressed that: "Our goal is clear: to erase Israel from the map." Ahmed Shukairy, president of the Palestinian Liberation Organization, proclaimed: "The Jews in Palestine shall have to leave... the surviving members of the former Jewish population in Palestine may remain, but my impression is that none of them shall."(9)

Under these circumstances, the Jewish state launched a preventive attack on June 4th, 1967. During the first three hours of this offensive, fifteen years' worth of Nasser's achievements and hopes were dashed. In effect, 300 Israeli planes flying at low heights over the desert to avoid Egyptian radars, attacked in the early hours of the morning. By midday, over 80% of the air force that Nasser had been able to gather with such effort, pride and hope, were destroyed in the Egyptian bases without even having set flight.

The powerful Egyptian army land forces of over one hundred thousand men strategically located in the Sinai Peninsula had lost their air protection. In this manner, they were left defenseless faced with the attacks of the Israeli airforce and were quickly annihilated. On the third day of the invasion, the Jewish army had occupied the Sinai Peninsula and had reached the shores of the Suez Canal. Nothing was in the way between this and Cairo. However, Israel deviated its attention to the armies of Syria and Jordania, Nasser's allies. These were also efficiently and swiftly swept away, leaving the Golan heights - from where Syria periodically bombed the Jewish population in Upper Galilee - in Israeli hands.

Thus, the Suez Canal that had been snatched from the hands of the British, was now threatened by the even more hated Jewish army. The Muslims whom Nasser had called to the holy task of Islamic restoration, lost even their sacred sites in Jerusalem. The great Aswan dam that was about to be concluded thanks to Soviet backing, was now defenseless.

In conclusion, during the short time space between the 4th and 9th of June, 1967, the Jewish forces led once again by General Moshe Dayan, inflicted the most complete defeat to the combined armies of three nations, which not only were triple their number, but were also heavily armed with modern warfare supplied by the Soviet Union. The outcome of the operations was so swift that the forces being speedily sent by Iraq, Algeria, Morrocco, Sudan, Kuwait and even Saudi Arabia to help the desperate Egyptian army, never had time to arrive at their destination. The military action described in the previous lines was called the "Six Day War".

While all this was happening, the Arab people continued to believe that their armies were triumphing over the hated enemy. Finally, on June 8th, Nasser was forced to publicly announce defeat. Before the distressed public listening to the dramatic broadcast on Radio Cairo, he accepted personal responsibility for what had happened and stated that he had made up his mind to resign and to designate Zacharias Mohieddin, the Vice President, as his successor.

The French daily Le Monde described the scenario in Cairo thus:

"In the semidarkness of the streets, hundreds of thousands, some men still in pajamas and women in nightdresses, came out of their houses crying and yelling: 'Nasser, Nasser, do not leave us, we need you.' The noise grew like a storm approaching. The entire population seemed to be mourning. Dozens of thousands met at the National Assembly, shouting 'Nasser, Nasser' and threatening to kill any congressman who would not vote for Nasser. Half a million persons thronged the five miles from Nasser's residence at Manshiet el Bakri in the center of Cairo to watch out for Nasser during the night, to make sure that he would go the following day to the National Assembly to withdraw his resignation. Millions more started to arrive at Cairo from all parts of Egypt to ensure that Nasser would stay."(10)

Since nothing blocked the way for the Israeli army to enter Cairo, Nasser, fearful of the Jewish advance, decided to resort to a tactic that he had successfully used in 1956: to block the Suez Canal with mines and sunken ships. The Arab nations declared an initial oil embargo against the U.S. and Great Britain, presumably allies of Israel.

Thus Nasser from the abyss of defeat imposed an historic change, the scope of which would be of tremendous consequences for world economy in the future. Professor Benjamin Shwadran, an eminent oil historian in the Middle East, stated that:

"This development of establishing an oil boycott against consumer nations due to political considerations constituted a radical innovation in modern Arab history."(11)

Petroleum: "The Sword of Islam"

Hydrocarbons in the Arab world became from that time on a political weapon. For the Arabs, petroleum was transformed into a political instrument, economic considerations taking second place. Thus, with Nasser, oil became the sword of Islam. This was a sword that had not yet been controlled but that in time would come to terrorize Western democracies, placing the world at large more than once on the brink of a new world war.

In effect, as time would prove, the Suez Canal Crisis unleashed an Arab action and hardened that people's attitude towards the Western hemisphere.

In an unprecedented act of political juggling, Nasser politically survived the thunderous failure represented by the Six Day War. The Arab masses themselves were clamouring for him to stay in power.

During a brief period a substantial part of oil shipments from the region to the Western world were interrupted. Nasser attempted by all means to convince the governments of the region's oil-producing nations to continue the embargo. His followers also tried to sabotage oil installations to force a decrease in the flow of crude.

But other Arab governments did not have the same respect for him. The Saudi government arrested 800 pro-Nasser workers suspected of sabotage and started to deport Palestinian workers.

The same measure was adopted in other nations subjected to uprisings supporting Nasser's position.

Soon afterwards, Arab producers reinstated their shipment of crudes to the Western world, stipulating in principle that these shipments could not be destined to the U.S. nor Great Britain. Concerned about the swift increase in production ordered by the Shah of Iran and fearful of losing his markets to that nation for ever, King Faisal of Saudi Arabia decided not to follow Nasser's game and ordered the ARAMCO to increase production without this being announced.

Thus, the oil embargo that the Arabs attempted to impose for the second time ended up a failure. According to Abdulaziz al-Sowayegh, a Saudi Arabian oil expert (who later became the Vice Minister of Information in that country), this failure was due to the following reasons:

"1.- The U.S., the fundamental target of the Arab oil weapon, was immune to the oil embargo because at the time it was fully self-sufficient in terms of oil supply coming from the Western hemisphere.

2.- International oil companies carried out an exceptional effort to compensate the shortage of Arab petroleum due to the closure of the Suez Canal, with oil coming from other sources...

3.- No production ceilings were imposed as a result of which no real physical shortage of oil was created.

4 .- There was no unanimous interpretation regarding the scope of the embargo..."(12)

A conference of ministers of Arab countries met in Khartoum in August to define two positions: one the one hand, Egypt, Syria, Algeria and Iraq proposed a "war economic plan". Even

Iraq came to request the complete shutdown of oil production until such time as Israel withdrew from the occupied territories. The more radical Arab nations insisted that the growing dependence of Europe on Middle East oil that had tripled between 1956 and 1967, placed the former in an extremely delicate situation. European industrial production would become paralyzed if the proposed embargo was kept. Saudi Arabia, Kuwait, Libya, Jordan, Morrocco and Tunisia were opposed to this proposal. The balance finally leant in favour of the latter, when Minister Yamani of Saudi Arabia, convinced the attendants that the oil boycott was harming the Arabs more than anyone:

"The only ones benefitting are Iran, Venezuela and America, that are busy occupying the markets abandoned by the Arabs." (13)

One month later, in September 1967, a new conference was held in Khartoum, this time involving the chiefs of state, during which, it was officially decided to end the boycott.

Once again resorting to an incredible political instinct, Nasser realized that in Khartoum his Pan-Arabian aspirations had been destroyed. It was no longer possible to convince the oil producing states to sacrifice themselves through a boycott or an oil embargo. Therefore, he resignates himself to getting the best he possibly could for his country. To achieve this, he undertook a new role. He knew he could not continue being the leader of all the Arabs, at least for the time being, nor the leader of the more radical Arab nations. He therefore took on the role of moderator in the disputes that arose among the conservative monarchies and the radical dictatorships. In this manner he finally convinced Saudi Arabia, Kuwait and Libya to grant Egypt and Jordan an annual contribution of 378 million dollars to reconstruct their destroyed economies. At the time this was an appreciable sum that represented an important percentage of the revenues from the countries giving this grant. Syria, however, maintained its radical stance previously defended by Nasser and was awarded nothing.

To ensure that the future destiny of the Arab oil nations would not be tied to eventual political adventures undertaken by Nasser or other radical leaders, King Faisal promoted during the meeting the constitution of the Organization of Petroleum-Exporting Arab Countries (OPEAC) which at the time was constituted by the three greatest oil monarchies in the Arab world: Saudi Arabia, Kuwait and Lybia. The articles of incorporation of the organization excluded de facto the more radical Arab countries such as Egypt and Syria, which had no oil, and other non-Arab oil nations such as Venezuela and Iran. The OPEAC was finally put into force in Beirut in January 1968.

Despite the evident differences between the conservative monarchies and the more radical Arab nations, the truth was that the Khartoum meeting saw the rise of a policy strengthening the use of hydrocarbons for ideologic purposes. This policy consisted in applying the revenues from the oil to achieve the goals of the Arab nation. In conclusion, oil would continue to be waged as a political weapon.

Nasser was not an easy bone to chew. Him being a cunning player, he had assimilated his defeat, dodged its consequences and fine-tuned his new strategy. From his overwhelming defeat before the Jewish armies in 1967, little by little he had reconstructed his position of leadership. In fact, not only did he count on Soviet backing but he had also managed to divide the European nations, positions that varied from a passive powerlessness to active stances such as France, the common denominator being the fear of the damage wrought by a new conflict in the Middle East. In effect, after the Six Day War, De Gaulle had embraced the Arab cause. For the French president this represented not only one more chapter in his traditional anti-American attitude but also a guarantee that his nation would not be affected by the periodic Arab-Israeli crises. In fact, on June 16th, 1969, France proposed consultancy meetings among that country and the U.S., the USSR, England for the purpose of seeking a solution to the growing tensions among Arabs and jews.

The positions were now defined. The USSR and France supported the Arab petitions that Israel withdraw unconditionally to the frontiers existing before the Six Day War. In practice, however, there was no way that Israel would voluntarily accept this imposition unless the four superpowers guaranteed in turn a permanent peace and safe borders. This was another story. Nasser's promises were vague at best but did not seem willing to accept final commitments.

The U.S. did not seem too willing to stand the consequences of an agreement. Kissinger sums up in his memoirs the American position:

"Our dilemma was that if we put pressure on Israel we would promote the Arab radicals and the Soviet customers that would see it as a vindication of their intolerance and their relations with the Soviets; for the same reason, this pressure could also lead Israel to extremes or at least to dig their heels in and concede nothing. If, on the other hand, we failed to pressure Israel, the fault of this stagnation would lie on us. In case Israel were to agree to set conditions, the palestinians probably would block the agreement with syrian and iraqi support"... "In other words, given the influence and intolerance of the Soviets, Nasser's activism and the power of the fedayeens" Kissinger argumented, "the Middle East was not ready for a full American initiative."(14)

In the meantime, tensions in the Middle East reappeared frequently. In effect, Nasser mantained up to 1970 a wear-and-tear war against Israel. Skirmishes occurred daily throughout the Suez Canal. In an attempt to end this situation, Israel decided to initiate air attacks in January 1970, bombing the outskirts of Cairo. In this manner that nation pretended to put in evidence before the entire world but above all before the Arabs, the helplessness of the Egyptian leader.

Prime Minister Golda Meir came to believe that peace could not be possible so long as Nasser ruled Egypt. The situation became increasingly conflictive with clashes between Israel and Syria in the Golan heights. Attacks by fedayeens became commonplace and also Israeli retaliations. In the midst of this endless situation, the two great powers became ever more involved. In effect in January 1970, Nasser secretly visited Moscow to try and get more support from the USSR.

The result was immediate. On January 31st, 1970, Alexei Kosygin, the Soviet premier, sent a letter to President Nixon, warning him that Israel had recommenced military operations against the Arab states. If the attacks continued, the letter said, "the Soviet Union shall be forced to make sure that the Arab states have means available to definitely repeal the arrogant aggressor." Kosygin likewise asked that Israel be "forced" to cease its attacks and to withdraw its troops from the occupied Arab territories.

During the analysis meetings that the president held with Kissinger at the White House, the Middle East subject came up time and time again. In one of his memoranda, Nixon stated that:

"We have been rejoicing in the Soviet defeats in the Middle East in '67 - and the State Department and its collaborators said that the June war was a defeat for the Soviets -. But it wasn't.

They became friends of the Arabs and the United States became their enemy. (In) the long term (this) is what suits their interests."(15)

Nixon was right, at least regarding some Arab nations. Despite the pressures exerted by the States on Israel - that led that nation to finally accept a ceasefire against the Arabs on March 17th, 1970 - the USSR had already committed its support to Nasser and considered that this would give it a growing influence over the Middle East.

In effect, the Soviets had sent not only 1,500 military consultants to Egypt but also a great cargo of weapons that included SA-3 land-air missiles, deemed to be the most advanced Russian antiair system. This type of weaponry had never been given by Moscow to any other foreign nation, not even to North Vietnam. However, Nixon did not want to provoke a scaling in this situation so he kept his previous decision of keeping in suspense an arms supply package to Israel.

"In this manner" Kissinger stated in his memoirs, *"the Middle East crisis became more acute. On May 1st, Nasser directed an open message to Nixon during a speech whose peremptory tone highlighted the weakening of our position. The United States 'must order Israel to withdraw from the occupied Arab territories'. If we could not achieve this, Nasser demanded that we abstain 'from giving any new support to Israel so long as that country continued to occupy our Arab territories, whether it be political, military or economic aid'. Otherwise, 'the Arabs shall have to arrive at the unavoidable conclusion that the United States wish Israel to continue occupying our territories..."(16)*

It was thus evident that Nasser was skillfully maneuvering the situation. Moscow was offered a growing influence in the Middle East. The Arabs were given the possibility of revenge against Israel with backing by the USSR. Simultaneously, he put in a spot the situation of pro-Western Arab rulers such as King Faisal of Saudi Arabia, whose position was evidently weakening in front of his own people, by insinuating that he was an ally of the U.S., who in turn was an ally of Israel. To counteract this impression, moderate Arab rulers were once again forced to fall into Nasser's game, putting at his disposal the economic aid he required to reconstruct his own influence as well as his armies, in order to prepare for a new confrontation with Israel. In this manner the bases were being set for a new chapter in the unavoidable and endless conflict in the Middle East.

On September 28, 1970, Gamal Abdel Nasser died due to a heart attack. He was 49 years old. The effects of his actions would last however for a long time. After his disappearance, many Arab leaders have tried to emulate him. The new conflict gestated by him would follow its unstoppable course until finally, in the autumn of 1973, a new crisis of dire consequences would explode.

Upon his death, Nasser was succeeded by Anuar al-Sadat, barely known at the time although he had been part of the group of officers that had overthrown King Farouk in 1952. The new head of state had a difficult task before him. Succession of a figure of the stature of Nasser was an almost impossible task; therefore it was thought that he would be no more than an interim figure. In fact, during the first moments two different reactions took place throughout the Arab countries. On the one hand, the population was disillusioned when they saw that the new Egyptian ruler lacked the eloquence that fired the masses to a paroxism of nationalistic fervour. On the other hand, the conservative monarchies breathed more freely once left without that uncomfortable leader whose infinite political resources kept them in his power. Let us once more resort to Kissinger, an exceptional eyewitness to these events that would relate the reigning impression. In his memoirs he referred to Sadat in the following terms:

"He gradually consolidated his internal situation and his freedom of action in the international sphere. Even then few observers (myself not included) became aware that his courage, vision and decision would in the future carry his nation and his region towards an international political revolution, thus showing himself to be one of the great leaders of our time."(17)

On the other hand Sadat could not and did not wish to stop the course of Arab vengeance that his predecessor had set in motion. In this regard, one must not forget that Saudi Arabia, the richest country in the region, though conservative, was ruled by a theocratical monarchy that could not see with good eyes that Islam's sacred sites in Jerusalem had fallen into jewish hands. That is why a new Arab-Israeli conflict was unavoidable. However, in the future, those monarchies would play the game by their own rules, without being led astray by a populistic leader like Nasser that endangered the stability of the Arab ruling houses in the Persian Gulf. This however did not change the basis of the thesis expounded by the Egyptian leader. Nevertheless, destiny would not allow the author of this thesis to see the success with which oil, the "sword of Islam" would be wielded in a not too far future by its coreligionists not only of the Arab world but from Iran as well. In conclusion, it seemed as if Nasser's prophesy would become true in achieving a unified criterion of those whom he called

"our brothers, those who, wherever they are, pray in the direction of Mecca." (18)

The Closure of the Suez Canal

In any event, as a result of the Six Day War, the Suez Canal had remained closed to international navigation and would stay so for eight years until 1975. The Canal could not be reopened because since the conflict a state of impending war between Egypt and Israel was maintained and each side controlled one of the shores of the canal.

To understand the trascendence of this fact, suffice it to mention that by the '60s over 15 percent of the world's maritime traffic passed through the Suez Canal. The close of this canal brought about specially serious repercussions in the international oil markets. One must not forget that the hydrocarbons coming from the abundant fields of the Persian Gulf and mainly Iran, Kuwait and Saudi Arabia - that at the time held close to 50% of known proved oil reserves - reached Western markets through the Suez Canal. In fact, about three million barrels of crude went through the canal daily.

Once the canal was blocked the oil tankers were forced to take a considerably longer route going to to the cape of Good Hope, bordering the entire African continent before reaching the markets in Western Europe. This implied an added round trip distance of close to 9,500 nautical miles. Now therefore, since more time was needed to cover this route, the existent tankers were insufficient to transport the volumes of oil needed by the final markets thereof.

The industrialized nations finally solved the economic dilemma that they were facing as a result of the conflict. To decrease dependence on Nasser's policies and his allies, the oil companies had been developing since 1956 due to the first close of the canal new supply sources of oil located in areas closer to the European markets, such as the case of Algeria, Lybia and Nigeria. By 1960, North African oil had achieved a 4 percent share of oil consumption in the Western European countries. By the end of the '60s this share had reached 30%.

However it is worthwhile mentioning that the second closure of the Suez Canal did not take the Western consumers by surprise. Knowing the risk that Nasser represented, they had already taken steps in case of emergency. Thus, the European nations decided to create crude reserves for this possibility. Whereas Great Britain, to give an example, had oil reserves for up to six weeks in 1956, by 1967 the average inventories in Western Europe could last for over four months. Other producing countries such as Venezuela, Iran, Indonesia and the United States increased their production to make up for the deficits in Europe, in such a way that the tankers that previously used to cross the Suez Canal simply modified their routes.

Likewise, to decrease dependency on the Canal and Syria's pipelines, new supertankers were designed and built with capacities of around 200 to 300 thousand tons. This decreased freight prices. These new tankers were so huge that they could not go through the Canal. Some of them could transport up to three and a half million barrels of oil in just one trip.

The implementation of the entire set of solutions required however several years. While this was achieved, the world once again faced an energy crisis. During that time, Venezuelan oil once more took on a starring role in the world markets.

For purposes of illustration we can confirm that between 1956, the nationalization of the Suez Canal and 1970, the year in which the industrialized world had adapted to the maladjustments of the closure of the canal, Venezuelan oil production increased continuously from 2.4 million barrels per day the first year mentioned to a production of 3.7 million barrels by 1970.

Although oil prices did not experience increments during that period - except for a short time - the increased production volumes and the enormous revenues collected by the country as a result of the concessions granted in 1956 and 1957, gave Venezuela an extraordinary mass of monetary resources, that, if properly applied, would have placed our country in the position of achieving the economic development goals corresponding to our potential of wealth.

One cannot deny however that during the '50s the country accomplished significant economic achievements.

Notes

1.-Gamal Abdel Nasser. THE PHILOSOPHY OF THE REVOLUTION.

2.-Jack Anderson with James Boyd. OIL, THE REAL STORY BEHIND THE WORLD ENERGY CRISIS. page 170.

3.-J.K. Galbraith. THE AFFLUENT SOCIETY.

4.-Stephen E. Ambrose. EISENHOWER, SOLDIER AND PRESIDENT. page 416.

5.-Shoshana Klebanoff. "OIL FOR EUROPE: American FOREIGN POLICY AND MIDDLE EAST OIL". page 251.

6.-Jack Anderson with James Boyd. OP.CIT. page 170.

7.-Jack Anderson with James Boyd. IDEM. page 179.

8.-Gamal Abdel Nasser. OP. CIT.

9.-Paul Johnson. MODERN TIMES. page 668.

10.-Jack Anderson with James Boyd. OP. CIT., page 176.

11.-Jack Anderson with James Boyd. IDEM. page 179.

12.-Abdulaziz al-Sowayegh. ARAB PETRO POLITICS. page 99.

13.-Zuhayr Mikdashi. THE COMMUNITY OF OIL EXPORTING COUNTRIES. page 85.

14.-Henry Kissinger. MY MEMOIRS. page 255.

15.-Henry Kissinger. IDEM. page 397.

16.-Henry Kissinger. IBIDEM. page 401.

17.-Henry Kissinger. IBIDEM. page 877.

18. Gamal Abdel Nasser. OP. CIT.

CHAPTER III
THE LIBYAN CRISIS

The Libyan Alternative

Since the nationalization of the Suez Canal in 1956 oil companies made great efforts to diversify their sources of hydrocarbon supply. These companies were in fear of the growing influence of Nasser's ideas in the Middle East and in particular the effects that his increasingly virulent anti-Western position could have on the region's producing nations.

By the year 1959 Standard Oil of New Jersey discovered an important oil reservoir in Libya. From that time onwards, the investments for new reserves multiplied with great success, with the discovery of vast hydrocarbon deposits in Cirenaica and Tripolitania. In effect, by 1961 Libya exported just about 20,000 barrels of oil per day. However, by 1968, its production was in excess of 2.8 million barrels per day, reaching 3.1 million in 1969. At that time Libya was covering 45% of the oil requirements of Germany, 28% of Italy, 22% of the United Kingdom and 17% of France. Nowhere else in the world had such an accelerated growth taken place in the production of hydrocarbons.

The result of this extraordinary expansion was a parallel decrease in Europe's dependence on Persian Gulf oil. Thus, in 1960, over 70% of the oil imported by Western Europe came from the Persian Gulf and barely one decade later these imports had fallen below 50%. In this manner, the hydrocarbons from the Middle East were gradually replaced by those produced in the north of Africa. In effect, while Lybia and other north African oil producers contributed barely 4.5% of the oil required by Western Europe in 1960, its share of the market experienced an accelerated growth, thereby taking almost 42% of these requirements by these nations by 1969.

According to the estimates of the Western oil companies Libyan production could exceed 5 million barrels of oil per day before 1973. In other words this north African nation was on the road to becoming a producer equivalently important to Saudi Arabia and Iran and evidently greater than the other nations in the Persian Gulf.

Libya also had an even greater advantage due to its strategic geographical location. It was ruled by a monarchy headed by Mohammed Idris al-Senussi, better known as King Idris I, who had ascended the throne with the blessing of the Allies after the Second World War. As a result, Idris I was openly pro-Western and enthusiastically welcomed the prospects of prosperity that oil offered its desert nation, a country with barely 2 million inhabitants and an extension of over 1.7 million square kilometers, of which about 1.6 are part of the Sahara desert.

However, spurred on by the country's advantageous situation, King Idris requested a 10-cent increase on the price per barrel of oil. This evidently was a reasonable petition since with this Libya hoped for a compensation for lower transport costs, inasmuch as the country is located ony 700 miles from the European markets, whereas the oil coming from the Persian Gulf while the Suez Canal was closed had to go round the entire African continent to get to those markets. Even though the oil companies were opposed, they were aware that the monarch's request was acceptable and would have probably been heeded, since the abundant oil coming from that country gave relief to the tensions in the production in the Middle East.

Nevertheless, the hopes for the industrialized Western nations of having a new and abundant oil maná were suddenly cut short from 1969 onwards. The strength of Nasser's message gave a violent historic twist and Libya embraced the cause of the more radical Arab forces.

Historical Background

To understand this situation, we should, though briefly, review Libya's history. Inasmuch as it has coastline in the Mediterranean, phoenicians, greeks and romans took turns in the past to found and dominate its main towns. From the seventh century onwards the Arabs had conquered the nation and by the middle of the sixteenth century, while the cities on the coast recognized ottoman sovereignty, the interior was ruled by the Beni Mohammed dynasty founded by the shereef of Morrocco and whose last sovereign had been murdered in 1811 by order of al-Mukkeni, the pasha of Tripoli, who proclaimed himself sultan of Fezzan. The Italians occupied Libya in 1914 and in 1920 recognized the chief of the Senussi as the emir of the bedouins. The country becomes independent in 1951 and Mohammed Idris al-Senussi becomes its ruler.

With such an ancient and varied history the Libyan population constitutes a mosaic of ethnic mixtures. However, long centuries of Arab dominance determined that this mix would profess the sunnite Muslim faith. Thus it would be no surprise that the Libyan masses, like the rest of the Arab nations, would vibrate to the call of Gamal Abdel Nasser's fiery rhetoric.

A Bloodless Coup

In effect, on September 1st, 1969, a dozen young officials, none of which had the rank of captain, decided to take advantage of the opportunity of a trip King Idris had made to Turkey, to organize a banquet for higher-ranking officials. In the middle of the party the officials were surrounded by soldiers and summarilly jailed. A simultaneous operation was under way to detain that same night one of the other chiefs of the Libyan armed forces favoured by the king.

That is how in one coup coded under "Operation Palestine" and without shooting a single bullet, the self-named "Revolutionary Command Council" of young officials deposed the mandate of King Idris, the last representative of the Senussi dynasty that had exerted their influence over Libya since the middle of the 19th Century.

The revolution immediately brought about the dissemination of its principles. The first measure was to abolish monarchy and proclaim the constitution of a republic known as Arab Libyan Socialist and Popular Jamahiriya (al-Jamahiriyah al-Arabiyah al-Libiyah al-Ishtirakiyah). Likewise parliament was dissolved and the antizionist principles preached by Nasser, the greatest heroe and mentor of new rulers was embraced under the motto "Socialism, Unity and Liberty".

From the reigning confusion of the first days of the revolution a fundamental leader sprang up, a lieutenant barely 28 years old. His name: Mu'ammar al-Qaddafi. This was a young man of bedouin descent, whose philosophy centered around three main features: a deep religiousity, a profound xenophobia particularly against all Western things and a fervent admiration for Nasser. Two powerful forces seemed to drive most of his actions: idealism and hatred. He therefore embodied the essential conditions to consider himself a new prophet of the Arab world.

With the new government in office, the Arab countries experienced a realignment. Libya no longer was to take part in the future of the pro-Western nations. Now it would take its place beside nations with radical attitudes and an aggressive Arab nationalism, such as Algeria, Syria, Egypt and Iraq.

Soon, the new Arab military dictatorship headed by Qaddafi went from words to action. Christian churches and synagogues alike were closed down and transformed into mosques; dozens of thousands of persons, were expelled, not only the foreigners but also Libyan citizens that had originally been Italian, Jewish, Greek, etc. and property of the trade activities was restricted solely to Libyans of Arab descent.

Simultaneously Libya's international relations experienced an important transformation. Its pro-Western position was modified and the country leaned towards the USSR. Suleiman Maghrebi was elected Prime Minister. This man had obtained his pH.D. at the George Washington University and had briefly worked with Exxon but was openly against the Western hemisphere. He had become an outstanding agitator who had organized strikes and manifestations in 1967 in order to put pressure on the Libyan government to join the Arab oil embargo that Nasser had attempted to put in motion after the Six Day War.

Middle East Economic Survey, a well-known oil magazine stated that the military coup

"... could very well mean a decisive realignment of the forces in the Arab world. Up to the present, the inner dynamics of inter-Arabic policies had been regulated by a precarious balance between the so-called 'progressive' or 'revolutionary' states on the one hand and on the other, traditional monarchies that included most of the oil producing states... Now, with Libya's abrupt change to the field of 'revolutinaries'... the aforementioned balance between the two groups has been dramatically modified. And this will probably bring about important long-term implications... for the remaining oil producing monarchies, for the oil industry and for the Arab struggle against Israel, together with the connected strategic interests of the superpowers." [1]

Before delving on the revolution, Qaddafi understood that it would be necessary to expulse the anglo-American forces that had set up bases there since World War Two. The United States in effect had the Wheelus Air Force Base towards the east of Tripoli, an important air base, that acted as a training center for the NATO. Likewise, the British had similar bases in Al-Adem and Tobruk. One of the first goals of the new Libyan government was to shut down those bases. Not a year since the date of the coup had passed and had placed Qaddafi in a position of power, that the Lybian government requested and was granted the evacuation thereof.

The Price Revolution

However, at the beginning Qaddafi did not threaten the oil companies since he did not wish to risk the success of his revolution by putting them face to face. But he had not the slightest doubt that Libya had been cheated by those companies and their turn was coming now. Thus trying to avoid a direct confrontation, Minister Ezzedinal-Mabrik defined the oil policy of his government under the following terms:

"We do not wish to dig up the past, nor to bring it to mind. What we wish to emphasize with absolute clarity and frankness is that Libya's new revolutionary regime shall not be content with the old passive methods of problem-solving... The just demands we pursue are not for the purpose of bringing about basic changes in the existing structure of the oil industry worldwide, nor specifically in the system of prices. This does not mean that we approve of the existent system or that we believe it is fair. Libya shall continue to support the collective efforts taken by OPEC for the purpose of modifying the conditions in this regard." (2)

Libya sustained besides that its oil was worth much more than was being paid for it by the oil companies due to its very particular characteristics. In effect, besides the lower transport costs, the oil of that country was low in sulphur and this made it very valued at that time when anti-polluting regulations against fuels with sulphur content were being put in place. Once it was refined, Libyan oil produced advantageous proportions of particularly highly-valued products such as gasoline and heating fuels.

Though expressed in terms that in principle did not spell anythin to the oil companies but more or less arduous negotiation periods, the fact is that a radically different situation was about to occur.

On the other hand, the remainder of the demands requested by the new Libyan revolutionary government did not have the Western nations too concerned. In the beginning they saw Qaddafi as simply another episode in the continuous process of relatively unimportant political changes that used to happen periodically in the Third World. That is why nobody was too worried or mourned old king Idris' departure. On the contrary, many thought that this would be a positive change that would enable Libya to leave behind a situation of backwardness imposed by a medieval monarchy. Perhaps those others who showed more concern were the other oil monarchies in the Middle East, who understood that they could count no more on the Western hemisphere's solidarity in case of a similar situation. In regard to the latter, Henry Kissinger stated the following:

"By accepting Qaddafi's revolution, the political relations of the Western world with the oil-producing conservative states would also be affected. Libya taught those rulers a fatal lesson: that industrial democracies would not protect friendly rulers (as Idris' government) insofar as its hostile and radical successors did not endanger the access of democracies to the oil. Therefore, there would be no interest in attempting to buy the approval of the Western nations by trying to keep oil prices low..."(3)

We thus see that the deep geopolitical transformations produced by the Lybian revolution on the oil-producing Arab nations did not generate too much uneasiness in Washington. Even further, at a specific time, a group of exiled supporters of the monarchy, tried to promote an expedition and resorted to mercenaries with the purpose of freeing the imprisoned officials and thus organize a countercoup that would return power to king Idris. However, U.S. government officials warned the authorities of what was being planned, therefore the plan was discovered. Later on the State Department would explain that they did not wish the Libyan government to believe that the U.S. was associated in any way to any anti-Qaddafi complot. In fact, the American government continued to believe that the revolution would not affect the security of the oil investments in that area. To this regard Kissinger came to state that according to the criterion in force in the American administration:

"Balance of payment income and the safety of American oil investments would constitute our primary interests. We wished to keep our military facilities but not at the cost of threatening our economic interests."(4)

Once he felt more sure, Qaddafi, who had by then been promoted to Coronel and had been given the title of Prime Minister started to negotiate with the oil companies. He started by calling the 21 companies operating in Libya and demanded an unprecedented price hike in the history of oil negotiations by January 20th, 1970. If this petition was not voluntarily accepted, Libya would take unilateral measures and would rescind the oil contracts existing at the time and restrict production. This strategy was a novelty. Up to that time no oil-producing state individually or collectively through OPEC had attempted to improve its oil revenues by pressing the prices to go up. Participation increases had always been sought for this.

CHAPTER III

Simultaneously Qaddafi publicly committed himself with Nasser to place all Libya's resources to aid in the Arab conflict against Israel. In effect, as Paul Johnson confirms in his book entitled Modern Times:

"From the begining of his dictatorship, Qaddafi stressed the importance of oil as a weapon to strike the 'Western imperialists' because of their support for the cause of Israel". (5)

Libya's oil demands were definitely facilitated by King Idris' initial strategy in starting to locate the petroleum in that country. Hoping that production would rapidly increase, that former government had given preference to independent oil companies that did not feel the need to produce in other countries where they had initially made investments. In this regard, Fuad Kabazi, the oil minister during the King's mandate commented the following:

"I did not wish my country to be in the hands of one only company... We wished to discover oil quickly... That is why we initially preferred independent companies, since they had few interests in the eastern hemisphere outside of Libya. In this manner, Kabazi added, competition among the companies could be stimulated: "... If in one surface we found that any independent (company) had employed more energy and found oil, this enabled me to speak to the neighbouring companies and tell them: 'Look here, your neighbour discovered oil. You are almost in the same structure. Come on, hurry up and drill!..." (6)

Among all the independent companies operating in Libya the most aggresive one was undoubtedly the "Oxy" (Occidental Petroleum). In a short time that company had made sensational discoveries, coming to be Libya's greatest producer. However, its dependency regarding that country's production placed it in a difficult position of greater vulnerability at the time of negotiating with Qaddafi's government.

That is the reason why Oxy was the first company chosen. A 40 cents per barrel increase was demanded. The other companies were subsequently called and the same proposal was made.

At first, the companies rejected Qaddafi's request and presented a counterproposal: they were willing to pay an additional 5 cents maximum per barrel.

Qaddafi's initial threats were not even taken very seriously by the oil industry except for Occidental Petroleum. In effect, at the time the Libyan government presented its petition, the exploration efforts being carried out by the companies after the Suez crisis had beared fruit and the prices of the hydrocarbons in the international markets were going down. Thus we see that the crudes from the Persian Gulf that in 1965 were sold at 1.60 dollars per barrel, had gone to a price of around 1.20 and 1.30 dollars. Besides, despite the surplus offer that temporarily flooded the markets, oil was still being found in different areas such as Western Africa, Alaska, Indonesia, South America and the North Sea.

Despite the latter, by the mid '70s, the Libyan government ordered the Occidental to reduce its production from 680,000 to 500,000 barrels per day. This imposition was a severe blow for that company, since in contrast to the large international companies, it had no other sources with which to supply the requirements of its refineries in Europe and to make matters worse, Oxy's less-than-healthy relations with other companies did not help its possibilities of procuring the oil it needed to cover its urgent demands at reasonable prices. In effect, in the private club of the oil industry of that time, Occidental was an unwelcome partner. Animosity against Occidental arose in Peru, where the government had expropiated Exxon. Convinced that no other company could take charge of its facilities, Exxon hoped to be called once more; however Occidental reached an agreement with Peru and although it obtained the concessions, it won itself the enmity of the major international oil companies. Under these circumstances, those companies denied their help to OXY so as to keep its European refineries running, thereby obtaining a better negotiation base with the Libyan government.

In his book "The Seven Sisters" Anthony Sampson narrates the vicissitudes of Dr. Armand Hammer, President of Occidental, facing the Libyan demands:

"Dr. Hammer, therefore, was left alone to face the situation. He himself in person negotiated with the revolutionaries during the entire month of August, arriving back every night by private jet from the oppressive heat of the desert to his home in Paris. The struggle, despite it all, lacked warmth, since the two parties knew perfectly well that Hammer could not do without that oil. Finally, he accepted to pay thirty extra cents and to increase two cents per year for five years. Taxes for his company also increased from 50 to 58 percent." (7)

The depth of the increase accepted by Occidental together with the increase in taxes represented a total that scandalized the other companies. Nevertheless, two weeks later, the Libyans closed a similar deal with the Oasis consortium, made up by three independent companies: Continental, Marathon, Amerada-Hess and Shell. A decrease of some 125,000 barrels per day had been imposed on this consortium.

To ease the negotiations with Libya the production cuts ordered by that country were tied together with the 'accidental' damages suffered by the Trans-Arabian pipeline (Tapline) during May 1970. This circumstance represented the temporary exit from the market of some 500,000 barrels per day of oil that Saudi Arabia exported to Europe. On his part, Syria would not allow companies to enter its territory and make the necessary repairs to the pipeline. New production decreases were imposed: 110,000 barrels per day for Exxon, 55,000 b/d for Mobil and 120,000 b/d for Amoseas Consortium (Texaco-Socal).

In its most critical moment, the flow of oil to Europe coming from the Arab countries was reduced by about 800,000 barrels per day, the result of the production cuts imposed by Libya and by 500,000 barrels per day because of the Tapline 'accident'.

All in all, Europe was being deprived of 1,300,000 b/d of crudes. This was not a figure that could not be handled by the oil companies. In this case however a set of circumstances favoured the Libyan aspirations. In Nigeria for instance, a civil had broken out that worsened even more the situation in Europe, where, to make matters worse, a particularly cold winter was expected. The closure of the Suez Canal in 1967, still in force, had created a shortage in the number of available tankers, which had not been solved by 1970 and prevented a temporary restructuration in their route in order to cover Libya's production deficit with crudes from other countries. Other Arab nations also seemed willing to collaborate and were intently following the results of Coronel Qaddafi's audacious actions.

The large companies that Sampson referred to as "The Seven Sisters" were definitely reluctant to accept similar agreements to those arrived at with Occidental. They knew that if they did so, that it would immediately affect their relations with the other OPEC nations.

On the other hand, if they did not come to an agreement with the Libyan conditions the Western European markets would be affected by a great shortage of oil. After prolonged discussions, the great companies, starting with Socal and Texaco, little by little acceded.

As was to be expected, the demand for higher prices rapidly extended. Iraq, Algeria, Kuwait and Iran immediately demanded an increase in the taxes for up to 55%. "The Libyan success was an embarrasment for other OPEC nations. It made it virtually impossible to shut it up."(8)

The XXI OPEC Conference was held in December 1970. Resolution 120 approved during that conference recommended:

"-The setting of a minimum tax of 55% on the net revenues of the companies;
- A uniform reference price in all the member countries, equal to that of the most favoured nation;
- A uniform increase in the reference prices, capable of reflecting the favorable trends of the prices in the world markets;
- The adoption of a new system to calculate the qualities and differential locations affecting market prices,
- The elimination of all discounts offered in the export price of crudes as of January 1st, 1971."(9)

Not a month had gone by since the XXI OPEC Conference had approved the aforementioned resolution when, on December 3rd, 1971, Qaddafi's revolutionary government presented new demands to the companies. At the time, these included:

-A 5% increse in the fiscal taxes, effective retroactively.

-An increase of 30 to 39 cents per barrel on account of a differential freight compensation (given the lower transport costs of Libyan oil due to the proximity of its markets).

-Taxes payable monthly instead of quarterly.

-Mandatory increases in investments for an amount equivalent to 25 cents per barrel of oil exported.

If these demands were not met, mandatory production cuts would be imposed or the companies would run the risk of being nationalized.

Qaddafi's policies progressively led him to use oil more as a political weapon than as a national source of wealth by means of which revenues could be collected that could benefit his people. The truth is that his objective was to confront the oil-producing Arab nations with the Western nations. To this effect, Newsweek commented that Qaddafi's measures: "threatened with unleashing an oil war between the rich Arab world full of oil and the Western industrialized world thirsty (for oil)". Thus oil was used once more as a sword at the service of Arab political interests. This was ratified by the Libyan president himself, who declared that:

"It was about time that the Americans received a strong slap on their arrogant face. American imperialism has overstepped all the marks... American support to our Israeli enemy threatens our security with their aircraft carriers and from time to time they threaten our territorial waters."(10)

Now therefore, although it had been difficult for the consumer nationsto accept the price increases, the truth was that as a result of the oil offer exceeding demand since the end of World War Two, the prices of the product had stayed depressed for too long. The oil companies, spurred by the discoveries of new reserves in different parts of the world, were not capable of understanding that the market forces were starting to invert and that the time had come for producer companies as well as consumer countries to accept to pay a higher price for a product that was of vital importance to the world. The hesitancy in accepting this reality in its due moment produced several years later much deeper transformations in the energy market which would be translated into conflicts and would lead to price increases that would take on truly traumatic proportions for mankind.

The Confrontation with the U.S.

On the other hand, the true transcendence of the Libyan Crisis must not be seen in the increases created in the prices of hydrocarbons. The more serious consequences of this crisis are evidenced in the profound alterations it produced in the geopolitics of the oil markets. Libya had come to be part of the nations willing to use their oil as a political weapon against the industrialized nations of the Western world. In fact, in the coming years, it would become apparent that Qaddafi's proffessed radicalism would end up by placing the oil resources of that nation at the service of the most varied terrorist causes in the entire world.

Libya became an endless source of finance for radical causes. Libyan aid was not only aimed at the Organization for the Liberation of Palestine (OLP), the objectives of which were in fact fully in tune with a policy favoured by all Arab nations. This finance was not either limited to financing operations against Israel. The tentacles of Qaddafi's support of terrorist activities have extended throughout the world.

Qaddafi however never concealed his intention to use any means for the purpose of destroying Israel. The international press also commented that the Libyan president had begun construction on plants capable of producing chemical warfar and that all efforts were being undertaken to procure missiles capable of reaching enemy territory.

As was to be expected, the policies followed by the government of Libya led that nation to serious confrontations with the U.S. One of the reasons that brought on the progressive souring of relations between both nations were unilateral decisions on the part of Libya in 1981 to ascribe full sovereignty over the Gulf of Sidra, that lies between Tripoli and Bengazi north of Libya. Obviously the United States deemed these aspirations to be illegal and the fleet of that nation assigned to the Mediterranean periodically navigated those waters. To this effect, Caspar Weinberger, the U.S. Defence Secretary during the Reagan administration, sustained that:

"Our Mediterranean fleet for many years had maneuvered and exercised in all those international waters now claimed by Qaddafi. I felt it was vital that we continue to do so; that we not given any credence to the Libyan claim of jurisdiction over the Gulf. Such a claim, if honored, would have serious precedent for other bodies of international water around the world. Our forbearing to go into territories Qaddafi baselessly claimed as his own would signal that his absurd claims were being taken seriously."(11)

Qaddafi responded to the American attitude by threatening to destroy any type of U.S. naval or air units that penetrated the waters of the Gulf of Sidra. Thus, on the night of August 18, 1981, two American F-14 planes were confronted by Libyan SU-22 Soviet-made fighters. Although the American pilots advised that they were flying over international waters, they were attacked by the Libyan jets. The F-14 responded by launching AIM 9-L (heat-seeking) missiles which shot down both Libyan planes. Qaddafi reacted to this by renaming the Gulf of Sidra the "Death Zone" and ratifying his threats. He then proceeded to install SA-2 and SA-5 Soviet-made long-range antiair missiles.

The United States tried to impose economic sanctions on Libya. However, these were difficult to apply. For instance, by 1986, when President Reagan was trying to persuade his European allies to interrupt their trade with Qaddafi, five

American oil companies continued to operate in Libya, contributing with more than 40% of that country's oil production and employing over 1,000 Americans. At that time, close to 40,000 persons coming from Western European nations continued to work in Libya as well as about 50,000 people from east Europe. Eighty British companies were represented in Libya. According to David Lamb in his book entitled The Arabs, Journeys Beyond the Mirage:

"Trade between Libya and Italy exceeded $3.5 billion a year, and Libya owned 14 percent of Fiat, the Italian automaker. And where did Kadafi get the deadly materials needed to launch attacks on Americans, Europeans and Arabs? From none other than the United States." (12)

Trade between the U.S. and Libya, which had peaked at $7.6 billion in 1980, when more than six thousand Americans were working in that country, had fallen by 1985 to barely $300 million per year. In the summer of 1986 the administration of the United States, fearful of episodes similar to those of Iran upon the Shah's fall, ordered the American oil companies to liquidate their assets in that Arab country. At that time, Amerada Hess Corp., CONOCO Inc., W.R. Grace & Co., Marathon Oil Co. and Occidental Petroleum Corp. were still operating in Libya.

In 1986 incidents like the Gulf of Sidra would be repeated. On March 24th, American planes were attacked by SA-5 missiles at 8 a.m. The missiles missed their target. Later, that same day, two Libyan MIG-25 planes came threateningly close to the U.S. air patrols but were repelled. Two new SA-5 missiles were fired by Libyan forces but once more missed.

At 2.30 p.m on March 24th, an American A6 plane destroyed a Libyan fast-missile patrol boat that was approaching some of the American units patrolling the area. Another similar boat was seriously damaged that same afternoon but was able to reach the port.

In response, Qaddafi announced the setting in motion of a terrorist plan by means of which he pleaded "all Arab people" to attack any American target whether it be "an interest, goods, ships, plane or a person."

On April 5th, 1986, a bomb adscribed to Libyan terrorists exploded in a West Berlin discotheque, killing two persons and injuring 230, among them some fifty American military personnel. Other terrorist attacks were carried out in the airports of Rome and Vienna. As a result of those acts, the government of the United States started to plan its own retaliations. Five objectives were chosen by the Americans:

"1.- The facilities at Murrat Sidi Bilal, known to be a commando training school.

2.- The Azziziyah barracks, command and communications center for Libya's terrorist related activities.

3.- The Tripoli International Airfield, which had Libya's IL-76 / CANDID large transport planes and also identified as a terrorist logistics "node".

4.- The Benghazi barracks housing many of Qaddafi's elite guards and involved in terrorist activities.

5.- The Benina airfield, not directly tied to terrorist activity but targeted nevertheless to ensure that the Libyan air defense forces did not intercept the strike forces."(13)

The attack was to be carried out by F-111 fighter bombers based in England. This type of bombers had been chosen for its ability to drop two-thousand-pound laser-guided bombs which made them particularly effective in night operations inasmuch as their advanced technology guaranteed a high degree of accuracy in the destruction of the targets chosen. Likewise, numerous attack planes belonging to the U.S. Navy were to be used from aircraft carriers navigating mediterranean waters. It was planned that the raid would be carried out at 2 am (Libyan time) of April 14th. The F-111s would have to go a longer way since France had refused the use of its air space. They were refuelled while flying in the midst of a total "radio silence" in the south French coast, then veered near to Spain and finally north of Algeria just before the attack. Sentry planes from the Air Way Alarm and Control System (AWACS) were also used, with domes full of radars and sophisticated electronic equipment that enabled them to control the entire operation from a distance of up to two hundred miles.

"Feet wet" was the code used by the pilots to indicate that the mission had been successful. One hour after the attack only one of the F-111 planes had ceased to radio in this code.

According to Caspar Weinberger, the results of the operation were the following:

" *The Sidi Bilal military complex was severely damaged. The Azziziyah barracks received substantial damage. The Tripoli International Airport was hit hard, and the five IL-76/CANDID heavy transport aircraft on the apron were destroyed. The Benghazi barracks were hit and a warehouse in the complex, involved in MIG assembly, was destroyed. At the Benina Airfield many planes were damaged or destroyed; but most important, the Libyans were unable to launch planes from the airport during, or immediately after, the attack.* " (14)

According to press reports, a bomb fell on an apartment building close to the French Embassy building. Likewise an adopted daughter of Qaddafi died in the attack and Libya reported numerous civil casualties. Voices of protest rang out in various countries such as England, Germany, Holland, France and Italy. However the voice of Qaddafi himself was not heard. After the operation he disappeared from public sight for several months, giving rise to speculations that he was facing serious criticism from factions linked to his own advocates.

Notes

1.-MIDDLE EAST ECONOMIC SURVEY. September 5, 1969.

2.-MIDDLE EAST ECONOMIC SURVEY. June 30, 1974.

3.-Henry Kissinger. YEARS OF UPHEAVAL. page 861.

4.-Henry Kissinger. IDEM. page 861.

5.-Paul Johnson. MODERN TIMES. page 669.

6.-Jack Anderson with James Boyd. OIL. THE REAL STORY BEHIND THE WORLD ENERGY CRISIS. page 209.

7.-Anthony Sampson. THE SEVEN SISTERS. page 254.

8.-Abdul Amir Kubbah. OPEC. PAST AND PRESENT. Vienna. September 9174. page 54.

9.-Abdulaziz al-Sowayegh. ARAB-PETRO POLITICS. page 105.

10.-Abdulaziz al-Sowayegh. ARAB-PETRO POLITICS. page 125.

11.-Caspar W. Weinberger. FIGHTING FOR PEACE. page 176.

12.-David Lamb. THE ARABS. JOURNEYS BEYOND THE MIRAGE. page 71.

13.-Caspar W. Weinberger. FIGHTING FOR PEACE. page 192.

14.-Caspar W. Weinberger. IBIDEM. page 198.

CHAPTER IV

THE FIRST OIL SHOCK

The Yom Kippur (or Ramadan) War

The Arab nations impatiently awaited the moment to take revenge for the humiliation they had been subjected to after the defeat of the Six Days War. Israel, aware of this situation, knew that sooner or later it would be attacked. In fact, Prime Minister Golda Meir informed the American ambassador in Tel-Aviv on October 3rd, 1973, that an attack by Syria and Egypt was being prepared in two separate fronts: to the north, in the Golan heights and to the south in the Peninsula of Sinai.

Incredibly, this notice took the CIA by surprise. Only days before, that agency had advised President Nixon that an imminent war in the Middle East was not probable. The CIA affirmed that the movements of Egyptian troops in the area were merely practice exercises. It would seem that the agency was led astray by the attitude of Anuar al-Sadat, the Egyptian President, who abruptly had moderated his anti-Israel rhetoric and had announced that all reservists who had been mobilized in the previous six months would be released by October 8. Although the report of that intelligence agency seems surprising, even more surprising is the fact that Israel, aware of the situation at hand, was taken by surprise when the attack finally occurred. For the first time since 1948, the attack was initiated by the Arabs.

In fact, Israel was perfectly aware that Egypt had mobilized a massive concentration of equipment to the shores of the Suez Canal, which evidently presaged its imminent intention of crossing the channel. Ariel Sharon, the audacious israelí general, in analyzing aerial photographs, declared to his officials: "There's no question. This time it's war" (1). Despite all this, he decided to retire for the day to spend Yom Kippur with his family.

Thus, on October 6th, 1973, while Israel celebrated the day of Yom Kippur or Day of Atonement, and the Arabs in turn commemorated the sacred festivity of Ramadan, Egypt and Syria launched a coordinated, though hardly surprising, attack on the occupied territories. Israel had been taken by surprise. Since it was the most sacred day of the year, many of the troops were on leave spending the day with their families or attending the sinagogues. This negligence would cost the Israeli Defence Minister, Moshe Dayan, his post.

The initial success of the attack was considerable. This time it was Israel's turn to have most of its air force destroyed by Soviet-made land-air missiles. In the meantime, Syrian war tanks overtook all Israeli positions on the Golan Heights, and were poised to invade northern Israel.

At the Sinai, the defence of Jewish forces was under the command of General Avraham Mandler, who, with a division made up by 294 tanks, was suddenly attacked by Egyptian forces comprising five infantry divisions, three mechanized divisions and two armored divisions. In sum, these forces had 1,400 tanks. Mandler died during this battle.

After the hostilities broke out, the U.S. undertook diplomatic efforts to stop the conflict. Henry Kissinger, Secretary of State, got in touch with the Syrian, Egyptian and Israeli governments. He likewise called an emergency meeting of the Security Council of the United Nations. However, no-one seemed particularly interested in foreseeing the outcome. The USSR objected to this call. In fact, Moscow seemed to be convinced that the Arabs would swiftly win the battle. The French and the English, also members of the Security Council, preferred to keep their distance. They knew very well that if they intervened, oil reprisals would be taken by the Persian Gulf Arab nations. Nixon himself, as confessed in his memoirs, came to be convinced that the imposition of a ceasefire would leave the area in such an upheaval that any future negotiations towards achieving a permanent compromise would become impossible. Furthermore, Nixon seemed to believe that Moscow had incited the Arabs to attack, seeking to gain political advantages in the region.

The success of the Arab attack was so overwhelming that Prime Minister Golda Meir ordered an immediate plan to evacuate the Jewish population from the more threatened regions in the country. On the Western front, Egyptian tanks passed the so-called Bar-Lev Line where the Jewish armies had stopped in their advances in the Six Day War and established a fourteen-mile beachhead. The damages inflicted to their army had been so great that Moshe Dayan, the Israeli Defence Minister and hero of the Six Day War, was ready to accept defeat.(2)

Likewise Golda Meir, panic stricken, rushed to ask the U.S. for massive support, especially tanks and planes, urgently needed to repel the attack. During the first three days, Israel had lost over 1,000 men and about a third of its war tanks. Israeli casualties had doubled by the sixth day, with over 2,000 men dead. The powerful Jewish lobbyists pressured the White House and Congress to answer these petitions urgently.

Arab diplomacy was also active, not only in the United States but in Europe as well. The governments of those nations were being warned by all means possible that any action in favour of Israel would bring about serious economic consequences for the world at large.

In fact, King Faisal of Saudi Arabia, traditionally pro-Western, had made a petition before Washington since April 1973 to pressure Israel into withdrawing from the territories occupied in the Six Day War. The saudi attitude was a serious reason for concern since between 1970 and 1973, that country's participation in the international oil markets had increased from 12.8% to 21.4%. Likewise, Yamani, the competent Saudi oil minister, had long been voicing sly threats that the oil concessions granted by his country might be nationalized if the American pro-Israeli stance was not modified. In two articles published on July 6th and 11th, the Washington Post stated that King Faisal himself had said that it would be difficult for his country to cooperate with the U.S. if a change in that policy did not occur. Was the King bragging?

In reviewing the events that occurred it becomes evident that the Arabs had been carefully preparing a scenario of psychological pressure. Reflecting on the result of this scenario the Washington Post once again published in its July 3rd, 1973 edition that an unprecedented level of tension had been reached between the United States and the Arab countries. "Henry Kissinger's most critical problem when he takes over the State Department shall be oil diplomacy" declared columnist Jack Anderson, "If the United States does not change its policy in the Middle East, the Arabs shall almost surely start to shut off production... the only alternative to diplomatic action shall be military action".

On August 23rd, 1973, Sadat secretly flew to Riyadh to have an interview with Faisal. Although the agenda of these meetings was absolutely confidential, it now seems evident that the attack being prepared by the Arabs for the following month of October was one item of discussion.

The night of August 30th, the NBC broadcast an exclusive interview with King Faisal who had decided to personally address American opinion. When asked if Saudi Arabia would restrict its exports to the U.S., he responded through an interpreter that:

"We do not wish to impose restrictions but it would be difficult for us to continue increasing production and even to continue having friendly relations with the United States if that country persists in backing Israel."

Returning to the hostilities that had been unleashed on Yom Kippur, the Egyptian armies continued advancing in the Sinai five days after the attack was begun. The Arabs were euphoric. Official Arab radio stations declared that the Jews would be finally "thrown into the sea". The leaders of these nations were expectant. Many of them, especially those who traditionally had maintained pro-Western positions, considered that their fate would depend on the attitude they adopted under such delicate circumstances. The rulers of Egypt and Syria, Anuar al-Sadat and Hafez al-Assad had won the Arab population's most fervent admiration for their efforts against Israel. King Faisal of Saudi Arabia in turn, persisted in his demands that the U.S. government change its policy towards Israel. In this regard, the Saudi sovereign demanded the backing of ARAMCO in order to defend his points of view before the American government.

On October 12 the chairmen of the four American companies associated to ARAMCO (Exxon, Mobil, Texaco and Standard Oil) addressed a memorandum to President Nixon through his assistant, General Alexander Haig. The purpose of this communication was to warn the head of state of the risk that the Arabs might agree to another oil boycott in the event that the U.S. acted in favour of Israel.

"We have been warned that the Saudis shall impose some oil production cuts as a result of the actions taken to present by the U.S. (backing Israel in the United Nations). Much more substantial actions shall be adopted by Saudi Arabia and Kuwait in the case of new evidence of an addittional American support to Israel's position... We are convinced of the seriousness of the

*Saudi and Kuwaiti intentions and that any initiative that the
U.S. government adopts at this time in terms of additional aid
to Israel shall have critical adverse effects on our relations with
the moderate oil-producing Arab states.* "(3)

For Nixon the crisis could not have happened at a worse time.
Vice President Spiro Agnew was being accused of wrongful
handling and tax evasion. It seemed evident that he would be
found guilty. Therefore, Nixon was facing the urgent need to
elect the adequate person to occupy the Vice Presidency. In the
meantime, the Watergate scandal was acquiring even greater
proportions as the days went by. His own position as president
of the United States was at stake. Congress also seemed set on
approving a law that would substantially restrict the president's
powers in case of war. This difficult domestic situation kept
Nixon practically paralyzed.

In effect, faced with the Arab-Israeli crisis, he had to take an
urgent decision since if he let time go by, it would be too late
for Israel. It was not easy to choose an option. Not only did he
have to deal with the opposing pressures of Arabs and jews but
also with those of the oil companies and the contrasting
opinions of his own advisors. He also had to weigh the reaction
of the Soviet Union, ever anxious to take advantage of any
opportunity to increase its influence in the Middle East. In this
regard, he kept in mind the 1970 pro-Nasser Soviet attitude
and his own fears that the present crisis had been spurred on
by Moscow. Likewise he had to bear in mind the position of his
European allies. These, with the sole exception of Holland, had
decided to freeze shipments of any military equipment to
Israel, even those that had been previously ordered. Moreover,
the European nations had participated their decision of not
allowing refuelling, or even air refuelling, of vessels transporting
military equipment destined for Israel.(4)

The 12th of October was an extremely complicated day for Nixon. He found out that day that the Court of Appeals had decided to force him to submit his tapes with some conversations that constituted decisive proof against him in the Watergate case. That same day Congress decided to present Gerald Ford as the candidate to occupy the Vice Presidency of the United States.

That same day Nixon finally pronounced himself in favour of Israel and ordered the immediate shipment of war material required by that nation. Some political commentators sustained that this decision was based on the intention of propping the president's popularity during these difficult times. The announcement was made public as notoriously as possible on October 13th. Nixon even sent a message to Congress requesting additional aid for Israel in the amount of 2,200 million dollars.

That day, Golda Meir addressed a letter to Nixon stating that:

"Early this morning I was informed of your decision to ensure the immediate flow of American material to us. Your decision shall have an important and beneficial influence over our combat capacity. I knew that at this time of urgent need for Israel, we could count on your deep sympathy and understanding."(5)

However, the differences between the President's advisers were still great. Secretary of Defence James Schlesinger was concerned over the reactions of the Arabs and did not wish El Al planes to land on American air bases to load the material offered. The planes to send the war material to Israel were likewise tied up because the insurance companies were not willing to insure the private charter flights hired to send the material, alleging the risk of flights to war zones.

In the meantime, the American government found out that the USSR had initiated a vast air supply program of war equipment for the Syrian and Egyptian armies.

Faced with all manner of obstacles that seemed to hinder his orders, Nixon in his memoirs stated that:

"I called Schlesinger and told him that I understood his concern and appreciated his precautions. I assured him that I was completely aware of the seriousness of my decision and that I would personally accept responsibility in case the Arabs got annoyed and cut off our oil supply. I told him that if we could not get private planes, that we would use our own military transport."

Nixon stated as well that disagreements with the Pentagon also arose as to the type of planes that should be used to transport the material. As a result, in his own words, completely exasperated, he called Kissinger and told him:

"Damn it, use anything we have. Tell them to send anything that flies."(6)

The air transport operation to Israel began on October 13th. A few days later, close to 1,000 tons were being sent daily and in the following weeks over 50 flights loaded with war material from the U.S. landed in Israel. Ten modern phantom planes were also sent. This was therefore a more important operation than the one carried out by the Americans in 1948-49 on the occasion of the Soviet block to Berlin.

The Russians likewise were sending close to 700 tons of war material per day to equip the Arab armies and to keep the posts they had conquered.

CHAPTER IV

While all this was taking place, the Israeli counterattack had begun on October 8th. The jews first concentrated on the battle front in the border with Syria, whose proximity with Israel represented a strong threat for the population. In the most important combat among war tanks since World War Two, the Israelis recaptured the Golan Heights and advanced into Syrian territory, where they stopped barely 32 kilometers away from Damascus. It is probable that Israel did not continue advancing for the sake of saving itself the infinite logistical problems implied by overtaking a capital.

Once this triumph had been achieved the Israeli forces focused the attention on the south. Initially they attempted unsuccesfully to displace the Egyptians from the beachhead established on the east flank of the Suez Canal. However, on October 16th, the forces commanded by General Ariel Sharon were able to introduce a wedge in Egypt: they crossed the Suez Canal and advanced up to kilometer 101 of the highway joining Cairo with the city of Suez. At the same time, they blocked the ports from which the Third Egyptian Army - that had days before crossed the Canal to enter the Sinai Peninsula - could have received help. In this manner the Egyptian forces of over half a million men became isolated in the desert. Thus, Damascus and Cairo were practically defenceless. The prudence of the Israelis alone kept them from advancing.

General Ariel Sharon, referring to the bold crossing of the canal by the troops under his command on October 16th, stated in his autobiography:

"Six days earlier Sadat had considered the Israeli crossing a "television operation", staged only to make a momentary dramatic effect. Now, with the Third Army almost isolated and with my forces sixty miles from Cairo and at the gates of Ismailia, the Egyptians were in a panic."(7)

Hemmed in by the Jewish armies, Sadat, the Egyptian president - who in July 1972 had expelled the Soviet mission installed in Egypt since 1967 consisting of over 15,000 consultants and military experts - requested help from the USSR. Under these circumstances, the Secretary General of the Soviet Communist Party, which at the time was Leonid Brezhnev, sent Nixon a message warning that it was possible that Soviet troops would be sent to the area. (8)

In this manner, Nixon's initial fears were confirmed and he was forced to take the extremely serious decision of sending a "state of alert" to the American forces in the entire world.

Inasmuch as the events were so trascendent and so filled with possible danger they shall be detailed by chronological order:

On October 17th, Nixon met in the White House with the ministers of foreign affairs of four Arab nations. The attitude of the Arabs was now evidently different. They now wanted a ceasefire. On October 18 Moscow attempted to request a meeting with the Security Council of the United Nations to propose an end to the hostilities and a withdrawal of the Israeli forces up to the frontiers existing before the 1967 war. This time, Washington was opposed, alleging that this proposal was not realistic.

On October 19th, Nixon received a comuniqué from Brezhnev stating that the situation in the Middle East was becoming increasingly more dangerous. As a result of this, since the USSR nor the U.S. wished their relations to be damaged, a suggestion was put forward for both superpowers to put forth their best efforts to avoid a "dangerous escalation" in the events in the Middle East.

On October 20th, Kissinger flew to Moscow to have a direct interview with Premier Brezhnev. The following day both drew up a draft agreement to cease the hostilities which was to be presented by Moscow to Sadat and Assad, and Washington would do the same to Golda Meir.

The agreement ended up by being imposed on the Arabs and Israelis. Both sides unenthusiastically accepted its terms and it was put in force on October 22nd. However, a few hours later, Tel Aviv accused the Egyptians of violating the agreement and hostilities once again flared up.

New differences between the Kremlin and the White House sprang up. According to their respective informations, the opposing band had broken the ceasefire. Brezhnev and Nixon used the emergency "red" line to seek a solution.

It was thus evident that the crisis had reached such transcendent proportions that the great powers, fearful of what might happen, decided to exert influence over the warring sides to stop the conflict from escalating. Thus, on October 24th a second ceasefire was signed. Despite the foregoing, the impression was that the USSR had decided to fish in rough waters and, though fearful of the consequences of an international crisis, was willing to take advantage of the situation to try and have a larger military presence in the Middle East.

In effect, intelligence reports received by the White House informed that the USSR was preparing seven air transported divisions and that it was ready to send over 50,000 men to the warring zone. 85 Soviet vessels, including several aircraft carriers and helicopter carriers were readying their positions in the Mediterranean.

These preparations coincided with a public request by Anuar al-Sadat to Brezhnev. Sadat requested a foreign joint force, capable of keeping the peace in the Middle East. The maneuver was clear. If the request of the Egyptian president was attended, Moscow could send troops to the area, a situation that had actively been sought for a long time. For this reason, Nixon decided to address Sadat directly with the following message:

"I have just found out that a resolution may be introduced before the Security Council tonight, urging foreign military forces - including those of the U.S. and the USSR - to be sent to the Middle East to impose a ceasefire. I must tell you that if this resolution is placed before the Security Council it shall be vetoed by the U.S. for the following reasons:

It would be impossible to gather a foreign military force of enough magnitude to counterbalance the local forces at war in the Middle East.

If the two nuclear superpowers were called to provide such forces, they would enter into a potentially extremely serious situation due to the direct rivalry among these two powers in the region." (9)

In effect, that same day, Moscow advised Washington that Israel would continue to fight despite the ceasefire ordered by the Security Council. It was therefore imperative that the U.S. and the USSR immediately send forces to the region. If Washington did not act on this, Moscow was willing to act unilaterally.

The confrontation between Washington and Moscow was therefore the most serious threat for world peace since the crisis of the cuban missiles that had occurred eleven years previously.

In this manner the local problems in the Middle East once more threatened to extend and create a conflict of unforeseeable consequences that could involve not only the super powers but the entire world. Some analysts have wanted to highlight the drama lived by mankind in those moments, stating that the President of the United States could have adopted decisions that were not wise nor prudent due to his altered state of mind on account of the increasingly serious Watergate scandal. Perhaps Nixon himself was fearful of that possibility since in the crucial moments he delegated the handling of the crisis on the Secretary of State. Thus, it was Kissinger and not Nixon who chaired the meeting in the White House that responded to Brezhnev's message. Likewise, it was Kissinger who under the circumstances gave the "order of alert" to the American forces.

The aforementioned "order of alert" probably made the leaders of the Soviet Union recapacitate. Soon afterwards, the White House received a new message from Brezhnev, stating now that Moscow had decided to send "seventy observers" to the Middle East. This was an entirely different situation. No longer were there menaces of military contingents nor anything related to the intelligence reports that mentioned aircraft carriers and seven divisions. The crisis between the two super powers seemed therefore to have been dispelled.

The Arab Oil Embargo

Nevertheless, the chapter of the Arab-Israeli conflict that had originated in the Yom Kippur war was a long way from being over. The hostilities had lasted barely 18 days but the chain of events for the entire world had not yet seen its last day.

The new humiliation suffered by the Arab nations exasperated the spirit of its people and rulers. This time even King Faisal of Saudi Arabia, himself affronted by President Nixon's position despite his warnings, exerted all his influence in pro of his Arab brothers. His example was followed by the remaining Arab oil exporters, even those who called themselves moderate.

Under the circumstances, those nations once again resorted to the strategy attempted by Nasser in 1967: an oil embargo against Israel's occidental allies. Likewise, a reduction in oil production was decided and a strong hike in the prices of the product. In contrast to the first try, this time the embargo was rigorously applied.

The steps adopted by the Arabs against the Western world were originally drawn out in an emergency conference held by the Organization of Petroleum-Exporting Arab Countries (OPEAC) in Kuwait from the 16th October, 1973, i.e., as soon as these nations realized that the so-called Yom Kippur war was not going according to planned and that the United States was openly backing Israel. Two positions were adopted in that conference regarding the way the Arab nations should use the oil as a political weapon. A first position defended the convenience of carrying out production cuts that would affect fundamentally the U.S. The second, more radical, position fostered the nationalization of foreign (and particularly American) oil interests in the Arab countries.

When defending the first of the positions, Ahmed Helal, Egypt's oil minister stated:

"We hope for a gradual reduction of Arab (oil) production that in its first phase would be aimed against the U.S. and that would progressively expand to other areas of the world. At the same time we wish to invite the nations that proclaimed their neutrality in the struggle (against Israel) to change their positions in favour of our cause."(10)

Iraq and Libya in turn sustained that the foreign oil companies operating in the Arab world and particularly the American ones should be immediately nationalized. To this effect Dr. Sa'doun Hammadi, Iraq's oil minister, sustained that the Arab countries should:

"-Nationalize all American oil interests in the Arab world;

-Withdraw all Arab financial reserves from the U.S.;

-Break diplomatic relations with the U.S."(11)

Libya's position in the Kuwait conference was even more radical. The oil minister of that nation proposed the following measures:

"-To Immediately deny crudes, natural gas and other products to the U.S."

"-To reduce Arab oil production in an amount equivalent to that previously exported to the U.S. and persuade the non-Arab producing nations (Iran, Nigeria and Venezuela) not to supply oil to the U.S."

"-To withdraw Arab financial reserves from the U.S. and send orders to Arab financial experts to seek ways to use these reserves in Europe for the purpose of sabotaging the U.S. financial position worldwide."(12)

After intense deliberations, the Arab oil ministers decided to adopt the position of a gradual reduction in production. The official statement issued on the occasion of the closing of the Kuwait Conference stated:

"The Arab oil ministers having met on October 17th in the city of Kuwait have decided to immediately initiate a production cut in all the Arab oil countries of no less than 5 percent for the month of September. This same procedure shall apply each month and production shall be reduced in the same percentage regarding the previous month until the Israeli forces have completely evacuated all occupied Arab territories since June 1967 and the legitimate interests of the Palestine people have been reinstated."(13)

Oil prices, which had practically remained stable in the previous two decades, immediately shot up. In just one day, October 16th, the Arab oil producers of OPEC increased the prices of their crudes in over 70% from 3 dollars to $5.12 per barrel. As traumatic as this situation could be, Saudi Arabia, the supplier of more than 20% of the free world's energy requirements, went one step further and ordered an additional oil production reduction of 10%. But the bad news had not yet finished. In effect, Saudi Arabia as well as the other Arab oil producers of OPEC announced on October 21st, 1973, that all oil shipments to the U.S. and other Western allies of Israel as well as Trinidad and the Bahamas - that could serve as intermediate reshipment points - were from that moment on paralyzed.

The first Arab state to announce a full oil embargo against the U.S. was the United Arab Emirates. Emir Mana Saeed al-Otaiba, oil minister of the UAE declared:

"... my government has no other choice but to declare its desire to put all its capabilities at the service of the battle (against zionism)... We believe that the use of oil as a weapon shall bear fruit if all the Arabs use it... The government of Abu Dhabi has decided to cut off oil supplies to the U.S. until this country changes its aggresive stance against the Arab nation... This

step shall be extended to any country that adopts the same aggressive position against the Arab nation..."(14)

Thus, for the first time in Arab oil history, the Yom Kippur war (or Ramadan war as the Muslims called it), gave rise to a unanimous support to common political objectives. Under the leadership of Saudi Arabia, it was decided to use oil as a "political weapon" in pro of the Arab cause. Of the ten members of the Organization of Petroleum Exporting Arab Countries, only Iraq abstained from supporting the decisions of the October 1973 Kuwait Conference, and this was only due to Iraq favouring an even more radical position.

In turn, the White House was also getting ready for what could happen. By October 15th plans had been announced to conserve energy and a series of voluntary measures were suggested. Plans were put forward to reduce the speed of cars, domestic heating, to close gasoline stations on weekends, to improve energy efficiency in industrial plants, to decrease fuel consumption in planes by 29% and reduce the volume of heating fuel to be distributed for domestic, commercial and industrial use. It was estimated that these plans would jointly save around 1.6 to 2 million barrels per day. Additionally, programs substituting coal for oil were suspended and on October 29th of that year, Congress approved the construction of the pipeline from Alaska.

It seemed evident that King Faisal who was traditionally pro-Western was, at that moment, most influential in the decision to sponsor the oil embargo. Two versions, not necessarilly oppossed, have been given regarding the attitude of the Saudi sovereign. On the one hand, some well-informed analysts on Middle East policy and its complexities consider that the embargo was the only alternative left to Faisal to avoid a nationalistic conflagration which could have consumed the conservative nations in the Gulf, swept away by the vengeful vehemence of those who, having had no luck defeating Israel, would decide to point their fury against the less radical rulers in the Arab states. Thanks to this clever maneuver, Faisal was able to calm his Muslim correligionaries, assuring them that the just weight of Arab vengeance would fall on the allies of the Jews.

The second version refers to problems of a technical nature that apparently affected production in Saudi Arabia, as a result of an overproduction in its fields. In this sense, some oil analysts stated that strong tensions had arisen between ARAMCO and the Saudi government, whose technicians accused the company of permanently damaging some fields because of a policy of overproduction. This policy had created a marked decrease in the internal pressure of the fields which could only be partially reversed through expensive investments in water injection and secondary recovery programs. In effect, a prudent handling of the oil reservoirs would force the inner pressure to be kept above certain levels so as to push the oil to the surface. It was even said that ARAMCO's figures on discoveries and reserves in that country were not reliable. In conclusion, it was thought that the only solution to the problems was a strong temporary decrease in Saudi oil production in order to carry out urgent and undelayable repair work in the wells. To execute these works, it was necessary to interrupt production.

According to the previous statements, King Faisal could have very well taken advantage of the situation due to the result of the Yom Kippur war to order production cuts and an embargo that in practice enabled his country to thus solve its technical problems. These circumstances were extensively dealt with in the meetings of the Subcommittee of multinational companies adscribed to the U.S. Senate Foreign Affairs Commission chaired by Senator Frank Church.

In this regard, the declarations of the senator himself on August 7th, 1974, at the moment of publicly announcing the minutes of the sessions corresponding to the investigations that the Subcommission had been advancing during seven months are very interesting. Among the more prominent declarations the following are worthwhile mentioning:

-*"In May 1973 the Saudi government made quite a severe suggestion in the sense that Aramco as well as its partner companies should launch a campaign to try and change America's pro-Israeli policy. The companies took in the suggestion, followed the instructions and later informed the results of their efforts to the king. The corollary of their efforts was a joint memorandum signed by Aramco's top executives and sent to president Nixon, urging him to modify the position of the United States"*...

-*"The Saudis trusted Aramco and partners with the handling of the embargo, acknowledging that the Saudi government lacked the capabilities to manage it properly. Aramco fulfilled the wishes of the Saudis, including primary and secondary embargo operations on the American army."*...

-*"The general impression that oil production in Saudi Arabia could increase by simply opening a tap is totally false. The great demand for oil that started in 1972 led to enormous efforts to quickly increase Saudi production. Those efforts were thwarted by serious technical difficulties and construction delays. Massive capital investments were required."*...

-*"If it had not been for the Saudi embargo, Aramco could have been forced to restrict production for technical reasons, in order to preserve the eventual recovery in the oil fields. The embargo "saved" Aramco and turned the technical reasons for the oil shortage into political reasons."*...

-"*Mr. Anderson made a series of statements regarding Aramco, many of which were substantiated during the sessions and through the documents obtained. He stated that, if the embargo were to be lifted, Saudi Arabia was not going to be able to produce the quantities of petroleum that were expected.*"... "*that the increased production had freed enormous amounts of natural gas that had to be burned*"... "*that King Faisal had ordered and Aramco had carried out a direct and indirect embargo on the American army*"... "*that the executives of Aramco supposed that the company was going to be nationalized*"... "*One way or another, all these statements were substantiated during the sessions of the Subcommittee*".(15)

In any event, the consequences of the Arab oil embargo for the Western world were dramatic. The full force of actions unsuccesfully attempted by Nasser years before was being applied. Oil had been converted into a powerful weapon in the hands of the Arabs, who in this manner publicly announced to the world their decision of using it each time it would serve their political purposes.

In fact we see that in December 1973, Zaki Yamani, the charismatic oil minister of Saudi Arabia, visited the U.S. Showing himself to be a consummate politician and skillful diplomat, on the one hand he threatened the U.S. and on the other he offered continued help from his country to meet the America's energy demands, and also appealed to the sense of "fair play" of the Americans. He even requested the backing of the U.S. to keep the royal Saudi family in power. On December 9th, in the "meet the press" TV program Yamani stated that Arab oil would come to the U.S. once a complete withdrawal of Israeli forces from the Arab territories occupied in 1967 had been effected and this decision had been guaranteed by the United States. Attempting to awaken a greed for energy sources among the Americans he even calmy stated that:

"It is still feasible that Saudi Arabia could double or triple its oil production... that a production of 20 million barrels per day can be reached".(16)

Evidently, Yamani was bragging. As became evident later on during the sessions of the Subcommittee of multinational companies, Saudi Arabia was in no condition to increase its production. In fact, even by 1990, the experts consider that Saudi Arabia will find it difficult to keep up production much longer over the 9 million-barrel-per-day mark.

Curiously, the industrialized nations that had been preparing to face the consequences of the closure of the Suez Canal in 1967, were this time taken by surprise.

The Price Hike

In its most outstanding moment the oil deficit in the Western markets was over 4 million barrels per day including production increases from Canada, Iran, Venezuela and Indonesia. This was not really an unmanageable amount if, at the time, plans had been in place to share stored oil reserves and to handle mechanisms capable of avoiding nervous purchases in the markets. Since these previsions did not exist, the results were not long in coming. Panic flooded the oil markets and prices started to suddenly increase in the spot market.

The Shah of Iran, attempting to sound out the market, organized an auction in December of that same year with astounding results. Oil reached a price level of 17.40 dollars per barrel that had been unheard of.

Likewise, on December 28th, an OPEC meeting was held in Teheran, the purpose of which was to fix the new oil prices. Iran had considerably increased its production to make up for the deficit caused by the embargo and the production cuts of the Arab nations. The Shah of that nation therefore proposed that the price be fixed at US$ 14 per barrel. The Saudis suggested a price of US$ 7.50. The meeting finally agreed on an intermediate price of US$ 11.65 per barrel. (17)

The consumer countries awoke one day from the sweet dream of a world centered around cheap fuel. Long lines started to form at the gasoline stations where powerful cars thirsty for fuel awaited with their empty tanks, sometimes for hours on end, to buy a few gallons of the prized liquid. A particularly crude winter was felt that year and subsequently heating bills were sky high. Family economies were strongly hit.

The domestic situation in the United States was now critical. As a result of the Watergate crisis, Nixon had been forced to resign. For the first time in the history of the country Gerald Ford, a president not elected by the people, took office. In fact, Ford, Vice President until then, had not even been elected for that post by popular vote. Congress had elected him after the resignation of Vice President Spiro Agnew, who had been sentenced by a federal court in Baltimore to three years under probation and to pay a fine of 10,000 dollars.

American farmers demanded that their nation respond to the actions by the Arabs by applying an embargo on their substantial purchases of food. Ford, anxious to win the votes he hadn't been awarded at the ballot boxes, stated: "Throughout history, nations have gone to war over natural advantages such as water or food." These words hid a clear threat. As Business Week reported, some West European bankers were even privately pressing the U.S. to resort to military force to solve the problems arising from the oil embargo.

Finally, as a result of the so-called Arab Oil Embargo, in less than one year the average price of the product increased by 438%. The 34º API crude marked as "light Arab", for instance, went from 2.70 dollars to US$ 12 per barrel.

Oil consumer nations' invoices increased between 1973 and 1974 in over ninety-five billion dollars. Revenues for the eleven main OPEC countries increased from 24 billion dollars in 1972 to close to 118 billion dollars in 1974. Thus began, that year, the initial quota of the most massive transfer of wealth ever experienced by mankind. The rest would occur a few years later with the price hikes after the Shah of Iran's deposal.

The aforementioned oil price increase resulting from the Arab oil embargo translated into a deep alteration of capital flows in the world. OPEC countries collected much more money than they were accustomed to receive. Oil importing nations in turn were forced to put out much more money than they were accustomed to paying. Both groups of countries needed some time to adjust their economies to these sudden changes. In the meantime, OPEC members, particularly the Arab countries, treasured many more dollars than those they could spend whereas other nations were spending much more than was coming in. International payments were therefore not balanced. Hydrocarbon producing nations had high surpluses in their balance of payments whereas the other nations incurred heavy deficits.

In the four following years up to 1978, OPEC members would receive $603.5 billion of which $475 billion went to Muslim oil-producing countries.

The world would be forced to face critical situations. In this regard, it would be worthwhile to mention that the prices of hydrocarbons alone were not the cause of the crisis that came about in the years to come. In effect, the truth is that a world economic crisis had been in the works for a long time.

Background of an Economic Crisis

This crisis had probably started in the U.S. with a chronic fiscal deficit since 1958. In order to finance it, it was forced to issue money that in practice did not have the backing in gold that it had in theory. In any other economy this would have been enough to create a galloping inflation. However, the United States had an enormous advantage. Money surpluses generated from the growing fiscal deficit did not remain gravitating over the monetary mass, nor did they exert a pernicious effect on the economy. Rather, since the dollar was a currency welcome in all parts of the world, even to the extent of being a reserve currency very much appreciated by central banks, dollar surpluses were quickly drained toward other economies by means of growing deficits in their balance of payments by means of which a practically independent monetary system was created. Thus the era of the Eurodollar was born.

In a very simplistic fashion, since we do not pretend to address experts in the field, let us see how the system works: Through the deficit in foreign accounts the dollar surpluses issued by the American monetary authorities passed to other nations whose central banks attributed functions equivalent to that of gold to the dollar, i.e. reserve functions. Now therefore, for them the dollar had an added advantage since it generated interest. In effect, with the dollars coming into their coffers, these central banks issued Treasury bonds which were then placed on the New York Stock Exchange and purchased again with funds coming from money surpluses generated by the American fiscal deficit. This therefore was a closed circle though it generated increasingly greater doubts regarding the parity or convertibility of the dollar as currency.

Aware of the foregoing situation, President Kennedy on arriving at the White House in the beginning of the '60s, made great efforts to reduce these deficits. However this policy did not last long. Soon afterwards, Kennedy was shot to death in 1963 and Vice President Lyndon B. Johnson took office. This president adopted a policy that little by little committed the U.S. into entering Vietnam until, by 1965, the country was involved in a war which did not have a successful outcome, despite having won most of the battles. The Vietnam war once again dragged the Americans into an ever-increasing policy of deficits.

To give us an idea of the magnitude of the deficit growth in American foreign accounts, suffice it to mention that this was being fed by an increasing import-export unbalance. From 1964 to 1971 imports grew by 147% and exports only 74%.(18)

At the same time, the continuously growing exit of dollars from the United States due to the need to drain monetary surpluses enabled the country to make huge investments in other economies, particularly in European countries where many businessmen were anxious to mint their capitals through the sale of property. With the purpose of generating interest, foreign central banks granted loans in pounds, marks, French francs, lire, florins, and other local currency to American companies by means of the mechanism already mentioned. These loans enabled these companies to carry out heavy long-term investments.

Already, by 1971, this phenomenon had acquired such great proportions that the situation had become intolerable for the European central banks, which then started to think that it was risky to accumulate dollars indefinitely since they feared that the deficit in the American balance of payment would end up by affecting the exchange parity of that currency or otherwise propitiate the unconvertibility of dollars into gold.

In practice, therefore, the U.S. was playing a double game: on the one hand, it was avoiding its own internal inflation and on the other, it was purchasing enormous assets in other nations. Both objectives, probably achieved without a premeditated plan, gave rise to the expatriation of undesirable surpluses of its own currency.

De Gaulle came to harshly criticize this situation by stating: "The United States is exporting its own inflation".(19) This was not far from the truth.

Japan's situation was different since at that time that country had barely opened up to American capital. The yen remained devalued for many years, thereby fostering a constant increase of exports to the U.S., which at the time absorbed a third of Japanese exports. In time, Japan, with the accumulated dollar surpluses from its trade with the U.S., would start to make great investments in American soil. In any event, the accelerated growth of the Japanese economy had already become a source of serious concern inasmuch as it was starting to threaten the equilibrium of the world economy.

Curiously, the Europeans and the Japanese were facing a situation difficult to solve. On the one hand they wished that the Americans could put order in their house, i.e., they could reduce their fiscal deficit. However, at the same time, they did not wish to give up the security Washington represented in their role as "international police" and which protected that oriental nation from the USSR's expansionary ambitions. On the other hand, they understood that the U.S. deficit policy would lead to a deterioration in the exchange parity of the dollar. Now therefore, a dollar devaluation was equally feared since this would affect the possibility of continuing to make lucrative exports to the large American market.

Alternatively, the high deficits in the trade balance of the United States arising from the growing volumes of imports made by individuals and paid in dollars went to fatten a practically independent monetary system. Thus, the era of the Eurodollar was born. British financier George Bolton understood that for the first time there was a currency that was being developed unsupervised by the monetary authorities, a circulating expatriate that could be used to provide collosal amounts for financing. Having decided to take advantage of the situation, he transformed London into the world center for the new system of Eurodollars.

Thus, the market of eurodollars in 1959 alone tripled and once again doubled in 1960. In fact, the attraction of this market generated such interest that the steps adopted by several governments, including the U.S., to destroy it were counterproductive. It was the case of a type of monetary "black market" that was convenient for international financiers.

By 1971 the mass of eurodollars was so vast that the American monetary authorities lost, or voluntarily abandoned, control over what was happening. Two years later, in March 1973, Nixon - officially recognizing what the entire world already had - eliminated the convertibility of gold that the dollar had in theory.

Nixon's decision was unavoidable and the world at large saw it coming. In effect, by the end of the '40s, the existing gold deposits in Fort Knox exceeded 20 billion dollars, approximately half of the world's gold reserves. By 1947 these reserves had increased to about 25 billion dollars. Nevertheless, as a result of the growing deficits in the U.S. balance of payments, by 1968 these gold reserves had decreased to about 10 billion dollars.

From the time that the unconvertibility of dollar into gold became official, the main currencies began to float in the markets. This flotation put in evidence the fragility of the American currency, that between February and March of 1973 had lost 40% of its value in connection with the Federal German Republic mark. However, the dollar continued to be the currency used in general in international transactions. It was therefore evident that something very serious was happening when the world at large was becoming attached to a currency issued by a government that had officially disowned it by withdrawing its backing in gold. The eurodollar is therefore a species of unrecognized illegitimate child of the American economy.

Sponsored by this enormous monetary mass that lacked controls, world economy initially experienced a boom. This boom was likewise driven by the low energy costs, the prices of which had spiraled downward in relative terms between 1951 and 1972 when compared to the price of manufactured goods.

Thus, one can safely state that by 1973, the economy of the main industrialized nations was "reheated". The growing mass of eurodollars was already having an effect on inflation. International financial markets were facing grave tensions and the monetary authorities of the main nations were debating among dilemmas that seemed impossible to solve. It was evident that stormy times were drawing near.

"In short", according to Paul Johnson in his book entitled Modern Times "in the autumn of 1973 the financial basis for the world economy was disintegrating. The only thing needed to unleash a disaster was a sudden shock. What happened was not a shock; it was an earthquake."(20)

In effect, the sudden increase in the cost of energy unleashed by the 'earthquake' in the Middle East dealt a severe blow to the U.S., whose economy fell into a serious recession.

Now therefore, suffice it to mention that during the early '70s, American industrial production represented in itself over 30% of the entire world's industrial production. This explained the quick propagation of the crisis towards other economies, that were already seriously afflicted by the same evil troubling the United States: a hike in oil prices. This therefore was a vicious circle where the cost of energy was not the only factor responsible for the damages being produced, although undoubtedly it came to represent more than the last factor in a chain of events.

Although the industrialized nations had been affected, the Third World non-oil producing countries had fallen into an even worse situation.

Meanwhile, urged on by the U.S., a group of oil consuming nations capable of taking action to protect themselves from OPEC decided to join up. Thus, in 1974, the INTERNATIONAL ENERGY AGENCY (IEA) was created in Paris comprising 16 nations: The United States, Japan, West Germany, Great Britain, Italy, Canada, Belgium, Holland, Spain, Sweden, Austria, Switzerland, Turkey, Denmark, Luxembourg and Ireland. The AEI's main objectives were:

1.-To give aid to any member of the group that suffered a reduction of at least 7% in their supplies due to some action imputable to a country of OPEC. To cover this emergency, the members of the institute were committed, if necessary, to adopting measures tending towards reducing their own consumption.

2.-To put forth their greatest efforts in developing new sources of hydrocarbon production in non-OPEC member nations.

3.-To promote policies capable of reducing energy consumption.

167

4.-To contribute to developing alternate sources of energy.(21)

In conclusion, the first oil shock was felt as a result of the Yom Kippur war. Western industrialized nations had never seriously considered the possibility of some day facing an energy shortage. However, all of a sudden, oil exporting Arab nations showed that they were capable of altering the life style of the main industrial powers, causing cracks in the Atlantic Alliance and precipitating the appearance of serious international monetary problems. In this regard, Ruth S. Knowles stated that:

"Never, since the Trojan Horse and the atomic bomb had a new war weapon been conceived that could be so devastatingly effective as the use of the recently acquired oil power by the Arabs... The sword of oil was politically and economically double-edged. The Arabs brandished it both ways." (22)

While the Arab embargo was wreaking havoc that spread like gunpowder in the spirit of the governments and companies alike, Venezuela once more showed that from the strategic viewpoint it was the Western world's most reliable supplier.

A wave of optimism invaded that country as a result of the added enormous revenues. "State Capitalism" and the paternalistic state achieved their maximum expression. Increased oil prices led to an abundance of resources as had never been known before. Everything could be subsidized and companies, regardless of their state of inefficiency, had sure markets by way of all manner of tariff barriers and protection measures. Unemployment was minimal. The additional resources from the oil led to the undertaking of great 'pharaonic' development plans as well as ambitious social programs. Venezuela came to be a sort of paradise, a mix of the best of capitalism with the best of socialism. In fact, the national territory did not seem large enough to absorb in itself the full action of the State; therefore Venezuela became an international benefactor. There were no reasons to doubt the bright future that was ahead of us inasmuch as the experts affirmed that oil prices would continue to increase permanently.

However, this was to be only a passing illusion. In the long run this policy set the bases for one of the deepest and longest crises ever felt by the country. The abundance of those years led fundamentally on the one hand to the State becoming the 'mega-owner' of companies mostly yielding 'mega-losses' and on the other hand, a group of individuals got rich quickly, that money ending up mostly in foreign bank accounts. Venezuela became a country of nouveau riche people. Although in those few years Venezuela's government revenues far surpassed the global amount of income received by all the previous governments throughout the entire history of the country, by 1983 the economic situation was in such a state as to forebode truly difficult times ahead.

In those initial years full of euphoria the president of the Republic, a skillful politician capable of pronouncing the most lucid speeches, did not cease to repeat that "we must manage abundance with a criterion of shortage." Soon after, the population with its characteristic humour, summed up the achievements of these years of bonanza stating that what had been achieved had been to "manage abundance with a shortage of criterion."

In spite of the foregoing, not everything was negative. Some public and private companies came to be 'islands of excellence', an example of which is Petróleos de Venezuela (PDVSA).

Notes

1.-Ariel Sharon. WARRIOR: AN AUTOBIOGRAPHY. page 288.

2.-Steven Emerson. THE American HOUSE OF SAUD. page 36.

3.-Jack Anderson with James Boyd. OIL. THE REAL STORY BEHIND THE WORLD ENERGY CRISIS. page 316.

4.-Steven Emerson. Op. CIT. page 37.

5.-Richard Nixon. MEMOIRS. page 480.

6.-Richard Nixon. IBIDEM. page 483.

7.-Ariel Sharon. OP. CIT., page 333.

8.-Paul Johnson. MODERN TIMES. page 670.

9.-Richard Nixon. OP. CIT. page 497.

10.-Mohamed Harb. OIL WAR: THE SECRET MINUTES OF THE ARAB OIL MINISTERS MEETING. pages 116-117.

11.-Abdulaziz al-Sowayegh. ARAB-PETRO POLITICS. page 129.

12.-Abdulaziz al-Sowayegh. ARAB-PETRO POLITICS. page 129.

13.-Press comuniqué of the meeting of ministers of the Organization of Oil Exporting Arab Nations. October 1973.

14.-Mohamed Harb. OIL WAR: THE SECRET MINUTES OF THE ARAB OIL MINISTERS MEETING. page 133.

15.-Jack Anderson. THE MIDDLE EAST: OIL DEALERS. page 184.

16.-Felix Rossi Guerrero. DIARY OF AN OIL DIPLOMAT. page 75.

17.-Jack Anderson with James Boyd. OIL. THE REAL STORY BEHIND THE WORLD ENERGY CRISIS. page 317.

18.-Raymond Aron. THE IMPERIAL REPUBLIC. page 436.

19.-Paul Johnson. MODERN TIMES. page 665.

20.-Paul Johnson. IBIDEM. page 667.

21.-Luis Vallenilla. RISE. DECLINE AND FUTURE OF THE VENEZUELAN OIL. page 401.

22.-Ruth S. Knowles. AMERICA'S OIL FAMINE. page 107.

CHAPTER V

THE FALL OF THE SHAH OF IRAN

The Islamic Revolution of Ayatollah Khomeini

The world had not totally adapted to the crisis resulting from the Arab oil embargo when it once again faced a new and even more violent oil shock. This time the reason was the fall of the Shah of Iran in 1979.

In effect, the abundance of resources befalling Iran from 1974 onwards, far from strengthening the Shah's regime, ended up by deeply destabilizing it. Already by 1978 there had been public demonstrations against the government, demanding the return of Ayatollah Ruholla Khomeini, who was exiled in Paris. Khomeini was the spiritual leader of the shiites, the Muslim branch to which nine out of ten inhabitants of Iran belong.

Public agitation worsened in subsequent months. Strikes became rampant and popular unrest could not be stopped despite the stern efforts of the Shah's secret police.

In January 1979, the Shah made a last attempt to pacify the masses by calling Shahpur Bakthiar, leader of the opposition, to form a government. It was too late however and no concession was to be enough.

On January 16th, the Shah and his family fled the country, leaving the government in the hands of a regency council. He travelled first to Egypt, then to Morrocco and from there to Mexico.

In order to understand the deep unrest that led to the fall of the Shah of Iran, it is imperative to analyze the country's religious and political history. This is a Muslim yet not an Arab nation, whose population in its majority fervently espouse the shiite doctrine, traditionally counter to the sunnites, the

Islamic majority, for religious reasons. Most of the population in the Arab countries, except for Iraq, are made up by sunnites.

The confrontation between shiites and sunnites goes back to the year 637. In effect the schism among both Islam groups occured due to the struggle for power after Mohammed's death between Ali's followers - who, apart from being the prophet's cousin, was married to his daughter Fatima - and the faction of the Sunna, that backed the old aristocracy of Mecca (the holy city birthplace of Islam) as the successors of Mohammed.

The shiites sustained that the right to the caliphate corresponded to Ali, being as he was a relative of the prophet. The Sunna in turn affirmed that the right to be chosen as a caliph was not only reserved to relatives of the prophet alone but also to all the descendants of the Quaraysh Arab tribe of which the Omeya (UMayyad) clan was a part.

The Sunna's position won, the dynasty of the Omeya was therefore begun and the first three caliphs were members of this branch. However, in the course of many generations, the shiites never ceased to claim the injustice committed by those who usurped Ali's right to succeed Mohammed, inasmuch as the the Caliph not only ruled over the people but was also their spiritual leader.

The abovementioned confrontation worsened one generation later when Hussein, son of Ali and grandson of Mohammed, once again claimed his right to the caliphate. In the end, Hussein was murdered by the followers of the Omeya. From that time on, Hussein's martyrdom became one of the focal points of the shiite doctrine. Thus, the enmity between these two groups has continued on throughout the centuries, passing on from generation to generation, up to the present times.

On the other hand, the shiites, fervent believers in the Koran, were never able to adapt to a Western lifestyle. As pious Muslims, they believe that the Koran is the source of all knowledge since it was inspired directly to Mohammed from God. For a shiite, his faith is more than a religion; it is a complete way of life. The Koran is a synopsis of all the laws and rules of family life and behaviour in the community, including regulations governing politics and the principles that must guide commercial activities as well as all punishments to be imposed on those who break the social norms.

In this regard, author David Lamb, a scholar of the problems in the Middle East, when referring to the religious concept of the Muslims, stated:

"Only faith is necessary. Inshallah. Indeed, in Islamic institutions, the very word "innovation" is heresy, because nothing can be new; all knowledge is already in the Koran... Even science is viewed as something of an atheistic tool..." (1)

On the other hand, for a devout shiite, submittance to a mortal only decries rejection of Ala's divinity. This behaviour is deemed barbarian ('jahiliyya'). Human beings face a clearcut choice: or they obey the Laws of Alla in their entirety or they accept the laws imposed by man to dominate others. In the latter case they are in a state of 'jahiliyya'. The alternative is obvious: believers must choose between Islam and jahiliyya. The objective pursued by the shiites is to restablish the Kingdom of God on earth.

Thus, the centuries-old trauma left by the usurpation of power committed by the first caliphs being an integral part of the basis of the shiite credo, and uncapable of adapting to the process of innovation and modernization imposed by the Shah on Iran, it is no wonder that the people finally came to regard the Shah himself as one more usurper of power. To accept the Shah's rule implied entering into a state of 'jahiliyya'.

Economic affluence resulting from the increase in oil prices after the Arab oil embargo actually aggravated the religious feelings against the Shah. The shiites observed the changes brought about day after day by the increasing oil wealth. Faced with the fear those changes inspired in them, they reacted by seeking refuge in their religion. This was how it was not difficult for Khomeini to convince the Iranians that the Shah was an apostate who was trying to eliminate the influence of Islam over the country's political arena. Apart from the application of laws that were different from those in the Koran, this constituted a domination ('hakimiyya') of man over man, with its evident rejection of God's divinity.

From the political standpoint, the Shah's position depended on a fusion of interests proposed in the '50s by John Foster Dulles, between the Baghdad Pact sponsored by Great Britain and the security agreements entered into by the Americans with Iran, Turkey and Pakistan. After the Suez Canal crisis, the British presence in the Middle East area was tending to disappear. The Arab countries were being ravaged one after the other by revolutions that geopolitically speaking, brought them closer to the USSR and led to progressively radical positions. The old Baghdad Pact had disappeared. Under these circumstances, the Americans increasingly started to trust non-Arab Muslim nations such as Iran, Turkey and Pakistan, and to renew old agreements under the name of the Central Treaty Organization. In practice, under the protection of said agreement, the Shah received full support from the United States, thereby becoming a "Middle East police". It was therefore no surprise that the shiites saw the Shah as a puppet that the Western world had imposed on the Iranians against their will.

The Shah had also adopted the Sassanid calendar instead of the Muslim one, and had resorted to pre-Islamic Persian symbols such as the 'Peacock Throne'; he had accepted the title of 'light of the Aryans' and in sum, had tried to Westernize the country, thereby committing sins that went against the shiite doctrine. The conclusion was unavoidable: the 'Pahlevi apostate' had to be overthrown and replaced by new leaders that would embrace the Koran's religious traditions. The kingdom of Alla on earth had to be restablished.

The Pahlevi dynasty did not therefore have religious support nor the backing of a longstanding tradition. The first member of the dynasty was Reza Khan, a soldier with luck, who took power in 1952. During World War Two, Reza Khan adopted an openly pro-Nazi position. Thereby the British and Soviet troops invaded Iran, forcing him to abdicate in 1941 in favour of the heir prince Mohammed Reza Pahlevi, the last Shah of Iran.

Ayatollah Khomeini returned triumphantly to Iran on February the 1st. Prime Minister Bakthiar was deposed and on the 11th of February, Khomeini designates Mehdi Bazargan to that post. By means of a plebiscite held on April 2nd, 1979, the Islamic republic was proclaimed within the Muslim orthodox current. Iran therefore came to be controlled by a theocratical government, in which the executive, legislative and legal powers were subject to the authority of the Islamic religious leader.

The Hostage Crisis

Some time later the Shah, who was seriously ill, went to the U.S. for medical treatment. In reprisal, Muslim fundamentalist groups assaulted the U.S. Embassy in Teheran on November 4th, 1979, taking sixty-six hostages. This crisis came to have serious international repercussions. The assault to the Embassy seems not to have been approved by the government nor by Khomeini himself. However, there is no doubt that the Ayatollah's vigorous criticism against the Americans prompted this attack. Neither the Iranian government nor the religious authorities did anything towards helping to free the hostages.

The United States was particularly affected by all this. In barely a few years, Americans had witnessed the murder of a president, the trauma of the Vietnam war, the Watergate crisis and two oil shocks. They now had to confront the Iran situation and knew not how to react. This would be a phenomenon that would bring about profound sociological effects. Few times before in the history of the United States had the people's morale reached such low levels. The Americans could not grasp their government's inability to rescue the hostages. A commando-type operation was attempted under the code name "Desert One" but it failed. Despite President Carter's efforts to free his fellowmen, his popularity fell to critically low levels.

Deeply concerned about the population's morale, President Carter felt obliged to address a televised speech to the nation in mid-1979, stating that:

"I wish to talk to you now about a fundamental threat for American democracy... A crisis of trust. This is a crisis beating against the heart, the soul and the spirit itself of our national will... The trust we have always had as a nation is not simply a romantic dream or a proverb read in some dusty book... Trust has defined our course... We know America's strength. We are strong. We can recover our unity. We can recover our trust... We must altogether aim at achieving a rebirth of America's spirit."

After endless negotiations, finally Iran freed the American hostages in 1981. 442 days had gone by since the date of their capture.

In its zeal to achieve the freedom of the hostages, the U.S. government negotiated a series of conditions with Iran that would later on be harshly criticized:

"The agreement requires the U.S. to renounce any intentions of interfering in Iran's domestic affairs, to lift the trade embargo against Iran and to request its allies in Europe to do the same... The U.S. also pledged to help locate any assets of the deceased Shah and his family in America and to freeze them until such time as Iran puts forward legal claims before the American courts... The more complex provisions (of the agreement) refer to Iran's assets frozen by Carter at the beginning of the hostage crisis and estimated by the U.S. at an approximate total figure of 12 billion dollars. These include: 2.4 billion dollars in gold, securities and cash, directly under the control of the U.S. government; 5.5 billion dollars in foreign branches of American banks; and 4 billion dollars attached in suits against Iran by American companies and individuals. Carter signed an order asking the Justice Department to request the courts to abandon those suits and allow claims to be decided by a jury of arbitrators (one chosen by the U.S., one by Iran and another chosen jointly). The U.S. also accepted not to seek compensation for the damages to their Embassy in Teheran and to forbid the hostages from filing suit against Iran."(2)

Caspar Weinberger, Secretary of Defense during Reagan's term, joining the criticisms brought against this agreement, considered that the conditions accepted for the liberation of the hostages were a mistake and stated his opposal to any agreement with the Iranian government. To this effect, in his book called Fighting for Peace, he asserted that:

"... I feel strongly that conduct of the kind Iran exhibited during the seizure of our Embassy completely disqualified it from any civilized intercourse with other nations. I feel that as long as the leadership in Iran remains as it is (and in my opinion it has not

changed substantively after Ayatollah Khomeini's death), it is futile to expect that any kind of agreements with such a government would be kept or would be of any value."(3)

The hostages were freed at the time when Reagan the president of the United States. Former president Carter, upon hearing the news, stated:

"These barbarian acts perpetuated against our fellow countrymen in Iran can never be excused. These criminal acts should be condemned by all the decent law-abiding people in the world. These were abominable circumstances which we shall never forget."

The Shah of Iran's fall generated in turn deep changes in the geopolitical structure of the Middle East. Up to that time, the Shah was undoubtedly a stabilizing factor in the region, despite his permanent insistence in progressively increasing the price of crudes.

The Iran he ruled, though Islamic, was not ethnically Arab and therefore did not answer to the same unrest that periodically altered the peace in the Persian Gulf. The Shah was a mature and well-experimented ruler, who after his youthful flirtations when he let himself get carried away by the nationalistic policies of his prime minister Mossadegh and which temporarily cost him his throne, now saw the opportunities open to his country by adopting a more balanced position. He was an intelligent man who understood that Iran was located in an extremely delicate geographical spot where the great superpowers were willing to pay high political stakes to gain control over one of the planet's richest regions.

Iran's vast frontier with the USSR and the enormous abundance of its oil fields made it into a coveted potential prize for the Kremlin's imperialistic desires, whose troops had already occupied the country up to 1946. The Shah therefore understood that his country's independence would depend largely on support by the U.S. After all, nothing could worry the American nation more than a Soviet presence in Iran, since most of the crudes coming from the prolific fields in the Middle East passed through the Hormuz Strait. Whoever, therefore, controlled Iran, would have the key to the Persian Gulf and the final control over the treasures of that entire area.

In order to keep its position, Iran had to be a strong nation. The Shah had become the "police" of the Middle East, thanks to an army that came to be one of the most powerful and wellstocked in the world. Backed by the "Nixon doctrine" that granted strong military support to certain chosen Third World countries capable of confronting communism, Iran was able to purchase the most modern war equipment from the U.S.

In a paper entitled The Iranian Revolution in International Affairs, internationalist Fred Alliday sustained that in the years prior to the revolution:

"... Iran continued to be an important part of the U.S. global military presence vis-á-vis Russia. Its armed forces were destined to play a limited role in any future war with Russia and the U.S. also lined up in 1970 a number of electronic sentry posts throughout the Iranian-Soviet border that were used to monitor radio and air traffic in the USSR..."(4)

The Shah also knew how to stand apart from the rest of the nations in the region. We thus see that Iran had recognized Israel since 1960. On the other hand, each time Middle East conflicts such as the Suez Canal crisis and the Arab oil embargo had affected the supply of crudes to Western nations, Iran, together with Venezuela, had come to the rescue by increasing its own production to cover the market deficits.

A mechanism capable of fostering a gradual increase of oil prices linked to a growth index in the price of manufactured goods had also been proposed by the Shah. If said proposal had been understood and accepted by the Western industrialized nations, its implementation would have saved countless suffering to mankind and serious traumas to world economy.

Now therefore, in spite of all his foresightedness, the Shah was not able to survive the social, political and religious upheaval generated by the immense mass of wealth suddenly entering the country after the oil embargo of 1973. Thus, the hurricane of contradictions and conflicts that repeatedly desolated the Middle East ended up by dragging down the most stable of the nations in the region.

The Second Oil Shock

One of the major changes resulting from the Iranian revolution was the sudden decrease in oil production in that country, falling from about six million barrels per day to less than two million. Repercussions in the international oil markets reached disastrous proportions. Cuts in oil supply had started since the end of 1978 due to anti-Shah strikes in the province of Khuzistan. The situation started to worsen from the beginning of 1979.

Despite the foregoing, the fall in oil production in Iran was not unmanageable. This is evident when confirming that over half of the deficit generated by the Iran crisis could have been compensated with oil production increases in other OPEC nations. Thus, during the first quarter of 1979, the most acute period in the crisis, OPEC oil production was barely 2.2 million barrels per day below levels existing during the last quarter of 1978.

However, a wave of panic swept the U.S. as well as other industrialized nations, greater even than that due to the 1973 oil embargo. Professor D. Rustow described the situation thus:

"Nervous buyers and hopeful speculators, convinced that the shortage would increase prices to sky-high levels, purchased as much oil as they could get their hands on and paid any price demanded. The result was a self-fulfilling prophesy. Frantic purchases worsened the situation, speculation made the prices increase and attracted more speculators and the subsequent price increase caused even more panic. While the exiled Shah travelled from Egypt to Morrocco and from there to Mexico, prices in the spot market doubled and tripled."(5)

The Petroleum Intelligence Weekly in its May 14th, 1979 edition reported: "The spot market for crudes is totally out of control with prices quickly going up to the 30 dollars-per-barrel mark, with surcharges of 8 to 10 dollars per barrel above OPEC official levels."

In this manner the existence of two parallel oil markets was put in evidence, and even though they had always existed, there had never been so great a contrast betwen them up to that time.

On the one hand, there was the official or contractual market with prices set by OPEC, moved by international oil trade among customary buyers and sellers. On the other hand there was the spot market sought out by incidental buyers. Most of the oil exporting countries preferred to sell their hydrocarbons in the first market, in view of the trade stability it provided.

However, as a result of the fall of the Shah of Iran, oil markets suffered deep changes. Thus OPEC crude marker - 34º API Light Arab - which, by the end of 1978 was quoted at 12 dollars per barrel in the spot market, increased to $16 in that same market in January, $22.50 in February, $35 in June and reached 41 dollars the barrel in the incidental market by November. In barely eleven months, it had increased by 340%.

In the meantime, the official price for the same light Arab crude that before the crisis was $12.70 per barrel, had been set by OPEC at the end of 1981 at 34 dollars.

The increasing diffence between the value of the crudes in the spot or incidental market and the official prices set by OPEC (contractual market) led several countries of the organization to see the chance to obtain added income by withdrawing important volumes of crudes from the second market to sell it in the first. This of course aggravated nervousness in the buyers, who then had to meet their requirements of hydrocarbons in a much more volatile market riddled with panic. It is worthwhile mentioning that in this regard, Venezuela maintained a conservative policy and avoided increasing its sales in the spot market.

Simultaneously, the oil companies had adopted a strategy similar to that of OPEC nations by increasing their share of sales in the spot market, where they could get greater revenues. This phenomenon was contemplated in an internal White House memorandum dated November 7th, 1979, prepared by analyst Terence O'Rourke:

"Most of the foreign oil taken from international markets and imported to the U.S. is controlled by a handful of large international companies. Other companies purchase all or almost all the foreign oil from them. In recent months, while there has been a shortage in oil supplies, these large companies reduced their sales to third parties in order to meet their own needs or otherwise deviate them to the spot market in order to benefit from the higher prices thereof... Its buyers had to resort to the spot market where the price bidding took them to

extraordinary levels. These buyers imported that oil to the U.S. at greatly inflated prices, thereby creating a double impact in pressing up the prices of domestic crudes as well as refined products."(6)

In reality, as already stated, Iran's decreased production could very well have been quickly compensated with production increases in other areas. The fear generated by the crisis had unleashed hysterical nervous purchases, which, as Professor Rostow has stated, were largely to blame for the violent price hike. Thus, by mid-1980, accumulated oil stock volumes were double those produced by the shutdown in production in Iran in 1979.

In the meantime, in Venezuela, the price of our crudes and products increased by 90% between 1978 and 1979, from an average of $12.50 per barrel to some 24 dollars by 1979.

It is not easy to understand the global impact the price increase of crudes had on world economy. The following lines shall illustrate some interesting data in this regard.

Non-oil producing Third World nations were most affected by the hydrocarbons price hike. Unemployment and inflation indexes reached unprecedented levels.

In fact, figures and statistics are far too cold to reflect the widespread misery and suffering in all the developed and underdeveloped nations alike. Undoubtedly, however, some felt these more than others. In terms of human suffering there is no way to express the consequences brought about by the sudden increases in hydrocarbon prices.

However, the responsibility of this impact cannot be exclusively ascribed to said increase. We have already mentioned an international crisis that had been brewing as a result of the chronic and spiraling fiscal deficits felt since 1958 in the U.S. economy, which led Paul Johnson to state that in the "autumn of 1973, the international financial system was disintegrating."(7)

Likewise, in a paper written by the economists Paul Hallwood and Stuart Sinclair published in OPEC magazine(8), the authors concluded that the effects due to inflation, economic growth deceleration and protectionary measures taken by industrialized countries had led to greater negative consequences in the developing countries than the increases in oil prices. However, one could argue that the phenomena quoted were at least in part the result of the oil price increases.

In any event, faced with the situation at hand, the Third World countries were left with no other choice but to resort to indebtedness to avoid total economic bankruptcy, with the subsequent social traumas.

Recycling the "Petrodollars"

OPEC revenues, that by 1970 had been $7 billion, increased in 1974 (a year after the first oil shock) to $72 billion, reaching by 1980 (after the second shock) the astronomical figure of $300 billion.

This phenomenal increase in income represented in practice the most massive transfer of wealth ever known in the entire history of mankind.

Now therefore, OPEC nations understood that this enormous monetary mass could not be immediately absorbed by the respective economies without creating distortions that would lead to an uncontrollable inflation.

Faced with this situation, these nations decided to place their money surpluses in the international financial system. We therefore see that in 1980 alone the members of OPEC made deposits and investments abroad in the amount of 110 billion dollars. Of course most of it was made by some Arab nations who, given their huge oil production and small populations, had no choice but to do so. This was the case of Saudi Arabia, Kuwait, the United Arab Emirates, etc.

The abundance of financial resources that came to flood the coffers of Western banks had to go somewhere, otherwise interest for the depositing nations would not be able to be cancelled.

Economists therefore coined a very adequate phrase in their complicated professional jargon: "Recycling of petrodollars". This recycling seemed to be the panacea for all the maladjustments created by the sudden increase in hydrocarbon prices. In simpler terms, the banks lent funds deposited by OPEC nations to third parties.

It was therefore a matter of recycling petrodollars no matter what. The entire world would thereby be happy. It was thought that in this manner OPEC's wealth surpluses could be distributed through international credits. The economists reasoned that OPEC countries would thereby receive the interests that wre their due; banks would get a juicy remuneration for acting as middlemen, and in view of the laws governing financial mechanisms, a multiplying effect would be felt by means of which, for each dollar received in deposit, several dollars could be granted in credit, thereby increasing the revenues of those institutions; importing nations could receive the financial attention they urgently needed to cancel their growing oil invoices and the entire financial system would count on abundant resources to grant credit aid needed by any country in order to achieve the desired goals of economic expansion.

It therefore seemed as though an almost magical solution to all problems had been found. It was even thought that this would end up by opening the doors to a new era of great expansion in world economic activities. Some experts were of the opinion that since modern economy is based on credit, the abundant economic resources could only presage an era of general prosperity, which, despite the growing cost of energy, would produce an increased generation of wealth that would benefit everyone.

The Financial System Crisis

Of course, many of those who sustained these opinions worked for the large banks. They had also forgotten that the arguments described were similar to those that had been used to defend the financial system that sprang up as a result of the appearance of the market of eurodollars.

Convinced by the foregoing arguments, lenders and borrowers alike embarked on a race that led to an accelerated and irrational indebtedness of the latter and serious risks for the stability of the former.

However, a phenomenon occurred that would have been easy to foresee. The accelerated increase in the circulating monetary mass together with the increased cost of energy and the not-so efficient destination that was being given to the financial resources in the prevailing eagerness to place them as soon as possible, brought about the appearance of extremely high inflation levels.

We thus see that inflation in the U.S. had reached 15% by 1979, its highest level since World War Two. To fight this scourge,

Jimmy Carter designated Paul Volcker as the president of the Federal Reserve.

Volcker was convinced that the only way to curb inflation was to impose stringent limits on the growth of circulating currency (M1). The results of this policy was an extremely high interest rate growth, which, by 1981, had reached 20.5%. This was therefore a bitter, but in the opinion of the Federal Reserve, indispensable medicine.

Obviously, the decision of the United States had necessarily to be followed by the rest of the industrialized nations. Otherwise the voluminous mass of petrodollars, attracted by the higher interest rates, would be fed into the American banks.

On the other hand, the international banking system was granting multimillion dollar financing to Third World countries to cover their costs of importing oil. However, the crisis in which these countries fell ended by placing them in a situation in which it was impossible to fulfill these obligations. Enormous sums for endless alternate energy projects were also granted as well as for the development of new oil-producing areas, where the costs far exceeded those known till then. However, the steep price fall experienced by the hydrocarbons in subsequent years made many of those projects antieconomical, and serious doubts were cast as to the possibilities of recovering the capital. In conclusion, many other activities in the U.S. and other nations were financed, which could have been highly profitable if a strong world economic depression had not been brought about and if the spiraling interest rates orchestrated by Volcker had not occurred, all of which led to the bankruptcy of countless companies that were never able to cover their financial obligations.

The situation described generated strong tensions in the international financial system. Evidently, this in turn produced another circumstance whose consequences could have been much more serious. In effect, once the aforementioned credits seemed irrecoverable, it was thought that a mass bankruptcy would ensue in many of the banks comprising the financial middleman system of the capitalistic world.

This phenomenon could have reached such vast proportions that banks and governments had to carry out important efforts to find solutions to the problem at hand, a problem which, to date, remains far from being completely solved. In fact, many nations are still embarked in a process of debt renegotiation.

According to the April 1987 issue of the Bank Safety Forum publication, by that date 10 percent of American banks were in the so-called "Problem List". At the beginning of the '80s the annual U.S. bankrupcy average in banks was 20. In 1986 alone, 138 banks went under. This publication estimated that by the end of 1987, a record figure of 250 banks would be bankrupt. (9)

Debt and the Third World Crisis

As a result of recycling the petrodollars, the world economy - and particularly that of the Third World nations - had been contaminated in a few years with a new disease: A debt of astronomic proportions. This debt, due to the increased interest rates, simply could not be paid off.

We thereby see that by 1983 Third World debt exceeded $500 billion, five times the rate of indebtedness in 1973. This figure represented annual payments in interest alone of close to $51 billion(10). The situation continued to worsen however and by 1986, the Third World public debt had reached the astounding figure of $1,040 billion.

For underdeveloped countries it was practically impossible to cover the cost of energy imports with their meager income, plus payment of their foreign debt, plus the cost of other indispensable import items. Even in the event that they had resources to cover the service of the debt, they would have had to do so by sacrificing any possibility whatsoever of domestic growth, which would obviously impose tremendous sacrifices on their respective populations, thereby creating very dangerous social conflicts.

Parallel to the increase in energy costs which led underdeveloped nations to pay thirty times the prices they had paid in the '60s for the oil being imported, an equally serious problem was arising. Resources from their own exports had fallen to the lowest levels in the previous thirty years.

The explanation of this phenomenon can be found in the fact that these nations were not only affected by the increase itself in the price of hydrocarbons but they also suffered the consequences of the indirect effect thereof on the industrialized nations. In effect, in the meantime that the cost of energy increased, industrialized consumers had increasingly lesser resources to purchase other products that they deemed less important. Thus, while developing nations were forced to pay giant additional invoices for their indispensable oil imports, the price of their exported products was falling to unprecedented lows. Inflation in the industrialized nations likewise made more acute the traditional deterioration in terms of exchange. Consequently, Third World economies were seriously affected by the lowest economic growth indexes in several decades.

Average inflation in Latin America reached 80% and in many countries of that region unemployment, including subemployment, included 45% of the active population. Inflation would exceed the four-digit mark in some Latin American nations. Enrique Iglesias, president of the

InterAmerican Development Bank, qualified the '80s as "the lost decade". During those years, the global Latin American debt increased by 75%. Each dollar increase in the barrel of oil represented for those nations additional expenses of $400 million per year. Years later, when the industrialized economies were upwardly recovering, many Latin nations had not been able to overcome the trauma and, to the contrary, their situation was worsening as time went by.

The Third World debt crisis officially broke out on August 20th, 1982, when Mexico announced that it was in no condition to continue fulfilling the obligations entered into by way of its international indebtedness, which amounted to the astronomical figure of $80 billion. It would subsequently be the turn of Brazil, Argentina, Venezuela and Poland. Regarding these last four countries alone, indebtedness with the banks exceeded the $230-billion mark. Thus, the Third World debt had become the most dramatic crisis inasmuch as it directly threatened the world banking system. Darrel Delamaide, in his book entitled the Debt Shock, referring to the need by debtors and creditors to renegotiate the amounts involved, stated:

"Renegotiation consisted, after all, in avoiding the banks from having to admit that those loans were not to be paid back. The banks have to cancel the loans that are not returned and these cancellations appear as losses in their accounting statements. Cancellation of such enormous loans might represent the disappearance of benefits and even the elimination of the capital necessary that constitutes the final obstacle on the road to bankruptcy."(11)

Crisis in the Industrialized Economies

In the industrialized economies, the effect of an increase in oil prices coupled with other structural factors that had been gestating from years before, brought about consequences of incalculable proportions. Suffice it to say that by 1983 the total share of unemployment in these economies was 33 million and since no recovery was foreseeable in the future, it was estimated that by 1985 this figure would be in excess of 35 million.

U.S. Inflation in 1980 had reached 15% and by 1981 there were 12 million people unemployed. Sales of automobiles had reached its lowest levels in 20 years. In 1982 the growth rate in the production of goods and services was negative.

In the Western European nations the average inflation rate had reached levels of 13% by 1983, for the third year running. By that year, economic growth was also negative and it was estimated at the time that by 1985 there would be around 23 million unemployed.

In 1982 international trade experienced a strong contraction for the first time since the end of World War Two.

The entire world suffered inflation levels that seriously damaged the economies of developed and developing nations alike. Both groups of nations were simultaneously affected by a deep recession. Economists diagnosed the symptoms as a "stagflation". Curiously, recession came hand in hand with inflation whereas the usual case is that both phenomena happen at very different times. In practice, the feared stagflation included the worst of both worlds, since in one critical moment, all the evils of inflation were being coupled with all the evils of recession. Stagflation is a sort of cancer of the economies and its cure is very difficult, since, inasmuch as the only way out from an inflationary process is recession, it would seem that the only way out of a stagflation would be a deep depression. Thus, the secondary effects of the medicine are sometimes worse than the illness itself.

Between 1973 and 1982, the problem of indebtedness was not limited solely to underdeveloped countries. In fact, during that period, the U.S. government alone contracted debts greater than the joint Third World debt. The accumulated fiscal deficit during those years reached $460 billion.

In conclusion, by 1971 the entire debt of all the countries in the world amounted to 3.6 trillion dollars. By 1981 this debt was increasing at an average yearly rate of 15% until it reached 14.3 trillion dollars. This change of phenomenal proportions was an indication that something very serious was happening in the world.

Steps for Saving Energy

Accosted by the increased energy costs, consumer nations started important energy-saving programs. Not without reason, a sort of mass hysteria for conservation of energy developed around the world. The success of these programs far surpassed the most optimistic government forecasts in the larger consumer nations.

Thus, for instance, the automobile industry reacted by producing smaller, more efficient cars that would consequently require much less fuel. New constructions were installed with thermal isolation systems that kept out the cold during the wintertime. At the same time, people started to lower their thermostats. In conclusion, the industry and the large consumers sought new, more efficient systems energy-wise.

Let us bring forth some examples of these statements. Between March 1979 and April 1981 oil consumption in the free world went down by 14%. As the economic recession worsened, demand for the product also decreased. In 1982 alone, the use of petroleum in the United States went down by

11% and the consumption of residual fuel by the American industry - of particular importance vis-a-vis Venezuelan exports - decreased by 41%.

In conclusion, the set of situations deriving from the two oil shocks had been translated into a decreased demand for hydrocarbons in the non-communist countries, going from 52.4 million barrels per day in 1979 to 45.5 million in 1982. Meanwhile, OPEC's participation in the world oil market decreased from 74% in 1974 to 44% in 1988.

Production Surpluses

Naturally, there had to be a reaction to the exaggerated increase in oil prices between 1973 and 1980. This happened shortly afterwards, leading to heavy surpluses in the supply of oil in the international markets with the subsequent fall in prices.

By 1980 some experts predicted that the price of petroleum would soon pass the 80-dollar-per-barrel mark. However, though the results of the efforts carried out to increase oil production were successful and the fall in demand for the product was abrupt, the May 25th, 1981 edition of Newsweek (less than two years after the fall of the Shah of Iran) reported that: "OPEC's immediate problems arise from a surplus of oil due to a global decrease in the economy that has curbed energy demands... Oil production now exceeds demand in approximately 2 million barrels per day and according to some estimates, this surplus could increase to 4 million by the end of the year." "Nobody is buying petroleum today because everyone is sure that it will be cheaper tomorrow" stated at the time Wanda Jablonsky, editor of the Petroleum Intelligence Weekly.

On the other hand, the surpluses achieved by OPEC members in international trade had reached the astounding sum of $109 billion in 1980. Not less surprising is the fact that barely two years later, in 1982, those same nations had an international trade deficit of over $18 billion.

Besides, in an effort to keep up the price levels, OPEC was forced to impose production quotas on its members. Production decreased from some 31 million barrels per day in 1979 to about 15.5 million barrels per day in 1985. Quota setting for each member has come to be a factor of continuous friction and disagreements among the members of OPEC, most of whom openly violate the production quotas assigned to them.

At the same time, OPEC's sacrifice in restricting production has helped in good measure for other oil exporters not affiliated to the organization to increase their share in the international oil markets.

In conclusion, surpluses in oil supply in the international markets gave rise as was to be expected, to a brusque fall in prices of the product. Thus, by the summer of 1986 these prices had touched a low of close to 7 dollars per barrel. The old saying according to which all that goes up violently must come down in like manner was fulfilled.

In truth, despite the tremendous obstacles, pressures and interferences of all kind in the world trade of hydrocarbons, by consumers and producers alike, oil markets in the end are governed by the same laws of demand and supply that are the fundamental basis of any economic process. Thus, when an obstacle arises affecting the volumes of oil offered in the market, its shortage determines a price increase. When on the contrary, the prices of the product are too advantageous, initiatives will always spring up to take advantage of the situation. This, in relatively short time periods, translates into an increase in the volume of oil offered in the markets. As oil prices become higher, the amounts reaching the markets shall also increase, giving rise to an oversupply and consequently prices shall once again fall. In this manner, after some time, a new shortage phenomenon shall arise and the process shall continue.

Therefore, regardless of the efforts put forth by the oil producers, i.e. OPEC nations, to increase the prices of the product, in the end the market laws shall always prevail. Likewise these laws shall always be fulfilled, regardless of the strategies developed by consumer nations attempting to attain lower prices.

For these reasons, it would seem that the most sensible attitude would be that producers and consumers of oil, such a vital product for mankind, put forward their best efforts to arrive at a price that can remunerate producers and at the same time is fair for the consumers.

The foregoing goals seem difficult to achieve so long as the world depends in great measure on an oil supply coming from a politically unstable region such as the Middle East, where events periodically and dramatically affect the oil markets. The countries in that conflictive region of the planet have preferred to use their oil as an extremely dangerous political weapon.

Notes

1.-David Lamb. THE ARABS. JOURNEYS BEYOND THE MIRAGE. page 16.

2.-TIME. February 2nd. 1981.

3.-Caspar W. Weinberger. FIGHTING FOR PEACE: SEVEN CRITICAL YEARS IN THE PENTAGON. page 354.

4.-Fred Alliday. "The Iranian Revolution in International Affairs". OIL AND SECURITY IN THE ARABIAN GULF. page 20.

5.-Quoted by Jack Anderson with James Boyd. OIL. THE REAL STORY BEHIND THE WORLD ENERGY CRISIS. page 3.

6.-Quoted by Jack Anderson with James Boyd. IBIDEM. page 334.

7.-Paul Johnson. MODERN TIMES. page 667.

8.-Marco A. Angeli. THE INTERNATIONAL ECONOMIC ORDER AND THE PRICES OF PETROLEUM. page 30.

9.-Alfredo Toro Hardy. THE VENEZUELAN CHALLENGE: HOW TO INFLUENCE American POLICY DECISIONS. page 208.

10.-Marco A. Angeli. OP. CIT. page 19.

11.-Darrel Delamaide. THE DEBT SHOCK: THE ENTIRE HISTORY OF THE WORLD CREDIT CRISIS. page 17.

CHAPTER VI

THE IRAN-IRAQ WAR

Saddam Hussein vs. Ruholla Khomeini

Saddam Hussein came into power in the Republic of Iraq in 1979. An extremely ambitious ruler backed by the Baath party (the Socialist Arab Resurrection Party), he has a messianic vocation for power with aspirations of becoming the leader of the entire Arab nation. His designation occured on July 16th, after President Bakr resigned, officially for health reasons. That same day, Saddam was designated President, Secretary General of the Baath party, Commander in Chief and head of his country's Revolutionary Command Council.

The territory he governs lies between the Euphrates and Tigris rivers in ancient Mesopotamia. As Saddam Hussein has repeatedly stated, this is the birthplace of civilization. Its history has been one of the most violent and troubled in the entire world. During the course of many centuries Mesopotamia was successively conquered by Sumerians, Akkadians, Amorites, Assyrians, Persians, Parthians, Romans, Sassanians, Mongols, Turks and the British. Violence therefore is a historic and endemic disease for the populators of that region.

While Saddam Hussein was escalating to power in Iraq, the neighbouring country of Iran witnessed one of the revolutions that made the world hold its breath. In Iran, power had just passed into the hands of a theocratical government strongly inspired by the Islamic shiite fundamentalism professed by its maximum spiritual and political leader, the Ayatollah Khomeini, who had led the Iranian people in the uprising against the Shah, that caused the fall of one of the strongest and most stable regimes in the entire Middle East region.

Centuries of Antagonism: Endemic Violence

The contrast of personalities between the two leaders, Saddam Hussein and Ruholla Khomeini, seemed to forebode terrible times for the respective nations. Besides, Iran and Iraq had a longstanding history of confrontations going back several centuries. A new chapter in the bloody series of conflicts characteristic of the Middle East region was about to begin, once more dragging the entire world into a period of uncertainty due to the threat of a possible rupture in the flow of hydrocarbons from that wealthy oil region towards international markets.

To better understand what was about to occur, let us delve into the past. In effect, a historically deep mistrust had coloured the relations between Persia (present-day Iran) and Iraq. Throughout those centuries, both nations had mutually invaded one another hundreds of times and had been in turn invaded by others.

Our starting point is the year 637, a few years after Islamism was born. At the Jalula battle the Arabs ended Persian sassanian domination. This year was relevant in the Islamic world, since it also coincided with the schism that divided Muslims into two factions that would forever be enemies: the sunnites and the shiites. The former imposed the clan of the Omeya (Umayyad) of the old aristocracy as Mohammed's successors. The latter alleged that the Omeyas had usurped the rights of Ali, son-in-law and cousin of the prophet, to be his successor.

Towards the year 651, Arab domination had extended to the entire Persian territory and Islamism had been imposed. Later on, in the year 750, Abul Abbas, a descendant of Mohammed, defeated the Arab Omeya dynasty, and, backed by the shiites proclaimed himself Caliph and set up the Abbassides dynasty, transferring the capital of the caliphate from Damascus to Baghdad. Under the Abbassid caliphs, Muslim culture reached its height and this continued until the XIIIth century.

Between the XIIIth and XIVth centuries, Persia and Baghdad were invaded and devastated by the Mongol invasions of Hulagu and Timur Lenk. The Abbassides civilization was thus destroyed.

From 1501 onwards, a new dynasty, the Safavids, was established in Persia, and high levels of prosperity were reached. In 1508 Shah Ismail Safawi conquered Baghdad, which remained subjugated until 1514 when the Persians were once again expelled during the battle of Galdiran.

Once more Baghdad was conquered by the Persians in 1529 but this time were expelled by the Turkish sultan Suleiman the Magnificent, who took over Iraq between 1534 and 1535 and carried out three separate campaigns against Persia to conquer the region of Erzurur. Under Suleiman, the Ottoman fleet came to dominate the Mediterranean, conquering the north of Africa (except for Morrocco), the Arab Middle East and extending the empire from Tripoli to the eastern part of Asia Minor. In Europe he reached up to Hungary and was finally stopped at the gates of Vienna.

In 1623 the Persians conquered Baghdad and remained there until 1638. From that year until 1918, a long period of Ottoman domination prevailed in the present Iraqi territorry. However, confrontations with Persia were constant. Thus, in 1735, Persian navy forces took over the Strait of Shatt al-Arab, but soon after withdrew. By 1820 Baghdad was saved from a new Persian invasion because of a cholera epidemic. Twenty years later, the Persians conquered the city of Sulaimaniya and threatened to occupy the territories of Kuwait and Bahrain. After the occupation of Sulaimaniya, the Persians claimed the entire province of Khuzistan as theirs. In 1842 Persia dominated the eastern bank of Shatt al-Arab and occupied the city of Mohamarah, which was renamed Khorramshar.

The Ottoman conquerors in Iraq signed numerous treaties with the Persians between 1639 and 1913, each one of which was adjusted to the fate of the warring parties in the countless war conflicts. The last of these treaties was the Protocol of Asitana, signed in 1913, which set the eastern bank of Shattal-Arab as the frontier with Persia. The Ottomans also handed over all the islands in that body of water, including Abadan, to Persia. It is worthwhile mentioning that the Shatt al-Arab is a relatively narrow waterway where the Euphrates and Tigris rivers meet, in turn communicating with the Persian Gulf through the Strait of Khor Abdullah. This therefore is Iraq's only way out to the Persian Gulf and covers barely 9.3 miles of coastline.

The Ottoman empire was dismembered after the First World War. In 1918 the Iraqi territory was invaded by Great Britain and a mandate of the Society of Nations was issued in 1920 handing over administration of this territory to the British. In 1921, the British placed Emir Faisal on the throne of Iraq, thereby attempting to establish local authorities that could be accepted. In effect, Faisal belonged to the hashemites, connected by Islamic heritage to the al-Hashim, the descendants of Mohammed.

In 1932, Iraq finally became independent. A new treaty was signed with Persia in 1937 (that by then had already adopted the name Iran) and Iraq. Said treaty ratified the frontiers among the two nations demarcated in the 1913 Protocol of Asitana.

In 1969, Iran proposed a new protocol to Iraq that would substitute the 1937 treaty. Under this new protocol, both countries would have joint administration over the Shatt al-Arab. Iraq's opposal to signing the new protocol led Iran to revoke the 1937 Treaty and to foster the subversion of Kurdish populations in Iraqi territory. Finally, in 1975, the Treaty of Algeria was signed, setting forth an intermediate line in the waters of the Shatt al-Arab as the frontier between the two countries.

The Basis for the Conflict is Set

We thus arrive to 1979, the year of the ascension to power of two strongminded leaders in Iran and Iraq, each one driven by very different goals. One of them was Saddam Hussein, an Arab-style socialist, a leader with a violent past, willing to drag his nation into the riskiest adventures in order to achieve his goals of dominance over the Persian Gulf. Iran, on the other hand, had a theocratical government whose ruler is none other than the Ayatollah Khomeini, the spiritual leader of his nation, fervently shiite and deeply inspired by religion.

Khomeini was no less capable of violence than Saddam. For Khomeini, the Holy War or 'Jihad' is a morally acceptable weapon placed in his hands by Islam and he would not hesitate to use it if necessary. His incendiary religious rhetoric started to win adepts among the shiite population of the Arab nations.

Khomeini's hatred of Saddam did not start upon his ascension to power in Iran. While still exiled in France, a journalist asked him in 1978 who were his main enemies, and he answered:

"First, the Shah, then the American satan, afterwards Saddam Hussein and his infidel Baath party."

The centuries-old accumulation of hatred, mistrust and resentments between the two nations had another ingredient, which, though not new, was now fanatically thrust forward: religious confrontations.

In effect, as already analyzed in previous chapters, Islam is divided into two traditionally opposed factions: sunnites and shiites. Nine out of ten inhabitants in Iran are shiites. About 55% of Iraq's population is shiite, whereas 20% is sunnite.

For the fervent shiite, a socialist dictatorship is an unacceptable political doctrine. The Koran is the synopsis of all the laws; therefore, a government like Saddam Hussein's represents the domination of man over man and is thereby unjustifiable from the religious point of view, since mortals must only submit to Alla. The goal of the shiites is to reestablish God's kingdom on earth. The public powers must therefore be subordinated to the authority of the religious leaders.

The religious problem was acquiring greater proportions due to the fact that two of the holy cities and pilgrimage points for the shiites, the cities of al-Najaf and Karbala, were located in Iraq.

Ali, Mohammed's son-in-law, had been murdered close to al-Najaf and his remains had been buried there. Karbala in turn was the site of the martyrdom of Hussein, the prophet's grandson, which made it into a focal point in the shiite doctrine. In the Muslim month of Muharram, yearly processions were carried out to commemorate the death of Hussein and other martyrs by the sunnites. This type of ritual frequently degenerated into clashes between followers of both religious groups, which obviously had a great political potential for destabilization.

From the ideological point of view, there was an unsurmountable difference between the men who now controlled these two nations. The shiite religious leader was convinced that the ultimate goal of Islam was to "abolish nationality" and, therefore, Arab nationalism advocated by Pan-Arabism was fundamentally opposed to Islam. For hard-line Iranian revolutionaries, Arab nationalism in Iraq and other nations was a negative and obstructionistic philosophy that had to be eliminated before the Islamic revolution could be furthered.

Evidently, for a dictator like Saddam Hussein, the shiite doctrine constituted in turn an undeniable risk for the stability of his government. He could not forget that most of the population in Iraq was also shiite. Thus, the sympathies of that sector of Iraq's population to the Iranian revolution threatened the Baath party's goals of achieving full control over all spheres of the country's political life. This, therefore, was not only a religious struggle among two nations or among two systems of government, but also among two different types of social organization.

To diminish the risk of the threats, the Iraqi government started to expel its own citizens of Iranian descent and in turn welcomed all Iranian counterrevolutionaries with open arms.

But not only were there religious, political and ideological obstacles among the two countries. Old racial hatreds also compounded the divisions. Iraq is ethnically composed by various groups. Arabs and Kurds constitute the majority of the population; however, there are also Assyrian, Armenian and Turkish minorities. Part of the Arab population feels deeply rooted in a longstanding culture where Pan-Arabism plays a major role. The inhabitants of that nation still felt deeply moved with the impassioned eloquence with which Nasser had called for the unity of the great Arab nation. The Kurdish population is originally Indo-European and is therefore racially linked to the inhabitants of Iran. Nevertheless, contrary to the Iranian population, the great majority of Kurds embrace the sunnite credo.

An element of friction was the aforementioned link of the Kurdish population to Iran. This represented a serious economic threat for Iraq, inasmuch as the area inhabited by these contained vast oil reservoirs that yielded close to 50% of the country's production and more than half of the production of natural gas. Furthermore, this region was crisscrossed by the pipelines that pass through Syria and Turkey and carry oil from Basora to the Mediterranean. The Kurds had not given up their ancestral aspirations of autonomy, traditionally spurred on by Iran and strongly opposed by Iraq.

Iran in turn, though Muslim, is not an Arab nation. Its population is racially Indo-European and does not even share a common language with the Arabs, since the official language in Iran is farsi (Persian).

It is worthwhile mentioning that the reigning erratic policy in Iran tended to create increasingly greater fear and confusion among its neighbours. The first two governments after the fall of the Shah were in theory chaired by secular rulers: Abolhassan Bani-Sadr and Muhammad Ali Rajai. However, true power dwelled in the radical clergymen that praised Muslim fundamentalism. Thus, although the secular government attempted to reach stable relations with the neighbouring states, the ayatollahs and mullahs had not given up their aspirations of instilling their religious revolution in the entire Persian Gulf or at least their intention of stirring up the shiite minorities in other countries in the region. Iran therefore, had become a destabilizing element in the entire area.

We thus see that as a new political configuration was starting to appear based on the triumph of the Islamic revolution in Iran, Khomeini and his followers had no qualms about preaching their preferences and resentments against the rulers of the neighbouring states. They even came to the point of determining who were to be the rulers that would stay in power and who would be overthrown, once the revolution had spread. Thus, among those destined to be deposed were President Mubarak of Egypt, Sultan Qabus of Oman, King Fahd of Saudi Arabia, King Hassan of Morrocco, King Hussein, whom they called the "Shah of Jordan" and President Nimeiry of Sudan. Only Qaddafi of Libya and Hafez al-Assad of Syria were absolved.

As tensions mounted, isolated confrontations also started to multiply along the frontier between both nations. Iraq decided to give monetary aid and weapons to the Arab separatist populations in Iran. In turn, the latter started to foster an uprising of the shiite population in Iraq.

On the 4th of November of 1979, a group of Islamic fundamentalists seized the U.S. Embassy in Teheran. Thus began a period of strong international tensions, in which relations among the Arabs and the Iranians would increasingly spiral downwards.

Under the circumstances, Saddam Hussein saw the opportunity to strengthen his regime by exploiting the antagonisms provoked by the foregoing events and by taking on the role of defender of the weak Arab monarchies, who were in a quandary since they did not wish to set up alliances with Iraq's Baath socialistic party and neither with the shiite fundamentalism prevailing in Iran.

In December 1979, the political situation in the Persian Gulf became even more complicated with the Russian invasion of

Afghanistan, a Muslim country. The echoes of the bloody struggle of the Soviet soldiers against the Islamic correligionaries filled with anguish the hearts of all men who prayed in the direction of Mecca.

On April 1st, 1980, elements connected to the al-Daawa shiite Islamic party attempted to murder Tariq Aziz, Iraq's Vice Prime Minister. Although Aziz survived, other personalities linked to Saddam Hussein's government died in the attempt. Four days later, during the funeral for the victims the Al-Daawa party carried out another terrorist attack.

In retaliation, Iraq declared that the shiite party was illegal and that affiliation to the same would be punishable by death. Meanwhile, the deportation of shiites intensified. Also in April, Ayatollah Baqr al-Sadr, the religious leader of the Iraqi shiites, was jailed, tortured and murdered by hired assassins.

Referring to these facts, Christine Moss Helms, a researcher with the Brookings Foreign Policy Studies program, reported:

"Many clandestine opposition movements within Iraq are largely Shi'a in orientation. Of these, the Party of the Islamic Call (Hizb al-Da'wa al-Islamiya) or al-Da'wa, appears to be the best known in the West... Believed to have been formed in the late 1950s, al-Da'wa allegedly had early financial links to the shah of Iran but seemed to take its ideological impetus from Muhammad Baqr al-Sadr who had close ties with the Iranian clergy."(1)

The death of Baqr al-Sadr brought about great indignation in Iran. It was no secret for anyone that Khomeini was convinced that his revolution would finally be imposed in Iraq. Therefore, official radio transmissions from Teheran had already referred to the Ayatollah Baqr al-Sadr as the next ruler of Iraq. Khomeini declared three official days of mourning in Iran for the death of this most recent of martyrs of Islam. Afterwards, he addressed a message to the Iraqi military, inciting them to rebellion:

"I have given up hope on the upper echelons of the Iraqi law enforcement forces. But I have not given up hope in the officers, NCOs and soldiers and I expect them either to rise heroically and to destroy the foundations of oppression just as happened in Iran, or to desert their garrisons and barracks so that they will not bear the shame of the Ba'th Party's oppression."(2)

Personalities linked to the government of the deposed Shah of Iran started to meet in Baghdad to urge Saddan to act against Iran. They were all convinced that the deep purges carried out by the government of that country among the Iranian army officials had weakened their position to such an extent that it was now an easy target for Saddam Hussein's armed forces.

Thus, the Iraqi government arrived at the conviction that any attack against Iran would be no more than a swift intervention that would quickly put an end to Khomeini's regime.

Saddam Hussein therefore took for granted the following when he decided to attack Iran:

First: That Iran's military forces had been substantially weakened after the Shah's exile. The Imperial Guard, the elite corps of those forces had been dismembered. Officials ranking higher than Lieutenant Colonel had been purged and new commandoes had been set up, based on loyalty to the new regime and the convenience that the latter obey the new religious guidelines of the revolution.

Second: When the Americans withdrew, it would not seem possible that there could be enough technicians capable of repairing or servicing the sophisticated military equipment that had been provided to the Shah.

Third: That, once hostilities broke out, many armed officials and soldiers would desert inasmuch as they did not share the new regime's revolutionary ideology. He was convinced, in particular, that the pilots would be the first to fly over to neighbouring countries as soon as they could get into their planes.

Fourth: It was taken for granted that the Iranian leaders were so divided that a joint response in case of war would be impossible. Internal chaos would end up by defeating the revolution that had already shown signs of being unable to control the forces that drove it.

Fifth: It was also taken for granted that the Islam revolution did not have the full support of the civil population or that, at least, important sectors had become disillusioned and could deliberately conspire to weaken Khomeini's regime. Elite members, army men, officials and ethnic minorities such as the Arabs and Baluchis would undoubtedly be included and even conservative religious leaders. The growing rates of unemployment, the increasing scarcity of consumer goods and other evidence of maladjustment provided the bases to suppose that unease was growing and encompassing a wider sector of the population.

Sixth: The repeated declarations of Iranian religious leaders calling to export and disseminate the revolution to other Persian Gulf Muslim states, would undoubtedly contribute to isolate Iran and to promote other states in taking Iraq's position.

Seventh: That Iran's markedly anti-imperialistic position would also isolate that country from the superpowers who would therefore deny any aid. From the international standpoint, the taking of the U.S. Embassy seemed to have placed Iran on the fringes of civilization. Thus an attack against a nation that had committed such a barbarious act could only strengthen the prestige of whomever carried it out.

Saddam Hussein thus arrived at the conviction that he would reap an easy victory. In his opinion, the attack against Iran would bring about the expected results in no more than two or three weeks. The objectives pursued were the following:

a)Iraq's capture and preservation of the eastern bank of Shatt al-Arab, whereby this important water mass and its islands would remain under the exclusive domain of Iraq. Likewise, he proposed the "liberation" of some territories that had been annexed to Iran, such as Zain al-Qwas and Saif Sa'ad.

b)To induce the secession of the Arab inhabitants in the region of Khuzistan and eventually other non-Persian minorities populating various regions in Iran.

c)To precipitate the fall of the government in Iran.

On September 15th, 1980, Saddam Hussein addressed an impassioned televised speech to his nation. With his own hands he destroyed the Algeria Treaty signed in 1975, that had granted half of the Shatt al-Arab to Iran. Later on he asserted:

"The Iranian leaders have violated the agreement by means of an open and premeditated interference in Iraq's domestic affairs."(3)

The Gulf War

Iraq's offensive finally took place on September 22nd, with the invasion of Iran's extensive 800-mile border from Khoramshar in the south to Qas e-Shirin in the north. On the first day of war, Iraq attacked ten Iranian airports, attempting to destroy that country's air force before the planes could set flight. In October 1980, the Iraqis had crossed the Karum river and destroyed the Abadan-Teheran pipeline. On the 24th of that month, the forces occupied Khorramshahr and surrounded Abadan. Towards the end of 1980, the Iraqi forces had penetrated 20 miles into Iranian territory along the vast front they had chosen.

In the opinion of experts on the subject, the strategy chosen by Iraq in attacking along such an extended front made no sense whatsoever and could only be explained by the fact that Saddam Hussein, lacking military experience and formation, had decided to direct the war personally.

However, it soon became apparent that the situation was not working out according to Saddam's plans. On the one hand, the attack on the airports was not giving the expected results. Iran's air forces remained intact and were soon in a position to retaliate. On the other hand, though in truth Iran's armed forces were disorganized and in the beginning could not structure an effective resistance, the local population unexpectedly and fiercely defended its territory.

In conclusion, while Iraq showed a military superiority on land, Iran's air forces carried out effective attacks against numerous commercial and industrial facilities in Iraq, particularly in Basora. The Iranian air attacks finally decreased, not because the pilots were deserting but because there was a shortage of spare parts and servicing for the American-made planes. In spite of this, the result of these attacks was that Iraq could not continue exporting oil from the reservoirs located to the south of the country.

A few months after the war had broken out, it became evident that Saddam Hussein was not in a position to achieve not even his smallest goals. In effect, the failed attempt to capture Abadan kept him from occupying the eastern banks of Shatt al-Arab.

Thus, the Iran-Iraq war was indefinitely prolonged. Saddam Hussein in the end only strengthened the bases of the Iranian revolution inasmuch as, faced with a foreign attack, the population tended to join forces with the government in order to defend the nation.

On the other hand, as Saddam only too late discovered, the geography of his country had become his worst enemy. While Baghdad and other important Iranian population centers and industrial facilities were close to the frontier with Iran, Iranian targets were out of Iraq's reach. As a result of this geographical feature, Iran's air forces had few miles to travel to reach Iraq's main strategic targets. On the contrary, except for the Iranian facilities in Khuzistan, the Iraqi air force had to fly hundreds of miles in enemy territory to reach important targets.

Iraq's only outlet to sea was through the Shatt al-Arab strait, whose eastern banks were in the hands of the Iranians and which had been closed for navigation, thereby blocking Basora, the only port at Iraq's disposal, some fifty miles upstream. Iran, in turn, had thousands of miles of coast over the Persian Gulf and the Indian Ocean, so its outlet to sea was never threatened.

Umm Qasr, Iraq's only military port, located on the border with Kuwait, could not be used. The outlet to sea from Umm Qasr required passing through a narrow canal between the Kuwaiti islands of Warba and Bubiyan. Fearing Iranian reprisals, Kuwait did not authorize the Iraqi marine force to pass through that canal.

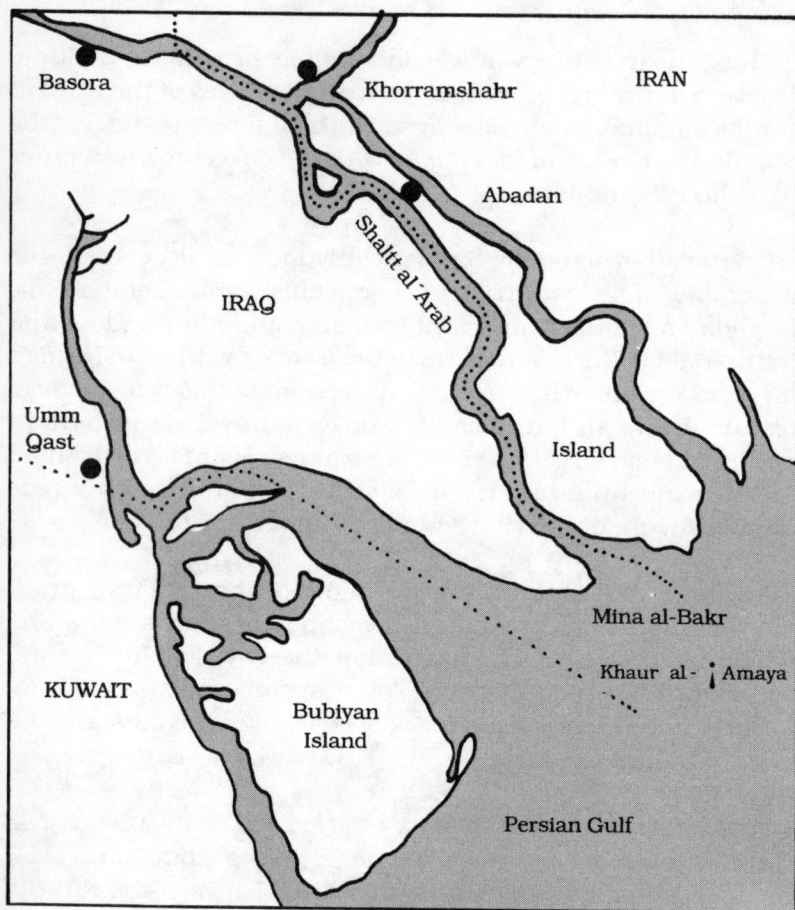

Iraq's Exit to the Persian Gulf

In this manner, soon after the war had begun, Iraqi oil could only reach foreign markets through the pipelines crossing Syrian and Turkish territory. Two new pipelines had to be built: one by Turkey and the other through Saudi Arabia. All of Iraq's imports had therefore to be carried by land. Thereby this nation came to strongly depend on Jordan, Turkey and Kuwait.

From March 1981 onwards, the Iraqi armies had lost their capacity to advance and were frankly in a defensive position. By September, they were forced to withdraw from the outskirts of Abadan. Finally, in September 1981, Saddam Hussein proposed a ceasefire with the excuse of the proximity of the Ramadan sacred festivities. His offer, however, was ignored by Iran.

On July 7th, 1981 Iraq was dealt a severe blow. In effect, during a surprise attack, Israeli planes bombed the nuclear reactor at Osirak, close to Baghdad, thereby forcing Iraq to give up its dreams of developing its own atomic warfare. President Ronald Reagan, in referring to this serious incident, stated the following in his memoirs entitled "An American Life":

"Israeli Prime Minister Menachem Begin, who informed us of the attack only after the fact, said that Israel had acted because of information it had received that the Iraqi plant was to be used to produce fissionable material for nuclear weapons for use against Israel. He said that a French shipment of "hot" uranium had been scheduled to arrive soon and that if he had waited longer, he could not have ordered the bombing because the resultant radiation would have drifted over Baghdad, Iraq's capital."(4)

In the meantime, the Iraqi leader had to face even greater adversities. Most of his military equipment was Soviet-made. Moscow had supplied over 50% of Iraq's weapons, the value of which exceeded $34 billion. Despite all this, the USSR had decided to interrupt its sale of weapons to Iraq soon after the war began. In order to get weapons, ammunition and spare parts compatible with their Russian weaponry, Iraq had to resort to Eastern European countries, China and Egypt.

In September 1981, Iran announced that it had a "secret weapon" that it would use to attack. This was a weapon as old as Islam itself: the Holy War. The Ayatollah Khomeini himself called for hundreds of thousands of ill-trained and lightly armed Revolutionary Guard volunteers to throw themselves at the Iraqi forces, thereby creating a devastating effect on the latter, but also suffering great losses themselves. These were fervent youngsters directed by clerics, all willing to die inasmuch as they firmly believed that heaven would be their reward. British historian Edgar O'Ballance describes thus what was told to him by an Iraqi officer:

"They came at us like a crowd coming out of a mosque on Friday. Soon we were firing into dead men, some draped over the barbed wire fences, and others in piles on the ground, having stepped on mines."(5)

In March 1982, Iran once again launched a strong offensive. These attacks culminated in May of that year with the Iraqis withdrawing from the City of Khorrasmshahr that had been taken at the beginning of the war.

By July 1982, Iraq suffered severe losses in the defense of the City of Basora that was about to fall into Iranian hands. The war was now developing on Iraqi soil. Khomeini had been able to transform the conflict into a national and religious crusade against Saddam Hussein, who had by then become the Satan that had to be defeated with Alla's help.

However, in the same measure as Iraq's forces were giving signs of their inability to defeat the Iranian forces, international concern and particularly that of the other Arab nations was starting to grow. The industrialized democracies considered that a triumph of Khomeini's government would imply grave difficulties in the entire Middle East region, which undoubtedly would lead to serious oil supply shortages. In this regard, the world was still suffering the consequences of the 1973 Arab oil embargo and the oil shortage due to the fall of the Shah of Iran. On the other hand, the oil-producing Arab nations were truly terrified by the possible triumph of shiite fundamentalism, convinced that an expansion of the Iranian influence in the region would seriously affect the political stability of their governments.

Only two Arab nations openly stated their sympathy towards Iran: Libya and Syria. Qaddafi, the rule in the former, seemed bent towards any cause that someway or another could damage the despised Western democracies. Curiously in Syria the socialist Baath party was also in power; however, the personal enmity between President Hafez al-Assad and Saddam Hussein had created an insurmountable obstacle between the people of those two nations that would be impossible to overcome as long as the two leaders remained in power. Syria even reached the point of closing the pipeline transporting Iraqi oil to the Mediterranean, with the consequent heavy losses that this implied.

In the meantime, the other Arab nations chose the lesser evil. Feeling more threatened in the short term by Iranian shiite fundamentalism than by Iraq's Baath socialism, they decided to create the so-called Gulf Co-operation Council, a group with political, economic and military purposes, comprising Saudi Arabia, Kuwait, Qatar, the United Arab Emirates, Bahrain and Oman. The nations associated to the Council gave massive economic support to Iraq and provided substantial loans to keep up the war against Iran.

We thereby see that the remaining Islamic nations' help tilted the balance in favour of Iraq. To solve the problems of the closing of the Iraqi port of Basora, Kuwait finally lent its own port facilities. During the conflict, Kuwait granted almost irrecoverable soft loans in excess of $16 billion. Jordan gave permission for Iraq to use its land to receive all the necessary imports by land. President Nimery of Sudan sent troops to collaborate in the war against Iran. Even Anuar al-Sadat, who professed a justifiable enmity against Saddam, not only sold Soviet-made weapons and spare parts to cover those not being supplied by the USSR, but even authorized Hussein to call Egyptian residents in Iraq to serve in the Iraqi army. Thus, in 1982, over 20,000 Egyptian citizens formed part of the Iraqi troops. The wealthy Persian Gulf states supplied all the economic aid required by Iraq in its war against Iran. Saudi Arabia granted soft financing of over 1 billion dollars per month(6). Turkey, taking advantage of NATO maneuvers in 1983, sent 15,000 troops to stifle Kurdish population uprisings in Iraqi territory, so that Saddam could concentrate on his struggle against Iran.

By September 1983, France decided to sell its most sophisticated war equipment to Iraq, including Mirage F-1 and Super Etendar planes, as well as the very modern Exocet missiles.

In the meantime, the crisis was achieving increasingly graver proportions. Support by the Arab oil nations and the Western democracies led Iran to threaten to block the Strait of Hormuz, navigated by tankers transporting close to 65% of the world's non-communist oil. Faced with these threats, the Commander of U.S. forces in the Middle East announced in December 1983 that:

"In the case of Iran closing the Strait of Hormuz the US will bring its forces into action... As the military potential of the six memmber states of the Gulf Co-operation Council is not adequate defence, should one or more members of this Council so request, the American forces will intervene."(7)

The U.S. was being progressively coerced into adopting a position similar to that of the Gulf Co-operation Council. Evidently, Iraq's attitudes had been openly against the American policies in the Gulf. However, President Reagan himself during a press conference held in London, stated that:

"... Iraq has not overstepped the mark as Iran has done."(8)

1985 went by without the war among the two nations reaching a head in favour of any side. On February 9th, 1986, however, Iran launched a new and effective campaign and resorted to the tactics used by Khomeini in 1981 and 1982. Over one hundred thousand voluntaries armed with light weapons and willing to die, overtook the Fao peninsula in the southermost tip of Iraq, with considerable casualties for both sides.

Desperate, Saddam Hussein, proceeded to apply a strategy that would force the conflict to become international. In effect, on July 1986 he started to attack Iranian tankers with the purpose of depriving that country of the incomes garnered from oil. Iran immediately responded by attacking Baghdad's allies' tanker vessels, particularly those belonging to Kuwait. According to declarations by George B. Crist, Commander of the U.S. Navy in the Persian Gulf, by January 1987, Iraq had attacked over 132 tankers, destroying or seriously damaging about 40 of them. Iran in turn had attacked 70 tankers and destroyed 11.

By December 1986 it was therefore evident that Iran had decided to concentrate most of its attacks against Kuwaiti tanker vessels. There was a reason for this. The only outlet to the Persian Gulf for Iraq was through the Shatt al-Arab, the Khor Abdullah Strait. Inasmuch as this had been rendered useless, Kuwait had lent its own port facilities to Iraq. For that reason, the Iranians were launching attacks against vessels of any nationality going towards Kuwait or sailing from that port. In this manner they also attempted to intimidate the small Arab oil states in the Persian Gulf to dissuade them from lending aid to Iraq. Navigation channels close to Kuwait were also mined.

Simultaneously, Iran started to strengthen the shores of the Strait of Hormuz with Seakiller and Chinese-made Silkworm surface-to-surface missiles. These highly explosive missiles were capable not only of damaging a large vessel but of even sinking it. Therefore the strategic strait was once again threatened with the serious consequent results for world oil trade. To this effect, Caspar Weinberger, the U.S. Secretary of Defense at the time, in his book "Fighting for Peace" stated:

"Clearly a factor that caused us great concern was the Iranian acquisition of the Silkworm surface-to-surface antiship missile... Now Iran had a large warhead weapon that could conceivably close the Strait of Hormuz. Intelligence had discovered a number of potential and actual Silkworm sites in Iran along the coast, both east and north on the Strait, that were ideally suited for targeting any ship in the Strait."(9)

Finally, apart from the naval attacks, Kuwait's oil facilities started to become the target of terrorist attacks. Rapid small-boat attacks were also launched by the naval arm of Iran's Islamic Revolutionary Guard Corps, a paramilitary organization more fanatical and more lethal than the regular military. At the same time, Kuwait started to suffer the consequences of increasingly frequent terrorist attacks and bomb explosions. For security reasons, the Kuwaiti police started a mass program of deportation of foreigners.

Approximately 25 percent of the Kuwait population is shiite. It was inevitable that the sunnite majority would start to mistrust the former, and consider them as threats that had to be closely watched and repressed.

Kuwait, in an attempt to protect the navigation of its vessels, requested help from the USSR. In principle they preferred not to resort to American cooperation because since the Yom Kippur War, the Americans were looked upon as allies of Israel. Besides, the U.S. had refused to sell some high-technology military equipment to Kuwait. Of all the conservative monarchies in the Gulf, Kuwait had the longest-standing friendly relations with the USSR.

That possibility of Soviet aid to Kuwait was a source of much concern for the Americans. For many years the Kremlin had attempted to increase its presence in the Persian Gulf. It now had the chance to do so. Obviously the USSR was free to send its fleet wherever it wished, including the Persian Gulf. However, this would have been very difficult without counting on bases in the area and the logistic support of local governments.

In November 1986, a scandal of tremendous political proportions broke out in the United States, which some people thought could reach the dimensions of another Watergate. It was thereby baptized as "Irangate". In effect, the American population was astounded to know that the U.S. and Israel had been secretly selling weapons to Iran and channelling the funds from the operation to back the rebels in Nicaragua. This scandal exploded like a bomb in Baghdad and other Arab nations.

On May 17th, 1987, the American frigate Stark was attacked by an Iraqi airplane, apparently 'by mistake'. This vessel suffered the impact of an Exocet missile. 37 U.S. marines died in that attack. Saddam Hussein immediately excused himself officially for the supposed mistake and undertook to defend the Gulf's "freedom of navigation", which was progressively being affected by Iraq's attacks and Iran's threats. To this effect, Caspar Weinberger, in his aforementioned book "Fighting For Peace", stated:

"Iraq was clearly concerned that we understand the tragedy was an accident. Its government issued an immediate apology and condolences to families of the victims for the fearful error, and offered to pay damages and appropriate compensation. In addition, Iraq asked us to establish military-to-military meetings to work out safeguards against future problems between our forces in the gulf. We agreed to hold meetings in Baghdad for that sole purpose. Those meetings were in no way intended to indicate that we had taken sides in the war or would assist Iraq in the war."(10)

As a result of this incident, several nations decided to increase their naval presence in the area to patrol and protect navigation in the Gulf. The U.S. sent 43 warships and about 25,000 soldiers to the region and many other military vessels were sent by France, Great Britain, Holland, Italy and Belgium.

From July 20th, 1987, the U.S. marine started to escort Kuwaiti flagged vessels so as to protect them from attacks from Iran. Many Kuwaiti tankers were also reflagged under American flagship.

Iranian and Iraqi attacks against the tankers continued unabated. Insecurity in the Gulf was rampant. By January 1988, close to 190 tankers had been attacked by Iraq, whereas Iran had shot at 171. The growing number of mines also endangered navigation in the waters of the Persian Gulf with its consequent vulnerability faced with the continuous episodes of violence in that region.

Interruption of oil transit through the Strait of Hormuz represented a danger of unforeseeable economic consequences for mankind as a whole. The world at large seemed to unite to stop this madness that had continued for almost eight years.

Proof of this was that on July 20th, 1987, the Security Council of the United Nations unanimously adopted Resolution No. 598, setting forth the following steps to reach an agreement to end the conflict:

-A cease-fire and withdrawal of the parties to internationally recognized frontiers.

-A U.N. mission to be sent to supervise the cease-fire.

-The liberation of war prisoners.

-U.N. mediation with Iran's and Iraq's cooperation to reach an acceptable agreement to the differences.

-Moderation by other states in order to prevent an escalation in the conflict that could hinder implementation of the Resolution.

-The exploration of ideas for the purpose of constituting an impartial committee to determine responsibilities in the conflict.

-The designation of a group of U.N. experts for the purpose of contributing to the stabilization and reconstruction of the countries involved in the conflict.

The Soviet Union in turn requested the immediate withdrawal of all foreign fleets operating in the Gulf, and their replacement by a U.N. peace corps.

Resolution 598 was immediately accepted by Iraq. Iran, on the contrary, did not take a clear position and the conflict therefore continued.

After taking a defensive stance for over six years, Iraq launched an attack on April 15th, 1988, and recovered the Fao peninsula in barely thirty-six hours. On May 25th the town of Salamejh was also recovered. The initiative appeared to be now in the hands of the Iraqis.

On July 18th, 1988, Ayatollah Ruholla Khomeini announced by surprise that Iran would accept the cease-fire proposed by the United Nations. This decision, according to Khomeini "was more lethal to me than poison." Yet he had no other choice. The morale of the Iranian people was at its lowest point.

The war that many thought would never end, finally came to an end without any official document being signed. This was a senseless war that left no clearcut results. From the beginning both nations successfully insisted on causing each other the worst damage possible. At the end, both sides were exhausted, demoralized, destroyed and indebted. The blood of hundreds of thousands had witnessed the futility of these human struggles. Let us hope that these lost lives at least attained the heaven for which they sacrificed themselves.

Chemical Warfare against the Holy War

Mankind had been horrified by the use of poisonous gases during the First World War. It was thought that chemical weapons of that nature would never again be used by any civilized nation, inasmuch as they far overstepped the limits of morality. The Geneva Protocol was thus adopted in 1925 to forbid forever the use of this type of chemical warfare.

However, in 1984, U.N. investigators proved that Iraq had resorted to chemical warfare. Mustard gas and nerve gas (Tabun) had been used against Iran. This, perhaps, was Saddam's response to the "Holy War" summoned by Khomeini.

In 1986, the U.N. proved that Iraq had once again violated the Geneva Protocol, this time more extensively than in 1984, causing more casualties for the enemy.

Once more, Iraq resorted to poisonous gases in its final campaigns to recover the Fao peninsula in April 1988. In June of that same year, the Iranian population in Mehran suffered the bombardment of chemical weapons.

Now therefore, the world contemplated with horror the use of this chemical warfare against the Iranian enemy and felt no less worse with the news that Iraq was attacking its own Kurdish population with poisonous gases.

The Kurds inhabit a region located between the frontiers of Turkey, Iraq and Syria, in a mountain range to the northeast of the country. They are shepherds who share an ethnic Indo-European origin with the Iranians and belong as well to the same linguistic family, although throughout the centuries their language has developed important syntaxis and vocabulary differences with the farsi, Iran's official language. However, from the religious standpoint, the Kurds are mostly sunnite.

The Kurdish people have always hoped to become autonomous and this of course led them into continuous clashes with the Baath government of Saddam Hussein. Moreover, they did not share the Iraqi motivation for war against Iran.

In April 1987, the entire population of Sheik Wasan died or became gravely ill due to one of many poisonous gas attacks ordered by Saddam against the people living in the mountain region of Kurdistan. On March 16, 1988, Iraqi planes dropped bombs with poisonous gases over the town of Halagja, that had surrendered to the forces of Iran, the casualties being over five thousand dead and ten thousand injured civilians.

The death caused by chemical weapons is so fearful and its application so unjustifiable, especially in the case of defenceless civil populations, that reports by newsmagazines such as Newsweek caused an international wave of indignation. Never, in the history of mankind had a government dropped poisonous gas bombs over great concentrations of its own population.

The Geopolitical Problem

In the war of Iran against Iraq, not only were the differences among the nations at issue but also supremacy among the three most powerful nations of the Persian Gulf - Iran, Iraq and Saudi Arabia - was at stake. A final triumph of any of the warring nations would have led to the imposition of conditions not only in the three aforementioned countries but also on other Persian Gulf states such as Kuwait, the United Arab Emirates, etc. This statement gives an idea of the importance of the conflict from a strategic standpoint. For this reason, the great superpowers took the stances that they considered best served their interests.

On the one hand, the U.S. followed the conflict with concern and interest. This war, though undesirable, seemed in principle to serve its immediate purposes. The enmity against Iran due to the hostage crisis in the U.S. Embassy in Teheran had not been forgotten. Also, until the Shah of Iran's fall, the Americans had deemed Iran the Persian Gulf "police" and for that reason had supplied that nation with the most modern warfare, in the hands now of a government capable of destabilizing the oil-producing Arab nations for religious and political reasons.

Despite the foregoing and even in the midst of the conflict, the United States did not wish to give up a possible future reconciliation or at least an improvement in relations with Iran, after the death of Khomeini. The Americans, when analyzing the situation, could not help but sustain an ambivalent position. This was made evident in President Ronald Reagan's words a few years later:

"Iran is located in one of the world's most critical geographical areas. Located between the Soviet Union and access to the mild waters of the ports in the Indian Ocean. The geography explains the reason why the Soviet Union sent its troops to Afghanistan... and if they could, they would send them also to Iran... America's long term goal in the region has been to help to preserve Iran's independence from Soviet dominance."

On the other hand, the U.S. could not trust Iraq, a country heavily armed by the Soviets. In spite of this, Newsweek in its August 20th, 1990 edition reported that:

"Since the restoration of relations with Iraq (1984), the U.S. government has granted guaranteed loans to that nation to underwrite the purchase of billions of dollars in American grains and manufactured goods."

In conclusion, despite the risk the war represented for a continued energy supply, the Americans considered that this conflict neutralized, at least temporarily, the two more powerful nations military-wise in the Persian Gulf, thereby reducing the risk that one or the other might intervene in the delicate political balance of Saudi Arabia, ruled by a pro-American moderate monarchy.

This latter nation, the wealthiest in the Gulf in view of its volume of production and crude reservoirs, was nevertheless weak compared to the military power of the foregoing. Thus, while Iraq had a population close to 14 million and Iran had some 34 million, the population in Saudi Arabia was about 7 million.

The interests of the Soviet Union were also threatened with this war. Let us not forget that that country shared an extensive border with Iran, the population of which is predominantly Islamic. The USSR, not without reason, feared the influence of Iran's shiite fundamentalism over the political and religious stability of its Muslim population.

To this effect, Moscow did not forget that in 1978 the Baath Party had violated the alliance it had signed with the Communist Party since 1973. Thus, 14 important communist leaders had been executed with the excuse that they had attempted to stir up the Kurdish inhabitants against the government.

Finally, Moscow seemed to be interested in an Iranian defeat and a discreet triumph by Iraq, that would not enable the embarrasing Iraqi leader to adopt attitudes whose effects would be harmful for the USSR's domestic policies. In fact, the Kremlin, aware of the sympathies Iran's Islamic fundamentalism awoke in the Muslim sectors of its own population, saw with concern the possible reaction of the latter in the case that, thanks to Soviet backing, Saddam achieved an overwhelming victory over Khomeini. For this reason, Moscow was relieved when the nations of West Europe and especially France supported the cause of Iraq by selling it the most modern and sophisticated military warfare.

As the conflict escalated and acquired greater international dimensions with the "war of the tankers", both powers however realized that they had a common interest: to end the war. In fact, the U.S. and its Western allies saw their oil supplies from the Middle East increasingly threatened. The USSR in turn saw with greater concern the increasing amount of war vessels sent by the Western nations to the Gulf region. The two superpowers thus understood that a continuation of the hostilities could possibly lead to a confrontation.

Evidently, however, there were numerous differences in the focus the U.S. and the USSR had of the problem. The Soviet Union, for instance, maintained relations with Iran and Iraq, by means of treaties that had been signed and were in force and at all times had been respected; the U.S., in turn, did not even have diplomatic relations with any of the two nations at the time the war broke out. The United States evidently was interested in safekeeping oil supplies from the Persian Gulf, whereas for the USSR this was not a problem. The U.S. saw with great concern the possible effect the war might have over the relations of the Arab states with Israel and its impact on the Camp David-sponsored peacekeeping process. The Soviet Union was unphased by this. But the USSR was truly anxious about the effect of this war on Afghanistan, where 99 percent of the population is Islamic and where over 100,000 Russian soldiers were waging a bloody guerrilla war. The U.S. was undaunted by this. Approximately 10 percent of the Soviet population is Muslim. Therefore, the effect of the course of the conflict over this population was a reason for deep unrest in the Kremlin. Of course, this uncertainty did not affect the U.S.

The Oil Problem

Before the Gulf War broke out, Iran had been exporting 1.2 million barrels per day of oil and Iraq over 3 million barrels per day. Both nations attacked each other's production and refinery facilities at the beginning of the war. Thus, the conflict immediately removed over 4 million barrels a day of crude from the market.(11)

Likewise, the world at large faced the fear that Iran would fulfill its threats of closing the Strait of Hormuz, the transit way to the supertankers carrying most of the Persian Gulf's oil production to consumer markets. This strait was a mandatory waterway for about 65 percent of the oil from non-communist countries.

The nations surrounding the Persian Gulf in turn hold close to 55 percent of the world's oil proved reserves. Suddenly their waters were infested with mines and hundreds of tankers had to suffer attacks by both warring sides and even the protection of nations such as the U.S., England, France, Holland, Belgium, Italy and the USSR turned navigation in gulf waters into a true nightmare. Patrol vessels many times were on the verge of creating accidents inasmuch as the operations were not being properly coordinated.

Many feared a new hike in the price of hydrocarbons. The situation, however, was very different from that of the Arab oil embargo or the Shah of Iran's fall. In practice, production surpluses that at that time flooded the international oil markets easily helped to compensate for the fall in crude oil production created by the Iran-Iraq war.

The joint set of measures taken by the industrialized nations in an effort to conserve energy plus the effect of new crude suppliers such as Great Britain, Norway, Mexico, Colombia, Angola, Egypt, Cameroon, Malaysia, etc. plus the substitution of oil for alternate sources of energy, plus a decrease in energy consumption due to the world economic crisis of the two previous oil shocks and the resulting crude oil prices, had now given rise to a surplus supply in the international oil markets. In conclusion, the objectives pursued with the creation of the International Energy Agency were bearing the results expected by the industrialized nations.

Once more, these nations had been able to defend their interests faced with the obstacles encountered in an unstable international oil market largely affected by the complex political scenario of the Persian Gulf nations.

On the other hand, Venezuela's strategic importance was once more put in evidence, inasmuch as it is the only large oil producer in OPEC located in the Western hemisphere with a reliable position as supplier of crudes and derivatives, not threatened by the conflicts characteristic of that region nor disputes of any other nature.

Notes

1.-Christine Moss Helms. IRAQ. EASTERN FLANK OF THE Arab WORLD. page 29.

2.-Christine Moss Helms. IBIDEM. page 157.

3.-Iraqi Embassy press release. London. September 17th. 1980.

4.-Ronald Reagan. AN AMERICAN LIFE. page 413.

5.-Judith Miller and Laurie Mylroie. SADDAM HUSSEIN AND THE CRISIS IN THE GULF. page 13.

6.-Dilip Hiro. "Chronicle of the Gulf War". MERIP REPORTS. No. 126/126. July/September 1984.

7.-Committee Against Repression and for Democratic Rights in Iraq. SADDAM'S IRAQ. REVOLUTION OR REACTION ?. page 233.

8.-New York Times. June 1st. 1984.

9.-Caspar W. Weinberger. FIGHTING FOR PEACE. page 395.

10.-Caspar W. Weinberger. IBIDEM. page 403.

11.-Martin Gárate. NUMERO weekly. June 10th. 1990.

CHAPTER VII

IRAQ'S INVASION
OF KUWAIT

The Third Oil Shock ?

In the years during which the Iran-Iraq war lasted, many international commentators affirmed that Kuwait was running a grave risk of being invaded by Iran. There were serious grounds, in fact, to suppose that this might happen, since Kuwait, fearful of the shiite influence over its own political stability, had become one of Iraq's most prodigal allies. In effect, Kuwait had granted generous loans estimated at some $16 billion, destined to help finance the expenses of the war against Iran. In addition, Kuwait had handed over its port facilities to Iraq in order to alleviate the tremendous logistical problems resulting from the port of Basora being closed due to the Shatt al-Arab blockage, the latter being Iraq's only commercial outlet to the Red Sea. Thus, Kuwait became the preferred target of Iran's outrage. In this regard, Caspar Weinberger, the U.S. Secretary of Defense at the time, stated that:

"By September of 1986 it had become increasingly clear to U.S. Defense Intelligence officials that Iran had singled out Kuwait as the focal point of the pressure it elected to use against the Gulf Arab states. Iran was launching naval attacks against shipping of all nations bound to and from Kuwaiti ports in an effort to intimidate that small country and its neighbors, and dissuade them from providing political and financial support to Iraq. Besides the naval attacks, lethal Iranian or Iranian-sponsored activities against Kuwait during 1986 included three bombing raids on Kuwaiti territory, mining of Kuwaiti shipping channels, deployment of Chinese Silkworm surface-to-surface missiles aimed at Kuwait and located on the captured Iraqi peninsula of Al Faw, and terrorist attacks on Kuwaiti oil facilities."[1]

We thereby see that there was reason enough to believe that Kuwait would fear reprisals or vengeful acts on the part of Iran. However, two years had not passed since the conflict had ceased, when Iraq invaded Kuwait. In effect, on August 2nd, 1990 the powerful Iraqi army in a Blitzkrieg-style operation took over the diminute but wealthy neighbouring state, with a total population of around 1,9 million inhabitants and a territory of barely 7 thousand square miles.

Iraq's president, Saddam Hussein, believed by so doing that he had solved all the economic problems affecting his nation as a result of the eight-year war with Iran. He would no longer have to pay his pending debt with Kuwait and in one stroke had seized the vast oil reserves of that extremely small nation and procured an outlet to the Persian Gulf.

After the prolonged conflict with Iran, Iraq had been left partially destroyed and with a foreign debt calculated between $70 and $100 billion, though in truth it was difficult to arrive at the exact figure, inasmuch as most of this debt was owed to other Persian Gulf nations, who knew beforehand that they were probably uncollectible.

Saddam however was not content with this. In his opinion, the Middle East oil nations had to compensate Iraq for the tremendous sacrifice of having confronted Iran, thanks to which he had avoided the Ayatollah's islamic revolution from spreading throughout the region. If that had been the case, none of the feudal monarchies ruling those wealthy lands would have survived. It was therefore time to collect payment for the devastation and losses suffered by Iraq. More than 120,000 Iraqi soldiers had been killed and close to 300,000 injured, witnesses to his country's heroic attitude.

But, not only the nations of the Gulf had a debt with Iraq. In Saddam's opinion, Western industrialized nations had to acknowledge Iraq's contribution to stability in the Middle East. If it had not been for the sacrifices of his nation, Iran's Islamic fundamentalists would have destabilized the entire Persian Gulf in such a manner that the Western world's oil supplies would have suffered grave setbacks.

In truth, the foregoing arguments in the case of the Arab nations and also the industrialized nations, had a ring of truth about them. Proof thereof is that despite their mistrust of the Iraqi government, both groups decided to back it in its struggle against Iran. However, this was carried out based on the premise that between two evils the lesser one had been chosen.

Saddam Hussein, in turn, was not willing to give up Pan-Arabian leadership, the recompense he was convinced was his due. He would have to get it by other means. He therefore needed to put together the most powerful army in the Middle East. To achieve his goal he had to have money and solve a big strategic problem that had asphyxiated him during the war with Iran. He needed an unencumbered outlet to the Persian Gulf. There was a quick way of reaching both objectives: to take over Kuwait.

Historical Background

At first, Saddam Hussein justified his action alleging that Kuwait had caused serious harm by violating the production quotas assigned by OPEC and by overexploiting the oil reservoirs shared by both nations with detriment to Iraq. He likewise announced in the beginning that the invasion had been brought about in response to the clamor of Kuwaiti citizens who wished to end the corrupion of the ruling royal family, headed by Emir Jaber al-Ahmed al-Sabah. It must have been difficult, however, to find citizens from Kuwait that would follow his game, since only a few days later he had told the world that Kuwait as a nation was about to disappear and was to become Iraq's nineteenth province.

To justify his violent attitude he resorted to historical precedents that had already been used in 1961, in stating that Kuwait had belonged to the dismembered Ottoman empire and should therefore belong to Iraq.

In this regard, it would be interesting to quickly review the historical bases to that claim, a rather complex affair much like everything related to the political situation in the Middle East. In effect, what is today called Iraq had been the territory of three ancient administrative districts or "wilayas" that had been part of the Ottoman empire, the capital of which had been Constantinople, later called Istambul. These three districts were called Mosul, Baghdad and Basra (Basora).

In turn, Kuwait's present territory had been occupied in the eighteenth century by a desert tribe from the Najd region of Central Arabia, the Anaizah, the originators of the al-Sabah and al-Jaber families, the present rulers of Kuwait.

In 1756, Kuwait sprang up as an autonomous territory when the founders decided to designate an emir from the al-Sabah family as their ruler. Finally settling in that land, they built a small fort, thereby giving rise to the name of Kuwait which is derived from kut (fort). The inhabitants were fishermen and traded pearls. The territory of present-day Kuwait is a magnificent natural port, which determined the progressive dedication to sea trade. Their small vessels reached such far-off places as East Africa, having to border the entire Arabian peninsula to do so.

Traders by nature and sailors by geographical circumstances, the Kuwaitis frequently sailed the Shatt al-Arab and carried out their trade in Basora a few miles upstream. During the second half of the nineteenth century one of the emirs of the al-Sabah family, in an attempt to foster trade with the Turks, swore faithfulness to the governor of Basora, one of the "wilayas" of Iraq's present territories. In this manner, Kuwait's emir received the title of "great Kaimakan" or assistant to the Grand Vizier, thus establishing affinity ties with the Ottoman empire. In practice, however, this submission was purely nominal since the Ottomans had little interest in that small village of fishermen called Kuwait. In truth, the al-Sabah did not consider that they had lost their independence. For them, it was simply part of a complex trading tradition, according to which some sacrifice had to be made in order to gain something.

A clear example of the peculiar game of chess with which the al-Sabah maintained their autonomy is found at the end of the nineteenth century. The Germans had stated at that time their intentions of extending the Berlin-Baghdad railway to the port of Kuwait. Realizing that this project would only materialize the symbolic sovereignty of the Ottomans over their territory, Emir Mubarak al-Sabah requested British protection against the Turks. The United Kingdom, very keen on thwarting German intentions, granted this protection in exchange for which, in theory, they would take control over Kuwait's foreign relations.

Nevertheless, when the British attempted to meddle in the affairs of the Kuwaiti nation, Emir Mubarak led them to believe that he was willing to bestow a coal station in Kuwait to their rivals, the Russians. Faced with this prospect, the British decided to leave their interference aside, in exchange for which, Mubarak signed an agreement in 1899, pledging not to receive foreign agents or representatives without London's consent. The British also granted him 15,000 rupees and assured His Royal Highness' good offices in pro of Mubarak and his heirs, as well as guaranteeing the protection of Kuwait.

In the future, Kuwait would appeal several times to this protection, inasmuch as it is a small emirate that in many regards can in fact be considered a city-state, surrounded by formidable landscapes such as the Najd (subsequently part of Saudi Arabia), Basora (later on part of Iraq) and Persia (later to be called Iran).

In July 1913, the British and the Turks signed an agreement recognizing Kuwait as an autonomous state apart from the Ottoman empire, thereby formally defining the frontiers of the Emirate. The Turks, however, urged on by the Germans, put off ratification of the agreement. The United Kingdom reacted by setting up a protectorate in Kuwait in 1914 and by officially recognizing its independence. In exchange for this protection, the British demanded Mubarak's cooperation against the Ottomans in the forthcoming conflagration: the First World War.

Mubarak, despite the commitments he had pledged, nonetheless kept up an active trade with both sides, thereby maintaining the tradition of the al-Sabah. This was not only an opportunity for reaping profits but was also a way of ratifying his own autonomy.

After the First World War ended, the Ottoman empire was dismembered. In 1920, Syria and Lebanon became French protectorates, while Iraq, Jordan and Palestine were ruled by Great Britain.

To decide the future of the present territories of Saudi Arabia, Iraq and Kuwait, a Conference was called in 1922 that ended with the signing of the Treaty of al-Uquayr, containing a rather arbitrary designation of frontiers, sometimes by drawing straight lines through maps and worse even, without taking into account ethnic or even geographical considerations. The frontiers between Kuwait and Iraq were marked off one year later, in 1923.

As a result of the foregoing agreements a "neutral zone" was created, located between Iraq, Saudi Arabia and Kuwait. Iraq was also assigned frontiers that isolated it from the sea. Its only outlet to the Persian Gulf was through a narrow body of water formed by the confluence of the Euphrates and Tigris rivers, carrying the name Shatt al-Arab. This decision would bring about serious consequences seventy years later.

In the meantime, Great Britain and France could not reach an agreement regarding the destination of Mosul, one of the administrative districts of the Ottoman empire. There were political reasons to assign this district to Syria, as well as to Iraq. To this effect, Christine Moss Helms, a researcher with the Brookings Foreign Policy Studies Program stated:

"There was some doubt about the fate of the wilaya of Mosul, disputed by both France and Great Britain. It remained a "dark incubus of uncertainty" until it was allocated to Iraq in 1925 after much international bartering."(2)

Had the French position been successful, as almost happened, the territory of the wilaya of Mosul, to the north of present-day Iraq, would have become part of Syria. In any event, in the midst of the negotiations, the great losers were the Kurds, inhabitants of a region between the cities of Mosul, Kirkuk and Sulaimaniya, an ethnic, linguistic and cultural unity different from the rest of Iraq's population, whose rights have been totally ignored. This would give rise in the future to countless problems, many of which would end in dramatic bloodshed.

Saudi Arabia was created in 1932, at a time when a series of independent territories and emirates sprang up at the banks of the Persian Gulf. The United Kingdom also granted Iraq its independence in 1932. The frontiers between that new nation and Kuwait were once again ratified at that moment.

However, soon after, tensions arose once more. In effect, in 1937, King Ghazi of Iraq, a fervent nationalist, started to sow the seeds of future uprisings in the area. From a private radio station he installed in his palace, he launched fiery accusations against the French ruler in Syria, as well as the zionist aspirations in Palestine and British intervention in the entire Persian Gulf. He was likewise the first to declare that Kuwait should become a part of Iraq. His arguments would later on be taken up by Abdull Karim Kassem and by Saddam Hussein.

On June 19th, 1961, the United Kingdom granted Kuwait its independence. Government of the emirate rested in the hands of Abdullah al-Sabah, who, in an attempt to make his mandate legitimate, designated a National Assembly and adopted a Constitution.

However, six days later, on June 25th, Abdull Karim Kasssem, the ruler in Iraq since 1958 after a military coup that had deposed King Faisal II, opposed Kuwait's independence, alleging that it was part of Iraqi territory, having been an administrative dependence of Basora during the Ottoman empire. Kassem also sustained that Kuwait and Iraq were one only country that had been arbitrarily divided by the British.

Thus threatened by Iraq, the Kuwaitis once again requested help from the British, who sent troops to protect them. On July 20th, 1961 the Arab League admitted Kuwait into its fold, recognizing its state of independence and refusing to accept Iraq's demands. To back its position, the Arab League also got ready to send troops made up of soldiers from Egypt, Sudan, Saudi Arabia and Jordania. Iraq indignantly withdrew from the Arab League.

Gamal Abdel Nasser played an important role in the aforementioned events. Kassem likewise was a charismatic politician that posed a threat for the Pan-Arabian supreme leadership aspirations of the Egyptian leader. Thus, in order to avoid an outcome that would have enormously strengthened his opponent, Nasser exerted all his influence for the Arab League to support Kuwait.

Kassem was overthrown and executed in 1963 in a coup directed by Colonel Abdul Salam Aref. After Kassem's death, relations among Iraq and Kuwait improved. On May 14th, 1963, Kuwait was accepted into the United Nations, backed by Iraq's favorable vote, who recognized Kuwait's independence in October 1963. That same year, both states signed an agreement marking their respective frontiers. The agreement set forth, among other items, the payment of an important sum of money to Iraq, as well as this latter country's commitment to provide water from the Shatt al-Arab to Kuwait. It is ironic however that at the time Iraq recognized Kuwait as an independent state, the Baath Party, the party of Saddam Hussein, was in power. In fact, the confrontation with Kuwait was one of the arguments used by that party to undermine Kasssem's political bases.

In conclusion, although it is true that in a relatively short period in Kuwait's history, it was nominally subjected to the wilaya of Basora, which today is part of Iraq, it is nonetheless also true that Iraq was a part of the Ottoman empire. Now therefore, it is evident that Kuwait had established itself as an independent political entity since 1756, much before Iraq in 1932. In addition, Kuwait's frontiers were defined through a series of historical agreements, for instance the 1963 negotiations which marked off the frontiers between Iraq and Kuwait, giving rise to a pact by means of which Iraq recognized the independence of Kuwait in October of that same year.

In this aforementioned agreement, Iraq could not have the excuse that it was an agreement negotiated in its name by colonial powers without its interests being taken into account. Iraq had regularly complained that throughout its history, foreign powers had determined its destiny by means of conquest. In the entire Middle East region in particular, problems abound due to the artificial creation of nations and the demarcation of even more artificial frontiers set by European negotiators at the end of World War One. Nevertheless, in confirmation of the foregoing, two independent states, Iraq and Kuwait, making full use of their sovereignty, had decided to negotiate their frontiers by means of a treaty entered into in 1963. This was, therefore, a legitimate act, institutionally ratified by the political and constitutional powers of both nations, by means of which commitments were established and recognized by international law. In this manner, Iraq had renounced any further claim based on historical precedents from the time of the Ottoman empire.

(Add here map of the Ottoman Empire).

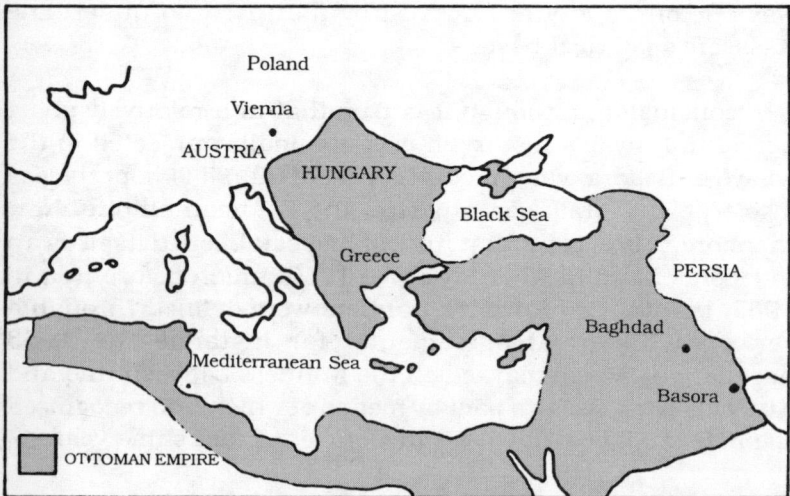

Ottoman Empire

In turn, the empire dominated by Istambul and ruled by Suleiman the Magnificent, had, by 1453, extended its domains to Asia Minor, the Balkans, Crimea and had reached the gates of Vienna. It subsequently extended to Mesopotamia (present-day Iraq), Syria, Egypt and the banks of the desert-like Arabian peninsula. Suleiman's heirs extended their control to the entire North Africa and formed a vast empire. The Turkish empire took sides with Germany and Austria-Hungary during the First World War which were defeated in 1918. This forced the dismemberment of the Ottoman empire, which was divided and transformed into several countries, whose frontiers were often arbitrarily and hurriedly set.

From the foregoing brief historical summary it can be surmised that having both nations belonged to the Ottoman empire, if Iraq had decided to annex Kuwait, the safety of the frontiers in the Middle East would have disappeared and the entire region would be filled with chaos. In effect, practically all the states in the area could use the same argument to present territorial claims against each other's neighbours. In fact, it is probable that Iraq could have been seriously affected by the subsequent instability, inasmuch as Syria, to give an example, could wager reasons to claim the entire territory of Mosul as theirs, this territory being not only vitally important due to its extensive oil reserves but also because it is crossed by pipelines transporting Iraqi oil to the Mediterranean.

The Basis for the Conflict is Set

Once the Iran-Iraq war ended, the latter country was left devastated and with an uncertain foreign debt figure, of probably up to $100 billion, largely contracted with the rich oil monarchies in the Gulf.

Saddam Hussein considered that his country had made great sacrifices thanks to which Arab feudal monarchies had been saved. Thus, he expected that the other Gulf nations not only pardon his debt but also, according to well-informed sources in the Middle East, wanted an additional $30 billion in fresh money. Moreover, according to the New York Times, in September 1990, Iraq claimed that Kuwait alone had to put out no less than $27 billion.

Apparently, Iraq required the money to reconstruct its economy. In practice, Saddam had embarked even more furiously in an arms race, the evident objective of which was to attain military preeminence in the entire region, for the purposes of backing his Pan-Arabian leadership aspirations.

In this regard, despite the fact that the war with Iran had ended, Iraq continued to make gigantic investments in the development of military programs including the construction of conventional weapons and the purchase of tanks, missiles, planes and the most sophisticated military collection that other nations wished to sell. Iraq was also spearheading the production of chemical and biological warfare, and for this purpose, research was being carried out to adapt those weapons to the heads of the Scud missiles purchased from the Soviet Union. According to U.S. and Israeli military intelligence sources, enormous sums were being spent on the development of nuclear weapons.

Western versions had it that Iraq had even started to build a giant cannon that could reach targets as far away as Tel Aviv, Haifa and other Israeli populations. This project was apparently discovered by the Mossad. In the following months, several components of what seemed to be sections of a colossal piece of artillery were confiscated in British ports. The official reaction of the Iraqi authorities was to scoff at what they alleged was no more than the product of a feverish imagination, inasmuch as the confiscated pieces were supposedly destined to build a petrochemical plant.

On the other hand, it was reported that companies from several European nations had been hired to build underground hangars that would meet the most stringent NATO security measures. These hangars could resist the most ferocious air attacks and the planes lodged in them were not only protected but could also take off in runways that began underground by means of takeoff techniques similar to those used in aircraft carriers.

While the Iraqi ruler's military plans were being discovered by U.S., Israeli and British intelligence agencies, it became increasingly difficult to purchase the equipment he required. Faced with this situation, he probably deemed that it would be necessary to adopt bold steps to present to the world faits accomplis which would be difficult to counter. In the opinion of some international analysts, that was the time when Iraq started to plan the invasion of Kuwait.

During the Arab Co-operation Council summit held in Baghdad in February 1989, Iraq requested that a demand be put before the U.S. to withdraw all its vessels from the Persian Gulf. A few days later, during another meeting held in Amman, Saddam ratified his petitions, reasoning that the progressive weakening position of the USSR would break the balance of powers in the Gulf, leaving the destiny of the countries in the region in the hands of Capitol Hill.

In April 1990, the Iraqi government initiated negotiations with Iran aimed at reconciliation. Evidently, plans to invade Kuwait could not be carried out if a war on two fronts had to be waged. In this regard, Saddam offered the Iranian president Hashemi Rafjsanjani the return of some territories occupied during the war as well as prisoners still held, inasmuch as an armistice among the two nations had never been signed.

Simultaneously the tone of his verbal attacks against Israel sharpened. Thus, on April 2nd, after the Mossad-ascribed murder of Gerald Bull, considered to be the author of the super cannon project capable of reaching targets in Israel, Saddam ratified that Iraq had binary chemical weapons and added:

"By God, we shall make half of Israel be consumed by fire if that nation attempts anything against Iraq."(3)

In June of that same year, before an OPEC meeting that was to be held the following month, Iraq stated that Kuwait and the United Arab Emirates had been violating their production quotas, with the ensuing weakening of oil prices that harmed the income of the other members of the organization. This circumstance was well-known and was a reason of frequent friction within OPEC.

On July 16th, 1990, Tarik Aziz, Iraq's Minister of Foreign Affairs, sent a communiqué to Chadli Klibi, the Secretary General of the Arab League, ratifying that not only was Kuwait continuously breaching OPEC's production quotas, but was also over-exploiting the Rumalia oil fields shared by both nations, with the subsequent damages in profits to Iraq in excess of $2.4 billion.

On July 17th, Saddam ratified his accusations against Kuwait and the United Arab Emirates. At that time, during a televised speech, he proferred military threats against those nations for the first time:

"If words fail to afford us protection, then we will have no choice but to resort to effective action to put things right and ensure the restitution of our rights."(4)

By July 21st, the CIA had informed the White House that Iraq had sent over 30,000 soldiers to the Kuwaiti border. The analysts of that agency concluded however that this was just a way to put pressure on Kuwait to fulfill its demands.

However, on the 24th of that same month, the U.S. decided to deploy six battleships to the area, with the purpose of counteracting Iraq's maneuvres. State Department officials sustained that the Bush administration would keep its pledge to support individual and joint defense actions of the friendly nations in the Gulf. However, Margaret Tutwiler, spokesperson for the Department, stated during a press conference that same day that:

"... we have no Defense Treaty with Kuwait and there are no special defense or security commitments with Kuwait."(5)

OPEC met in Geneve on July 26, 1990 and during that meeting Iraq ratified its threats against Kuwait for the violation of the oil quotas set by the organization. Never before in the history of that agency had a member threatened another with military action for not fulfilling commitments jointly agreed to.

In Venezuela this attitude would lead to severe criticism. A firm defender of respecting the quotas, Venezuela should have opposed Iraq's threats. The representatives of the nation should have stated their protest and should have left the meeting. This position was publicly assumed by Alberto Quirós Corradi, a recognized oil expert whose opinions were widely backed by public opinion.

On July 30th it was made public that Iraq had deployed more than 100,000 men to the border with Kuwait and had mobilized close to 30 tanks to that region. By August 1st, the CIA reached the conclusion that the invasion of Kuwait was imminent.

The attack occured on August 2nd, 1990. The Iraqi army started advancing at 2 am. Six hours later, the invasion had been completed. For each Kuwaiti soldier, the invading forces had 26.

Saddam's Assumptions

Saddam believed that in view of the swiftness of the action, the world would have no other choice but to accept the situation as an accomplished fact. Several suppositions apparently were the bases for the grave decision he had adopted, among which the following can be mentioned:

First: For many years, Iraq had been one of Moscow's most important "customers". In fact, the purchase of weapons from the USSR exceeded $32.4 billion. Saddam therefore supposed that although in recent days his relations with the Kremlin had soured, the Soviet leaders would still back his aspirations in the Middle East. In view of the serious domestic political and economic problems in the Soviet Union, the Iraqi leader did not think that the Kremlin would be in a position to intervene in the zone. Moreover, if throughout 1989 the USSR had abandoned its imperialistic aspirations in Western Europe, it would be even less inclined to face the consequences of an intervention in the Persian Gulf.

Moscow was in fact facing an even more serious immediate problem, the menace of disintegration of the Soviet Union itself. The declaration of independence of the Baltic republics, the insubordination of Russia itself under the leadership of Boris Yeltsin and the serious problem of lack of supplies expected during the forthcoming winter was enough to keep the Kremlin leaders busy. This did not mean however that they would be partial to an American intervention in the area.

Second: the U.S. in turn was going through equally serious economic problems with the ensuing fiscal and balance-of-payment deficits, as well as growing unemployment levels, the bankruptcy of numerous banks, the failure of the Savings & Loans system, the sudden fall in real estate values, the growing tensions in the financial system and, in general, the political problems resulting from the need to increase taxes in spite of Bush's emphatic promise to the contrary during his campaign. Based on these premises, Saddam thought that neither the government nor the people of America would be willing to get involved in a conflict requiring a military effort of astronomical costs and whose political consequences in the Arab world could not be predicted.

The Vietnam war, the only war that the U.S. had lost in its entire history despite having won all the battles, still echoed in the minds of the American population and this had created serious internal traumas. The soldiers of the American nation had not understood the reasons for which they had been sent to die so far away, in the defense of geopolitical interests that were so abstract that risking their lives for them seemed futile.

The Americans were even less inclined to give their blood or that of their children to defend the oil interests of companies that had benefitted from the sacrifices of the U.S. people. In effect, as a result of the Arab oil embargo and the fall of the Shah of Iran, the revenues of oil companies had been greatly increased.

Saddam was also convinced that the U.S. had lost its will to fight. During an interview held on July 25th, 1990, broadcast by the American TV channel ABC, he told April Glaspie, the American ambassadress that he considered the U.S. to be a society that "was not willing to risk 10,000 deaths in battle". Iraq in turn was willing to sacrifice hundreds of thousands of human lives.

Third: According to the Iraqi ruler's calculations, the end of the cold war and the closeness among the two super-powers would only facilitate an understanding according to which both nations would abstain from intervening, leaving the solution of the problem to the Arabs themselves. In conclusion, as long as one superpower did not enter the conflict, the other one wouldn't either.

Fourth: of all the oil monarchies in the Persian Gulf, the most anti-American was Kuwait. The emirate had been one of the first to adopt the oil embargo brought about by the Yom Kippur war. Already in 1984 David Ottaway, reporter for the Washington Post, had observed that Kuwait was "accustomed to blame the U.S. for all the evils afflicting the Arab world and the Gulf in particular."

In fact, in contrast to other states in the region, the emirate had no defense treaty nor security commitments with the U.S. To the contrary, Kuwait was the state that most cultivated relations with the USSR. However, continuing with its inveterate trading tradition and never losing the chance of making a good business deal with the superpowers, many times that state had threatened to resort to the opposing superpower to extract the best advantage from both.

Thus, during the Iran-Iraq war, Kuwait requested that its tankers be placed under American flagship to protect them from Iran's attacks. The U.S. only accepted this petition to avoid a similar petition being accepted by the USSR. Once this petition was accepted by the Americans, the Kuwaiti authorities declared that they wanted no part in any possible hostilities to protect these tankers, involving the U.S. This undoubtedly created serious resentment on the part of the Americans. This being the case, why was the U.S. to take on the expensive defense of a small state that had never sought its friendship?

254

Fifth: Kuwait's domestic situation could also be turned to Iraq's advantage. In the opinion of Saddam, a medieval government prevailed in Kuwait that behind the National Assembly approved after its independence in 1961, belied its feudal tendencies. This Assembly was simply the scenario for continuous insults among its members, although it could not be denied that nationalistic stances had been sometimes taken that had been recanted in the past. The Assembly had been dissolved in 1986 after some terrorist activities had scourged the city.

Over two thirds of Kuwait's inhabitants were immigrants that benefitted from the prosperity in the emirate, who carried out jobs that the Kuwaitis were unwilling to perform. Over 350,000 Palestinians lived in Kuwait, the greatest concentration in the Gulf, apart from 300,000 Egyptians, 200,000 Hindus, Pakistanis and Philipinos, all of whom complained about the discrimination they were subjected to, as well as all the other foreigners.

The Kuwaitis were zealous guardians of their nationality which was only passed on by blood ties. Only the children of Kuwaiti nationals received citizenship. Those born to foreigners in the emirate did not normally have a right to citizenship.

Kuwaiti nationals did not pay taxes, received generous sums from the government to purchase housing and lands, had their health expenses covered by the State, could study in any country under sponsorship by the government and enjoyed one of the highest standards of life in the entire world. These benefits of course were not extensive to foreigners who had the weight of work on their shoulders without the possibility of even buying lands or housing in the emirate. They were simply considered to be "inferior" workers with limited rights, who could be freely and arbitrarily expelled from the country by the authorities, as was frequently the case.

Saddam Hussein therefore supposed that the Iraqi troops would be received with open arms by the foreigners, an important portion of the population, who would thereby avenge the humiliations and discrimination they had suffered in the hands of the haughty Kuwaitis.

Now therefore, in the event that all these suppositions were to prove wrong, Saddam was aware that he had few choices left. Iraq's economic situation was in such a state that his government would be hard pressed to get on its feet. It was an economy based on promoting war. However, the falling oil prices, the high levels of foreign indebtedness and the refusal of other governments to continue selling sophisticated military weaponry constituted a series of factors that would hinder his course.

The Iraqi ruler was thus left with no alternatives. A change of direction towards peace would create insurmountable problems. What would he do with hundreds of thousands of soldiers with no possibilities of work ? How could his party stay in power, faced with the resulting economic crisis?

It was therefore better to face the consequences of war than the consequences of peace. To invade Kuwait would mean to burn his ships, as Tarik ibn-Ziyad, one of Islam's legendary generals, had done in the eighth century, the same leader who had taken Mohammed's religion to Europe. Upon disembarking in Gibraltar, this famous general had burned his ships while declaring:

"The sea is behind you and the enemy is in front. By God, there is no other way out for you than to save yourselves with courage and determination."(6)

It did not seem probable that Saddam had foreseen the world's reaction to his actions. The possibility of facing a powerful enemy evidently was part of his plans. However, considering the way the events took shape, his enemy was more formidable than powerful.

Backed by president Bush, the Saudis and the Kuwaitis, a Western Arab Alliance was formed headed by the U.S. and including over two dozen nations. It practically became a conflict of Saddam against the world. But nobody expected Iraq to defeat these collosal forces.

This being the situation, Saddam's goals could not be just to defeat his opponents. His objective was to defend himself long enough to acquire the stature of a hero in the eyes of the Islamic people. This would create a gap in the Muslim alliance which would increase if Saddam was able to drag Israel into the war. Could a soldier of Islam face a Muslim brotherhood to defend the hated invader of Jerusalem?

The religious conditioning of those who prayed towards Mecca was, for Saddam, a more powerful force than all the sophisticated war technology in his power. Sooner or later, the Muslims would have to answer to their consciences and decide whether their religion would allow them to maintain that alliance with the infidels. This was the moment that Saddam was awaiting. When it came, it would be the Muslim masses themselves that would end up treating as traitors those governments that had allowed the infidel U.S., the Great Satan, to trample on the holy grounds of the cities of Mecca and Medina.

To prolong the war as much as possible would have an added advantage for Saddam. How long could the varied interests of the Alliance stay together? Was the objective not to guarantee a more or less stable oil price? Now therefore, what would be the true value per barrel of oil if the cost of the war were to be added to the barrels produced in the area? Saddam was convinced that these considerations would finally be imposed and that an agreement would finally be reached in which Iraq, led by him, would start a new era of preeminence in the Arab world.

Arab history is filled with precedents where the best alternative was defeat. Gamal Abdel Nasser and Anuar al-Sadat are examples of this. After thunderous military defeats in 1956 due to the nationalization of the Suez Canal, in 1967 after the Six Day War and the 1973 Yom Kippur war, these leaders had transformed their failures into juicy political gains that had led them to the heights of glory. Cairo and other capitals in the Arab world are filled with monuments celebrating these "victories".

Operation "Desert Shield"

Saddam Hussein's political calculations failed in a fundamental aspect. He did not count on the joint U.S.-USSR front, two superpowers enjoying a post-cold war era of entente. Instead of agreeing not to intervene, both nations decided to oppose the Iraqi leader's intentions. Nevertheless, due to internal problems or because it would be convenient for Soviet interests once the region's geopolitical panorama had cleared up, the Kremlin preferred to leave the practical solution in the hands of other nations. In fact, probably Moscow decided to give public international support to Washington's position, in exchange for which two advantages were reaped: the material support needed by its troubled economy in the winter months and freedom to solve the problem represented by the uprisings in the Baltic states.

The United Nations likewise adopted a joint stance, the second time this had happened since the organization had been created half a century before, by approving an immediate condemnation of the invasion and urging Iraq to withdraw. In the following months, the U.N. approved 12 resolutions ranging from stringent economic sanctions and embargos against oil exports from Iraq and Kuwait to the blockade of all its imports and exports. Finally, on November 29th, 1990 the United Nations Security Council approved an ultimatum setting forth a deadline - January 15th, 1991 - for Iraq to withdraw from Kuwaiti territory. If, after this date, Iraq had not fulfilled the terms of the Resolution, the Security Council authorized the use of force. Of the 15 members of the Security Council, 12 (including the USSR) voted in favour, China abstained and only Cuba and Yemen voted against.

To guarantee the fulfillment of the ultimatum, an Arab-Occidental Alliance was formed, headed by the U.S. which immediately started to deploy a formidable military force to the Middle East. Nations such as the U.S., Great Britain, France, Italy, Spain, Holland, Belgium, Turkey, Argentina, Pakistan, etc. participated in this action. The Arab nations of the Alliance included Saudi Arabia, Egypt, Syria, Morrocco and other states and emirates of the Gulf, such as Bahrain, Qatar, United Arab Emirates, Oman, etc.

Iran took an ambivalent stance. At first it decidedly joined the position of the United Nations regarding the sanctions imposed against Iraq. Its attitude was somewhat "we had warned you", in remembrance of the cruel eight-year war it had suffered after Iraq's invasion of its territory. However, as time went by, Iran started to analyze the possible advantages of negotiating with its former enemy. Its attitude progressively changed, until it declared itself neutral.

In truth, Teheran's fundamentalist position seemed to interpret the feelings of the Muslim people. Although the rulers of many Arab nations had opposed Iraq, the population seemed to be sentimentally inclined in favour of Saddam

Hussein. Besides, understanding the advantages that Islam had set before him, the Iraqi leader had left behind his longstanding traditional baathist and socialist-inspired discourse to transform it into a fervent call to a holy war against the infidels.

The Iraqi ruler did not have the religious authority to call a holy war ("Jihad"). However, many Islamic leaders ended up by convincing the Muslim population that this holy war was fair, if not to defend Hussein, at least to back his position in favour of the Palestinians.

Aware of this, Saddam Hussein took every chance to attack Israel. To penetrate even further the soul of the Muslim population with his call, he had to stimulate the hatred of the Arabs against the Jews, whom he threatened to destroy if a war broke out. Saddam also had his own affronts to avenge. In this regard, he could not forget that in 1981, the Israeli airforce had destroyed the nuclear reactor being built with so much interest by Iraq.

In conclusion, two very powerful armies were on the verge of confrontation. On the one hand, Iraq, led by Saddam Hussein with over one million armed forces, skillfully honed and trained in eight years' war with Iran, apart from modern equipment purchased in the West as well as the USSR, such as Scud missiles and an arsenal of chemical and biological warfare that spread panic among its enemies.

The Arab-occidental Alliance in turn, though counting with a lesser number of men, was rapidly accumulating in the Middle East an impressive force with the most sophisticated conventional modern-technology weapons. A series of weapons never before used would be put to the test during this war. The technological superiority of the Alliance was evident. "Operation Desert Shield" was the name given to intimidate Saddam Hussein.

As the date of the ultimatum drew close, the world at large contained its breath. The menace of war carried with it the risk of a third oil shock. In fact, the embargo on Iraq's and Kuwait's production had already withdrawn approximately 4 million barrels per day of oil from the market. The result was not long in coming.

In effect, crude prices that had barely been kept up until the mid-80's and that had plummetted in 1986, once again escalated at the end of 1990. A few weeks before the invasion of Kuwait, OPEC had fruitlessly tried to maintain an official price of $18 per barrel and had imposed stringent quotas. However, by October 10th, 1990, the price of light crude quoted in the NYSE futures market was 41.15 dollars per barrel, the highest ever registered for a contract of that type in that market.

The threat of war and economic depression was spreading throughout the world, while the warring sides seemed to strengthen their positions. Iraq did not seem willing to withdraw from Kuwait. The Arab-Occidental Alliance was not willing to negotiate unless Iraq withdrew first. The date of the ultimatum was drawing close.

Finally the deadline was up and on January 16, 1991 the conflict exploded. That day, a perplexed world was able to see, like never before, the start of the war the minute it took place. Three CNN reporters (Arnett, Shaw and Holligan) transmitting from the ninth floor of Baghdad's Hotel Rashid informed the entire world that at 6.35 pm New York time, the bombing of the city had started.

On the other side of the planet, those who at the time were watching their TV screens, were amazed not only at the magnitude of the drama unfolding but also due to the technology of the telecommunications media. To witness a historic tragedy of such proportions the moment it started, represented an unprecedented phenomenon. With our hearts filled with anguish we heard the noise of the bombs and the thunder of the antiair cannons. Many of us came to believe that the world, as known until then, had reached a point after which everything would be different. From then onwards, we would have to face a new era filled with uncertainty.

But if the technology of the telecommunications astounded us, we were even more affected by the art of modern warfare used for destructive purposes. If only the imagination required to develop these devastation capabilities could be used to build a better world.

Operation "Desert Storm"

"Operation Desert Shield" whose purpose was to intimidate Saddam Hussein became "Operation Desert Storm" overnight, the purpose of which was to destroy this leader.

Two formidable armies entered the confrontation. On the one hand, Iraq's forces, one of the Middle East's largest armies at the time. Its land forces were overwhelmingly greater than that of its enemies, counting over one million regular soldiers and reservists. It had 5,500 war tanks, most of them Soviet-made T-54 and T-55 models of the '60s. Only 1,500 Iraqi tanks are modern and technologically more advanced. Iraq also had an important arsenal of rockets, though most of them were for defense purposes. This force included a vast number of Scud missiles with fixed and movable launch pads. Saudi Arabia's oil fields were within the target range of this kind of missiles, as well as Israel's main cities. Iraq also had vast numbers of Exocet missiles and sophisticated French helicopters, as well as 500 war planes, 70 of which were modern Soviet MIG 23s and 64 French Mirage F-1s. According to Western estimates, Iraq also had an estimated arsenal of 2 to 4 thousand tons of the following chemical agents:

-*Mustard gas, comprising the largest part of the chemical arsenal, producing a lasting garlic-scented cloud that burns the lungs, blisters the skin and in high doses can be fatal.*

-*Sarin, that if inhaled or absorbed through the skin, is lethal in a matter of minutes by paralyzing the nervous system even at low doses.*

-*Tabun, similar to Sarin, but slightly less toxic. This nervous agent can also quickly kill if inhaled or absorbed.*(7)

Perhaps one of the major advantages Iraq has is its army's level of training, having had enough experience in combat with Iran for eight years. Besides, the conditions of the terrain are well known and the difficult situations arising for men and equipment under the circumstances can be well handled.

When the hostilities broke out, and as was to be expected, the technological superiority of the Arab-occidental Alliance was immediately felt. Iraq's offensive capabilities were quickly and efficiently destroyed. The main targets of strategic importance were systematically bombed for several weeks, with close to two thousand air missions by day, without the planes of the Alliance encountering any resistance from the Iraqi air forces.

The following equipment was used in the ferocious punishment being exerted on Iraq: the legendary B-52s used in Vietnam and protected by F-16 fighter planes; A-63 Intruders and F/A 18s, escorted by F-14 fighter planes; Stealth F-117A bombers, practically invisible by radar, capable of dropping laser-guided 2,000-pound bombs, protected by F-15 fighter planes; Navy A-6E planes, dedicated to destroying the Scud missile launching pads; English Tornado jets, aimed at the landstrips of the Iraqi airports; EF-111 planes that obscured enemy radars to facilitate the destroy missions of the F-111 bombers; A-10 planes, sometimes dismissed for their slowness and aspect, but which resulted especially effective in the destruction of enemy tanks, as well as sophisticated Apache helicopters, designed for the same purpose. Tank KC-135 and KC-10 planes, capable of in-flight refueling of the entire airforce of the Alliance. Besides, this complex set of air operations was controlled by AWACS planes that from a distance of hundreds of miles were capable of supervising the theatre of operations. These were also backed by spy satellites, laser-guided smart bombs or heat tracking missiles, Tomahawk missiles, Patriot anti-missile missiles, night vision equipment, etc.

While Iraq was subjected to this phenomenal punishment, the entire world asked itself what was Saddam Hussein's strategy in allowing his country to suffer such devastating actions without even defending itself. With the sole exception of sporadic and futile Scud missiles aimed against Israel and Saudi Arabia, which most of the time were intercepted by Patriot anti-missile missiles, Saddam's forces remained out of sight. Its planes, initially hidden in the underground hangars, had resorted to escaping to Iranian territory, where, according to declarations by that government they were to be retained til the end of the war. What were Iraq's pretentions by withdrawing its most modern airplanes from its air space and by sending them to the territory of its previous enemy ? Could there be a secret pact between Iran and Iraq, by means of which both would announce an agreement and use their joint forces against the Alliance? This possibility was in the air. In fact, the

Iranian government had announced that it would abandon its neutral stance if Israel attacked any Arab nation.

On the other hand, the majority of military analysts considered that Saddam Hussein's strategy consisted in not fighting an air war where he had all the possibilities of losing. He apparently was willing to endure the systematic destruction of his nation by air, convinced that finally the troops of the Alliance would have to penetrate by land a territory that had been prepared for battle many months in advance. That would be the time when the Iraqi forces would start to act and the American army would suffer heavy casualties. That would also be the moment when American public opinion would exert its pressure against Bush's "warlike adventures". Thus, the numerous manifestations in Muslim countries would be added to the effect on the American population of the "return to the voting tables".

Finally, other nations like France, Germany, Japan, Italy, etc. started to reconsider the convenience of maintaining such a costly war and to analyze the possibility of negotiating a ceasefire with Saddam that would lead to a peace conference where a joint solution to the problems of the Middle East could be put forward. Evidently, a fundamental element to take into account in this conference would be the Palestine issue.

If this were to be the course of events, Saddam Hussein would become a new Nasser in the eyes of the Muslims and his influence in the Middle East would come to be a determinant factor in deciding the fate of the region. A solution of that nature evidently seemed to constitute the goal that Saddam had set for himself.

To this effect, researcher Barry Rubin of the Washington Institute for Middle East Policies sustains that:

"The United States shall defeat Iraq as far as it can or should. Saddam has to leave totally defeated, if not evicted from power. If he survives, the Arabs shall eventually consider him as the moral winner."(8)

On the other hand, if the final outcome of the conflict was Iraq's total defeat, the Alliance would have achieved its goal of eliminating Saddam Hussein as leader of that nation. This alternative would however bring about new and complex situations by creating a vacuum of power in the region.

Iraq has an important geopolitical role in the conflictive Middle East. A weak and devastated Iraq would open up the expansionary appetites of other leaders in the region, for instance Syria's Hafez al-Assad, or could tempt Iranian president Hashemi Rafjsanjani to extend his Islamic revolution, or fan Turkish president Turgut Ozal's aspirations of achieving the greatest benefits at the lowest cost for his country. Thus, Iraq's total destruction would sow the seeds for an eventual new chapter of violence in what has been called the "planet's most conflictive area". The possibility of this happening has led John Waterbury, Professor of International Affairs at Princeton University, to declare that the United States must "deflate Iraq and Saddam but not reduce to powder." (9)

When land operations began, the Arab-Occidental Alliance headed by General Norman Schwarzkopf, counted also with a collection of sophisticated equipment, among which were the following: M1 A1 Abrams tanks, apparently vulnerable under desert conditions, but whose capacity of destruction and advance speed make it a formidable weapon; M-2 Bradley vehicles, heavily armored and equipped with missiles; Apache AH-64A helicopters, with automatic 30-mm cannons and antitank missiles; MLRS movable rocket launchers, capable of shooting 12 missiles, each of which contains six persecute-

and-destroy bombs. In sum, on land, the technological superiority shall also be on the side of the Alliance.

Saddam Hussein's troops were no longer able to withstand the attack of the powerful war machine of the Arab-Occidental Alliance that was against the former's expansionary goals. Once the Iraqi will to fight had been broken after the devastating air attacks that took place during Operation Desert Storm, Saddam's once invincible army was in no position to thwart the advances of its enemy. Thus, in less than a hundred hours from launching the attack by land, Iraq's forces had been totally defeated.

In the meantime, the Iraqi high command and its leader had gone into hiding. It was said that once the command lines had been interrupted, the soldiers and officers on the battlefield were left to their own devices on how to react to the enemy's overwhelming onward march. It was also rumored that Saddam himself had refused to impart orders, fearful that the American ultramodern electronic espionage system was capable of detecting with the utmost precision the source of these orders, whereby a swift air attack would suffice to erase the Iraqi leader off the face of the earth.

And so, the Iraqi troops were forced to withdraw from Kuwait almost as swiftly as they had entered. However, the possibility of a withdrawal had already been envisaged. Explosives and mines were planted in all the oil wells.

A conflagration of monumental proportions ensued, after the withdrawal of the troops. The detonation of the explosives destroyed close to 900 Kuwaiti oil-producing wells and thousands of millions of dollars' worth of investments in the development of the oil industry of one of the world's wealthiest nations went up in smoke. The ecological damage of that catastrophe shall continue forever. The sands of the desert shall be coated for decades, if not for centuries, with oil-based residues resulting from the combustion of millions of barrels of petroleum.

The Persian Gulf waters will also be tainted by the Iraqi-provoked fires and devastating oil spills, carried out with the purpose of avoiding the troops from landing or commando operations to be carried out on Kuwaiti shores.

Kuwait was left totally devastated. The destruction of its oil industry was coupled with the systematic plunder of the wealth of that emirate during the invasion. Iraq was also destroyed as a result of the conflict. Its oil facilities, refineries, pipelines, industries, highways, bridges, ports, airports and the entire infrastructure in general of that nation were left in ruins due to the systematic bombing it had suffered at the hands of its enemy.

The scope of destruction far surpassed any periodic devastation experienced in those territories throughout the centuries, since the beginning of civilization. Somehow it seemed that a higher intelligence was bent once more on showing the world the futility of man's ambitions. The Euphrates and Tigris rivers had been the birthplace of civilization. However, advances in civilized life have somehow not been able to teach mankind the lesson that violence only breeds more violence.

Practically nothing stood in the way of the advancing Arab-Occidental troops which could easily have reached Baghdad and could have occupied the entire Iraqi territory if they had so chosen to do.

Finally, the U.S. as well as other Western allies, preferred to be cautious. A resounding victory with a minimum of casualties had been achieved. It was therefore decided not to run the risk implicit in the occupation of Iraqi territory.

In the meantime, the Kurdish inhabitants of northern Iraq - the location of the vast oil fields in the Mosul region - decided to stage an uprising and seek their autonomy. Saddam sent all the troops available to stifle this insurgency. To protect the population, the U.S. imposed an "exclusion zone" within Iraq, whereby any Iraqi plane flying over that area would be shot down.

Saddam Hussein was allowed to remain in power. Although undoubtedly a dangerous opponent, this leader continued to play a key role in the delicate geopolitical balance of the region. The possible success of the Kurdish uprising would have doubtless extended to Turkey, a good part of whcih is inhabited by these people, and would have thereby wreaked havoc on a government that was a member of NATO. This revolt could have also partially affected Azerbaijan, Armenia, Turkmenistan and even Georgia, still a part of the USSR at the time. The ensuing imbalance would clearly have affected Iran's interests, though undoubtedly this was less a matter of concern for the Western and Arab nations. However, the U.N. Security Council refused to lift the ban on Iraq's oil exports as well as other sanctions. As a condition to suspend these measures, Iraq was requested to totally destroy under UN supervision its Scud missiles and other offensive weapons. Likewise, an inspection of the country's industrial facilities was undertaken with the purpose of eliminating any possibility whatsoever of concealed chemical warfare or the completion of nuclear weaponry, as was feared by many.

Although the conflict had ended by early 1991, by October 1994, the date this book was sent to press, the U.N. has remained firm in its decision to maintain the embargo against Iraqi oil exports, despite the pleas of that nation, alleging that all the conditions exacted by that organization have been met.

October 1994: Saddam´s Attempted Brag

Exasperated by the United Nations' refusal to lift the economic sanctions against Iraq, or perhaps in an attempt to strengthen his image within his territory, the inhabitants of which had been suffering the rigours of defeat for several years, Saddam Hussein undertook a new adventure in early October 994, the objectives of which are difficult to comprehend. In effect, when least expected, the Iraqi leader decided to deploy close to 65,000 troops to the Kuwaiti border, backed by war tanks, in a clear threat against this minute yet opulent neighbour. Thus, Saddam has once again ratified his declarations that Kuwait is but a province of Iraq and has once again backed this allegation with reasons that have already been mentioned. Simultaneously, thousands of civilians undertook a march from Baghdad towards the frontier with Kuwait, bearing posters and placards in support of the Iraqi president.

The reaction of the former Arab-Occidental Alliance was not long in coming. Washington announced the immediate transfer of 28,000 soldiers to Kuwait and made hasty preparations to send some additional 20,000 men as well as placing 155,000 American soldiers in a state of alert. The Washington aircraft carrier was sent to the Red Sea and war vessels armed with Tomahawk war missiles, the devastating destructive capacity of which had been made evident during Operation Desert Storm, set sail for the Persian Gulf. Likewise, an impressive US air fleet of 500 tactical F-15, F-16, A-10 and Awac flying radar planes were made ready to intervene in the region.

The Kuwaitis also immediately transferred the bulk of their army to the northern frontier, while Prime Minister Saad Abdallah al-Sabah called for the population to keep calm, stating that "the military steps taken shall be enough to firmly halt a possible aggression".

The British in turn sent to Kuwaiti waters the HMS Cornwall, equipped with Sea Wolf missiles and manned by a crew of 237. Lynx helicopters are ready for action in the region, as well as a destroyer, auxilliary vessels and escort ships patrolling the Persian Gulf. The fleet of British Tornado planes stationed in the gulf and the Harrier combat planes in the Incirlik base in southern Turkey are also ready for combat.

France's lukewarn reaction differs however from its decisive attitude during Operation Desert Storm. Although Alain Juppé, the Minister of Foreign Affairs, announced the "availability" of the French military machine in the Persian Gulf, this time however, France has warned that it does not deem Irak to have violated any UN resolution. In fact, this European country had consistently mediated before the UN Security Council to lift the economic bans imposed against Iraq.

Bahrain also immediately sent several fighter bombers to add to the new international coalition. In the meantime, the Secretaries of Foreign Affairs of the six countries belonging to the Persian Gulf Cooperation Council - Saudi Arabia, Kuwait, United Arab Emirates, Qatar, Bahrain and Oman - met in Kuwait.

Curiously enough, this time round, with the exception of Bahrain, the remaining members of the aforementioned Cooperation Council have sent no special aid whatsoever. Many commentators have come to consider that the stance adopted by these nations indicates that they will allow the Western countries to incur all the expenses for the time being.

This operation shall undoubtedly be costly. William Perry, the U.S. Secretary of Defence, declared from Kuwait that the swift mobilization of vessels, planes, arms and troops to face this new emergency could cost his country close to one billion dollars, even if nothing comes out of it. "Our troops shall remain in Kuwait as long as the Iraqi threat persists" declared Perry, adding that "our pilots and marines are ready to enter into action if the Iraqis do not withdraw their troops to the positions occupied before the crisis."

In any event, faced with the formidable force of the U.S. and its British allies, as well as the eventual cooperation of France and other Gulf nations, Saddam Hussein does not stand a chance. At the time this book was sent to press, the Iraqi leader had started to withdraw the troops that had been concentrated in the border with Kuwait. Many are of the opinion that this was just a "brag" by Saddam, or a maneuver to call the world's attention to the refusal by the United Nations to lift the economic bans. It has even been said that this was a move to get the backing of the Iraqi population, after an attempted coup d'etat was unveiled.

Once the withdrawal of Iraqi troops is verified, the UN Security Council has warned that it shall not recommend that the embargo imposed after the 1990 invasion be eased until such time as Iraq recognizes Kuwait as a sovereign state and the frontiers between both nations are ratified. In this regard, Russia has proposed that once Kuwait's recognition is accepted, the UN should lift the sanctions against Iraq. This shall undoubtedly be a bitter blow for Saddam Hussein and shall weaken his leadership within Iraq. "We are under siege and the population is starving. To recognize Kuwait is to demand the impossible" stated the Iraqi chief of Parliament, Saddi Mehdi Saleh.

The American and British position is however even more drastic. In the opinion of the White House, after Saddam Hussein has once again threatened the entire world with a new crisis in Kuwait, "any consideration aimed at lifting the sanctions shall constitute a dangerous mistake". On the contrary, the U.S. has proposed a new sanction against Iraq and has urged the UN to approve a ban forbidding Baghdad from concentrating troops close to the frontier with Kuwait. The resolution proposed by the American government was finally unanimously adopted by the UN Security Council after lengthy talks had been held between Washington and Moscow.

Saddam did not count this time round on the backing of King Hussein of Jordan, nor of Yasser Arafat, the PLO spokesperson, who had supported him during the 1990 invasion. By 1994, both personalities are now committing their entire efforts to upholding the success of the Israeli-Palestinian peace negotiations. "Saddam's folly" undoubtedly would endanger these peace talks.

In any event, regardless of the final outcome of the action taken by Iraq, the truth is that this incident once more highlights the permanent instability in the Persian Gulf as well as the enormous expense incurred in maintaining peace in a region apparently condemned to unavoidable and recurrent violent outbursts.

Notes

1.-Caspar W. Weinberger. FIGHTING FOR PEACE. page 387.

2.-Christine Moss Helms. IRAQ, EASTERN FLANK OF THE ARAB WORLD. page 39.

3.-Newsweek. January 14th. 1991.

4.-Judith Miller and Laurie Mylroie. SADDAM HUSSEIN AND THE CRISIS IN THE GULF. page 16.

5.-State Department press conference. July 24th. 1990.

6.-NEWSWEEK. January 14th. 1991.

7.-NEWSWEEK. August 20th. 1990.

8.-El UNIVERSAL newspaper. January 19th. 1991.

9.-El UNIVERSAL newspaper. January 19th. 1991.

10.-NEWSWEEK. January 28th. 1991.

CHAPTER VIII

THE MIDDLE EAST: A REGION CONDEMNED TO VIOLENCE

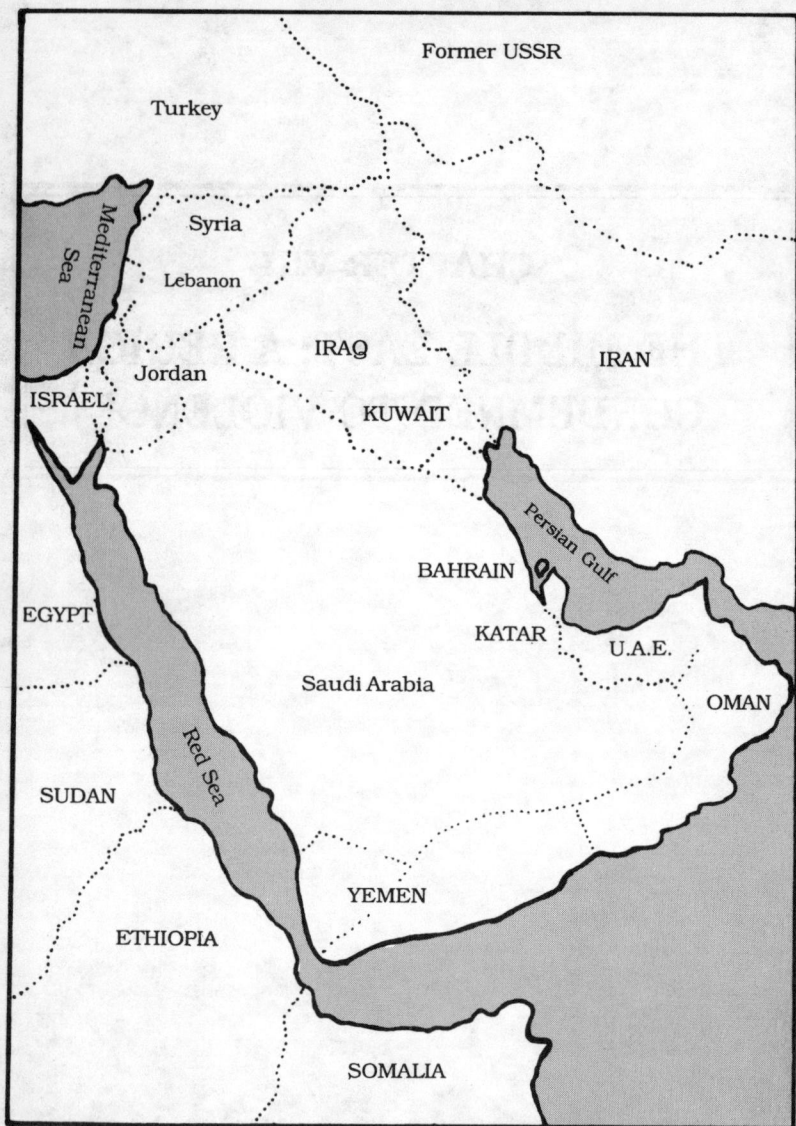

The Middle East

The Birthplace of Civilization

"As every President since World War II has learned, no region of the world presents America with more difficulty, more frustrating, or more convoluted problems than the Middle East. It's a region where hate has roots reaching back to the dawn of history. It's a place where the senseless spilling of blood in the name of religious faith has gone on since biblical times, and where modern events are forever being shaped by momentous events of the past, from the Exodus to the Holocaust."(1)

This is how Ronald Reagan, in his autobiography "An American Life", described his feelings towards the difficult circumstances he had to face as President of the United States, due to the recurring episodes of instability in the Middle East, the world's most convoluted area.

Undoubtedly history has shown that this region, the birthplace of civilization and the origin of the world's most important religions, is however an endemically violent area. Many centuries before our time, that region has witnessed countless invasions, conquests and devastations of the various cultures that arose, expanded and disappeared with spasmodic regularity in the Middle East. Sumerians, Accadians, Amorites, Assyrians, Medians, Caldeans, Arameans, Babylonians, Persians, Sassanians, Egyptians, Parthians, Cannanees, Hebrews, Macedonians, Mongols, Romans, Arabs, Turks, French and British are but some of the races, cultures and nationalities that took turns in desolating the region, spreading bitter violence but also, in many cases, creating flourishing civilizations that reached their pinnacle to be simply wiped off of the face of the earth by cyclical fanatical destructive passions that seem to emanate from these lands.

A comprehensive inventory of the history and reasons giving rise to the fanatism and ferocity felt by the inhabitants of that region of the planet would require many volumes and much investigation. Since the objective of this chapter is infinitely more modest, we shall attempt to simplify succintly some of the more relevant reasons why an era of lasting peace in the Middle East it not to be expected in the near future. Many of these reasons are so remote that we have no other choice but to forego analysis thereof. On the basis of these limitations, we shall quote some of the problems that at present gravitate over an extension of the planet's geography whose oil wealth has made it the center of the world's attention.

The Problems of Islam

The predominant religion in the Middle East and particularly in oil-rich countries is Islam, started by the prophet Mohammed who was born in Mecca towards the year 570 A.D. and who died in 632. Mohammed, an illiterate merchant, received divine inspiration from the Arcangel Gabriel (the same that announced the birth of Jesus to Mary) while in a trance. These revelations were transcribed into the Koran, the Holy book for the Muslims, that contains a synopsis of all the wisdom in the world. The Koran was written in classic Arabic which, for the Arabs, is the language of the angels.

It could be said that the Koran is a thorough colection of precepts for daily life. Its 114 chapters or suras encompass a series of dogmas and moral principles that constitute the only source of law, ethics, administration, etc. for the Muslims. This is a final revelation and as such, contains the final and most perfect solution to all questions. The Koran is therefore the origin of the "Shari'a", the set of Islamic laws that make no difference between what is religious and what is legal. The Shari'a, however, is not a formal code, according to Western world parameters. "The science of the law is the knowledge of the rights and duties by which man can lead his life properly in this world in order to prepare for the future life"(2). The principles sustaining the Koran are immutable and are therefore a source of divine inspiration for the "Shari'a".

Thus, for the pious Muslim, his faith is more than a religion. It is a complete system of life. The Law, the basis for community life, can be none other than "God's will revealed through the Prophet". The Islam is therefore, politics, laws, social mores and is so demanding in all its details that it even prescribes procedures for personal affairs, the organization of families (including marriage and divorce), property, trade activities, criminal laws (Muslim laws do not establish any difference between civil and criminal affairs), loans, wills, etc.

From the theological standpoint, Islam is in fact a simple religion. The Koran places everything in the hands of God. Everything is determined by Allah. Man has no reason to doubt nor to be worried. Every event, every change of fortune, every success or failure, depends on God's will. "Inshallah" (Alla's will). Islam is therefore a fatalistic religion. Everything is in God's hands and human beings must have direct contact with their creator, through intellect and faith, knowledge and will. To be in contact with God, man does not need middlemen nor clergy.

The Muslims accept the manifestations of modern Western civilization but reject their rules. They accept its technology but not its science. Science fills them with confusion since it is not included in the Koran, the synthesis of all knowledge. This cultural shock confuses them and leads them to take refuge in a simple religion full of content:

"God is most great.
I testify that there is no god but God.
I testify that Mohammed is the Prophet of God.
Come to prayer.

Come to success.
God is most great.
There is no god but God."(3)

Thus are the Mohammedans called to prayer and must all look towards Mecca for this purpose. This is a factor of unity and that promotes them to feel as if they were members of a great community.

However, not everything in Islam is unity. On the contrary, the first great schism in Islamism arose after Mohammed's death. This is a division whose echoes reach our days. In effect, during the prophet's last two years of life, practically all the Arabian tribes had submitted to him, and had pledged the adoption of the Muslim religion and the payment of tax.

However, in June 632, Mohammed died without leaving any instructions about an heir. Before dying he had said: "Oh Lord, I have delivered my message and have fulfilled my mission", and had delegated in Abu Bekr only the direction of public prayers. The prophet died in the arms of his friend's daughter:

"Aisha, the daughter of Abu Bekr, gently supported his head. He prayed in a faint whisper, "Lord, grant me pardon. Eternity in paradise. Pardon...' Suddenly Aisha noticed that his head had grown heavy in her lap. The Prophet of Arabia had gone to meet his Lord."(4)

In the beginning nothing happened, since the title of Caliph was granted to his faithful old friend Abu Bekr, who died two years later in 634. A struggle for succession immediately ensued. On the one hand were the representatives of the ancient aristocracy of Mecca, who announced that they would not accept any other leader but Umar ibn al Khattab, whom Abu Bekr had designated as his heir and who belonged to the Quaraish tribe. On the other hand was Ali ibn abi Talib, cousin and son-in-law of the Prophet (by marriage to his daughter Fatima). His followers proclaimed that succession belonged to him inasmuch as he was part of Mohammed's family.

Umar's faction prevailed and he adopted the title of "Prince of the Believers", beginning an intense campaign of conquests that contributed to rapidly extend Islamism. In the year 644, the new caliph was murdered while directing public prayers in the mosque of Medina. Othman ibn Affan, already 70 years old, was designated as his successor and ruled until he was 82 years old. He was also murdered by a mob of soldiers that shed his blood over the Koran manuscript he was reading.

With Othman's death everything changed in the Arab world. For 25 years, the Muslims had lived in a dream. God had chosen them to conquer the world, after which they would attain the unimaginable glories in paradise. Suddenly the dream had vanished and once again they found themselves surrounded by war, violence and bloodshed. A ferocious civil war was waged among the followers of Islam inasmuch as many leaders refused to obey Ali as the successor and accused him of conspiring against Othman.

Finally, Ali was also murdered on January 20th, 661. His death left the road free to his rival Muawiya Sole Khalif, belonging to the Quaraish tribe, who thus began the Omeya dynasty. Ironically, Muawiya was the son of Abu Sofian, who while the Prophet was alive, had been his most steadfast opponent.

These circumstances gave rise to a deep enmity between the Omeya and the followers of the house of Ali, who never ceased to claim that their rights to succession had been violated.

Muawiya died in April 680. Two possible candidates claimed the right of succession: his son Yezeed and Hussein, the son of Ali and Fatima and grandson of Mohammed.

On the road to Damascus, the capital of the caliphate transferred by the Omeya, Hussein, accompanied by a small group of followers, was attacked by over 4,000 men commanded by Yezeed. After courageously defending himself, he fell, mortally wounded. His head and those of his seventy-two followers was sent to Damascus.

Hussein's martyrdom awoke an impassioned devotion among his followers and produced a serious schism in the Muslim world that has lasted to this day. His supporters transformed his death into one of the most sublime religious episodes in the history of Islam.

Those who venerated Hussein and his father Ali came to be known as shiites, from the word Shia (party). The followers of the clan of Yezeed took on the name of sunnites, meaning that they had accepted the authority of the first three caliphs, Abu Bekr, Umar and Othman.

Thus began a fierce fight between these two factions. The hatred unleashed by those ancient events has never ceased and shiites and sunnites continue being mortal enemies to this date, over thirteen centuries after Islam's violent origins.

At present, the vast majority of Muslims are sunnites. The shiites however make up 95 percent of Iran's population and 55 percent of Iraq's inhabitants. There are also active and militant minorities in other countries in the Middle East.

After the fall of the Shah of Iran in 1979, power went into the hands of a shiite theocratical government headed by Ayatollah Khomeini. The fear that the Islamic fundamentalism preached by Khomeini would extend to other Middle East states was the determining factor in the 8-year long Iran-Iraq war that threatened to encompass the entire region and create a dangerous instability in the entire Persian Gulf.

The religious problems of the Middle East did not end with the war. On the contrary, hatred is still present. The shiites, a minority in other Gulf states, have always been discriminated against. They constitute however an important part of the labor force working in the oil fields of the Persian Gulf, thereby representing a potential threat for stability in the region.

Khomeini's Islamic fundamentalism has in turn taken on a special attraction not only among the shiites but has also contributed to worsen the religious sentiments of the sunnites. In fact, upon analyzing the events arising from the Iran-Iraq war, it would seem that an increasingly wider division is being felt between the Muslim masses and the pro-Occidental course adopted by the governments of the Arab-Occidental Alliance for survival reasons.

One must not forget that the nationalistic sentiments of the Arabs is one of its main features. Until the invasion of Kuwait by Irak, Saudis and Kuwaitis had always been reluctant to accept an American military presence in their territory for this same reason.

What shall be the reaction of the Muslim people when faced with this contingent of infidel soldiers headed by the Americans, that trample the soil of the country housing the holy cities of Mecca and Medina, the birthplace and burial grounds of the Prophet Mohammed? What will the Saudis think when they see American women who not only do not use chadors but wear military uniforms and share heavy duties with soldiers, are many times in a position to give orders to men by reason of their higher rank, bearin in mind that the Saudis deem women to be subservient creatures with no rights to driving licenses? How will a nation react to alcohol and other sinful Western customs being freely and happily enjoyed by the infidels?

Struggle among Muslim brothers was expressly forbidden by the Prophet and though evidently this prohibition was never obeyed, it is a factor that shall undoubtedly be exploited by those who wish to undermine the position of pro-Western governments in the Middle East. The conscience problem shall worsen when it is not just a case of fighting against a Muslim brother but a struggle to defend the interests of an infidel. For a Muslim, any type of alliance with the allies of the hated Jewish people that hold the city of Jerusalem, the most sacred city for Islam after Mecca and Medina, is an effort that would violate the deepest fibers of religious conditioning.

In conclusion, religious problems shall always be present in this region. The division among shiites and sunnites continues to this day and is a time bomb that sooner or later shall once again explode. The Muslim masses will be hard pressed to understand an alliance with infidels to confront their Islamic brothers, in view of the ongoing peace negotiations among Israel, the Palestinians and some neighbouring Arab countries. In the long run this problem could reach great dramatic proportions of misunderstanding. Apart from the theological or historical reasons separating shiites from sunnites, the radical fundamentalism of the former has had a formidable intellectual and social impact on countries where the latter predominate, namely Egypt, Syria, Lebanon and the monarchies of the Persian Gulf.

Abd al-Salam Faraj, an ideologist of the Jihad group that murdered Anuar al-Sadat, clearly expounded the confrontations arising in the Muslim world, in which fundamentalist groups can no longer tolerate the existence itself of pro-Western governments:

"There are some who say that the jihad effort should concentrate nowadays upon the liberation of Jerusalem. It is true that the

liberation of the Holy Land is a legal precept binding upon every Muslim... but let us emphasize that the fight against the enemy nearest to you has precedence over the fight against the enemy farther away. All the more so as the former is not only corrupted but a lackey of imperialism as well... In all Muslim countries the enemy has the reins of power. The enemy is the present rulers. It is hence, a most imperative obligation to fight these rulers. This Islamic jihad requires today the blood and sweat of each Muslim."(5)

The Arab-Occidental Alliance against Iraq has become a reason for serious concern for Muslim theologians. This Alliance has produced an intolerable degeneration or intoxication that progressively threatens Islam as never before since the times preceding the appearance of the Prophet. The religious sunnites and shiites, usually enemies, are now in agreement that pro-Western leaders have led the Muslim world to a state of apostasy and savagery (Jahiliyya).

For the pious Muslim, the only cure lies in the return of Islamic followers to the political arena they have abandoned. The systematic warnings and criticisms against the values of Western modernisation, openly opposed to the teachings of the Koran are continuously increasing.

From the political point of view, the result of Iraq's invasion of Kuwait shall be less transcendent for the Middle East than the trauma remaining in the Muslim conscience. The religious consequences shall come later. The fundamentalists shall have more arguments than ever to convince the Muslims that they have fallen into a state of jahiliyya. A disheartening panorama for the Western world could develop. As has happened in the past, cultural shock shall confuse the followers of the Prophet and it is probable that this will lead them to seek refuge in their religion, where everything is made simpler because everything is in the hands of Allah (Inshallah). Jahiliyya or the state of apostasy shall end when the kingdom of God is reestablished on earth and the public powers become subordinated to the authority of the religious leaders. This, according to the Muslims, is how everything will return to its normal state. The Koran shall once again be the compass guiding the policies of governments and the only source of law. This all coincides with the preachings of an increasingly expanding Islamic fundamentalism:

God is most great.
I testify that there is no god but God.
I testify that Mohammed is the Prophet of God.

The Arab-Israeli Conflict

A full analysis of the Arab-Israeli conflict would force us to go back to biblical times. At least a thousand years before Christ, the Hebrews founded a kingdom in Jerusalem that after Solomon was divided into two states: the state of Israel to the north and that of Judea to the south.

The following millenium was witness to the destruction and devastation of both states by the Assyrians and Babilonians. The entire region was controlled successively by Persians, Macedonians, Ptolomeans and Selucids. Approximately a century and a half before Christ, Simon reinstated the independent state of Israel which was once more lost to the Romans in the year 63 B.C.

By the year 135 of our Lord, the Romans had proscribed Jews from being in Jerusalem. The Jewish people were therefore forced to disperse. This was known as the Diaspora, which was not a new phenomenon, since it had started with the Assyrian invasions several centuries before.

The Arab conquest of Palestine began from the year 630 onwards. The Crusades took place between the years 1100 and 1300, during which the Christians intermitently imposed their domain with the intention of rescuing the Holy Sepulcher. From 1300 to 1517 Palestine was dominated by the Mamelukes and from that latter year to 1918, the entire region was controlled by the Ottoman empire.

In this extremely brief history at-a-glance, we thus see that the territories occupied at present by Israel never escaped the endemic violence that has characterized the entire Middle East region.

From the time they were expelled from the land of their ancestors, the Jews never renounced their hopes of returning to their Biblical roots. The phrase "Next year in Jerusalem" was never left out of their prayers.

On the other hand, from the VIIth century onwards, that territory has been occupied by inhabitants mostly embracing the Islamic faith. It would therefore be useless to devote an endless dissertation to who has the most historical rights to the land.

The truth is that that territory is at present called Israel due to a decision adopted by the United Nations in 1948. Another truth is that this decision implied that hundreds of thousands of Palestinians living there were forced to leave. The result of this is the Arab-Israeli conflict that impregnates the entire Middle East region, contributing in great measure to the recurrent episodes of violence affecting the entire area and touching the deepest fibers of Muslim religious feeling and the survival instinct of the Jewish people who for over nineteen centuries had patiently awaited the return to their ancestral land. This, therefore, is a struggle that will be difficult to end, more so since it entails the possession of Jerusalem, the current capital of Israel, a city venerated by Jews, Muslims and Christians alike.

In any event, foregoing the analysis of remote historical facts, we shall attempt to succintly review the events that led to the wave of violence rampant in the region since 1948.

For this purpose, we must at least go back to the year 1897, the year of the first World Zionist Congress held in Basil, Switzerland. As a result of this congress, the World Zionist Organization was created. A request was put before the Ottoman empire to give back Palestine that would therefore be inhabited by the Jews that had been scattered all over the world. As was to be expected, the Ottoman sultan refused to pay attention to this petition.

At the same time, England was starting to worry about the intense Jewish migration to that country as a result of the antisemitism rampant in East European nations. In view of these circumstances, the Fourth World Zionist Congress was held in London.

Some British leaders decided to offer a homeland for the Jews. Since at the time Palestine continued under the domain of the Ottoman empire, another colony was offered, in Africa: Uganda.

Initially, the World Zionist Organization accepted the offer. However, in the year 1907, it was rejected. The Jews had convened that they did not wish any other homeland but the "land of milk and honey" offered to Moses by the Lord.

During the First World War, the Ottoman empire became allied with Germany. The Arabs, wishing to free themselves from the Turkish yoke, offered their aid to the United Kingdom.

Thus, both nations convened that the British would back Arab independence and that the latter would rise up against the Turks. The Arab revolt started on June 5th, 1916.

A few months later, however, an agreement known as the Sykes-Picot Agreement was signed, whereby England and France convened that after the war the Arab territories would be divided into two areas of influence: Lebanon and Syria, under French domain, Iraq and Transjordania controlled by the British and lastly, Palestine, to be ruled by the British.

On the 2nd of November of 1917, Balfour, the British Secretary of Foreign Affairs, addressed a letter to Lord Rothschild, the most prominent British Jew, stating that his government had approved the following declaration:

"His Majesty's Government views with favour the establishment in Palestine of a national home for the Jewish people, and will use their best endeavours to facilitate the achievement of this object, it being clearly understood that nothing shall be done which may prejudice the civil and religious rights of existing non-Jewish communities in Palestine..."(6)

The Balfour Declaration and the Sykes-Picot Agreement were deemed an act of treason by the Arabs since both referred to lands that the British had offered them in exchange for their support against the Ottoman empire during the Great War and which definitely included Palestine.

Once the First World War was over, the Ottoman empire was dismembered. The United Kingdom took on the agreed mandate over Palestine and thousands of Jews started to emigrate to that land. In 1922, the League of Nations ratified the mandate granted to the British.

In the following years, the Palestinian Jewish population would dramatically increase from 5,000 in 1930 to 62,000 in 1935, representing by 1936 close to 28% of the population.(7)

As the Jewish population in Palestine increased, a strong uneasiness started to stir among the Arabs. Violence and acts of terrorism broke out in both bands. Between 1936 and 1939 a series of uprisings and strikes known by the name of the Arab Revolt, ended the peace and sowed the seeds of hatred among Jews and Palestinians. This was placated by the British. Concerned about the situation, the British government proposed the division of Palestine into two states: one Jewish and one Arabic. Jerusalem would remain neutral under British trust. This proposal however was rejected by both sides.

The British finally recognized in 1939 that the violent demographical changes being created by the Jewish immigration process was the cause of the Arab Revolt. His Majesty's government therefore approved a document known as White Paper, which set forth a reduction in Jewish immigration and the rights thereof to purchase lands in Palestine.

The approval of White Paper was linked by some to different motives. In effect, a new factor had appeared in the Middle Eastern panorama: oil. Some countries of the Persian Gulf started to envisage the existence of a vast source of wealth that in time would acquire fundamental importance in the entire region. Iran and Iraq were the first countries to discover petroleum in 1908 and 1927 respectively. Bahrain found oil in 1932, Saudi Arabia in 1936, Kuwait in 1938 and Qatar in 1939.

Some people thus believed that the British had decided to limit Jewish immigration to Palestine in order to cultivate goodwill with the Arabs, so as not to close the gates to the possibility of exploiting such vast wealth.

At the same time things started to change in Europe. The Nazi movement headed by Hitler had conquered Germany and Mussolini was the ruler in Italy. New winds of war started to threaten the world.

Finally the Second World War exploded in 1939. Hitler swiftly came to control practically all of continental Europe and turned against Russia. His influence was also felt in the Middle East where he would have undoubtedly reaped an extraordinary success if he had heeded Rommel's efforts in North Africa and had followed Raeder's advice.

The Nazi movement was strongly influenced by racist theories. The Germans belonged to the 'Aryan' race, which, in their eyes, made them superior. For Hitler and his followers, it was indispensable to foster a racial 'cleansing'. This could only be achieved by eliminating the Jews.

From 1941 onwards the Nazis systematically implemented the final solution (Endlosung) to solve the Jewish problem. Adolf Eichmann during his trial in 1961 stated that the final solution consisted in the "planned biological destruction of the Jewish race in the eastern territories". Several experiments were carried out to determine the fastest way to reach this objective. The execution of victims was deemed to be too slow and troublesome. Carbon monoxide poisoning also did not pass the test. After several experiments it was determined that a gas called Zyklon-B would be most appropriate for this purpose.

The final solution was implemented in the spring of 1942 in gas chambers in several camps that still raise terror in man. Belzec, with a capacity to kill 15,000 people per day, Sobibor (20,000 per day), Treblinka and Maidenek (25,000) and

Auschwitz, according to Rudolf Hess' words were "the largest facilities for human anhilitation of all time". Paul Johnson, in his book entitled Modern Times stated that:

"The figures are almost impossible to believe. In December 1941, Hitler exerted his domain over some 8.7 million Jews. By the beginning of 1945 at least 5.8 million had been murdered, of which 2.6 million were Polish, 750,000 Russian, 750,000 Rumanian, 402,000 Hungarian, 277,000 Checoslovakian, 180,000 German, 104,000 Lithuanian, 106,000 Dutch, 83,000 French, 70,000 Letonian, 65,000 Greek and Austrian, 60,000 Yugoslavian, 40,000 Bulgarian, 28,000 Belgian and 9,000 Italian. In Auschwitz, where 2 million were murdered, the process was a large-scale industrial operation. German companies offered bids to opt for the 'processing unit' that had an elimination capacity of 2,000 bodies in twelve hours."(8)

This human tragedy of overwhelming proportions and characteristics has come to be known as the "Holocaust" and evidently troubled the mind of an incredulous world.

After the Holocaust the Jews started to claim even more fervently the homeland that had been promised to them in the 1917 Balfour Declaration. In the meantime, the British, fearing that fulfillment of this promise would alienate the Arabs, tried to put a limit to Jewish immigration in Palestine that was already taking place in unstoppable waves.

In Jerusalem two main groups attempted to put pressure on the creation of the State of Israel. One was the Haganah that espoused the peaceful way. The other was the Irgun, directed by Menachem Begin, which became a formidable terrorist organization. On July 22nd, 1946 the Irgun blew up the King David Hotel, the largest hotel in Jerusalem, killing close to 90 persons. The Irgun's violent ways did not however stop there. In the following years the victims of the terrorist attacks of that feared organization would be counted by the thousands, including many British soldiers.

As violence became rampant, the English decided to wash their hands of the Palestinian problem and transferred the solution to the United Nations, requesting that the mandate be revoked. The unstoppable terrorism of the Irgun was irritating them. It was thought that if Great Britain withdrew, the Jews would be massacred and that the murder of British soldiers was being carried out by those whom they were attempting to protect.

In November 1947, a U.N. resolution divided Palestine into a Jewish and an Arab zone. Finally, on May 14th, 1948, the United Nations proclaimed the creation of the State of Israel. British mandate in that region expired at 12 o'clock midnight.

Six Arab nations immediately prepared to attack and destroy the new state, while Israel got ready to fight for its independence. The Syrian and Lebanese armies, 10,000 strong, had already taken positions in the north. The Jordan Arab Legion, with 4,500 well-trained and well-armed soldiers, got together with 3,000 Iraqi soldiers and were ready to attack the central region of Israel. The Egyptians with 10,000 regular soldiers were located on the frontier with the Sinai. The Palestinian "Arab Liberation" Army, also joined the attacking forces.

The Israeli Haganah in turn had 21,000 men but had practically no weapons, no armored cars and no planes.

Azzam Pasha, Secretary General of the Arab League, declared: "This shall be a war of extermination and a transcendent massacre". The entire world thought that the State of Israel would be swiftly annihilated, that the "Jews would be pushed into the sea" and that "Israel would be swept off of the face of the earth". The fiercest enemy of the Jews was the 'Mufti', the controversial leader of the Palestinians.

However, the Czech communists, responding to Soviet instructions, started a quick arms-supply operation to the new state, thanks to which the Jews were able to defend themselves.

The war finally ended with an armistice signed between the months of February and March 1949 by Israel on the one hand and Egypt and Lebanon on the other. Hostilities with Iraq and Syria ceased without a ceasefire being ever convened. The Palestinian territory that had been left in the hands of the Arabs was annexed to Transjordan and became the kingdom of Jordan. This country signed the armistice in April 1949.

Israel expanded its territories beyond those originally assigned in the United Nations-approved Palestinian partition plan. It is estimated that some 650,000 Palestinians fled the area.

Upon analyzing the operations, it would be difficult to understand the Arab defeat. This can only be ascribed to the division among their leaders. Paul Johnson gives us the following interpretation:

"It was a small-scale heroic fight... At the base of the Arab defeat was the hatred professed by the Arab Commander Fawzi al-Qawukji and the Mufti... The Iraqis and the Syrians had no maps of Palestine. Some of the Arab armies had good equipment but all except for the Jordans, were poorly trained and King Abdullah of Jordan only aspired to take hold of the Old Jerusalem and he achieved this. He did not have the slightest desire to witness the creation of an Arab Palestinian state, headed by the Mufti."(9)

From that time onwards, the Arab-Israeli conflict became a factor of permanent violence in the entire Middle East region. Wars have periodically erupted, contributing to the instability in the whole region and whose consequences however have not been regional but have taken on worldwide proportions. The conflicts of 1956 (nationalization of the Suez Canal), 1967 (The Six Day War), 1973 (the Yom Kippur or Ramadan War), 1979 (the fall of the Shah of Iran), 1982 (the Iran-Iraq war) and 1990 (the invasion of Kuwait) are all directly or indirectly related to the deep hatred promoted by the Arab-Israeli conflict in the Middle East.

For the Jews, the conflict is a problem of survival. They are surrounded by nations espousing the Muslim credo which believe that the cause against Israel is a holy war in which they shall triumph in the end, since Allah is on their side. For the Western world, the survival of Israel is in turn a geopolitical priority and a reason for deep unrest due to the increasingly stronger confrontation with the Arab nations. For these, the conflict is a reflection of the struggle for power between Western imperialism and Arab nationalism.

The hatred involved in this conflict has such deep roots that many generations would have to come and go before it can be appeased.

The Palestinian Problem

Prior to the First World War the land now belonging to Israel, the Western banks of the Jordan and the Gaza Strip, were part of the Ottoman empire. The Ottoman sultan, who in turn was the Caliph of Islam, was the ruler of a population organized based on religious communities made up by Christians, Muslims and Jews. Although the Muslims were the majority, the Ottomans recognized Christians and Jews as "People of the Sacred Book" and allowed them to practice their faith freely and to keep an independent legal system.

The foregoing situation changed when the First World War ended and the British were awarded the mandate to rule over the "Holy Land", which they called Palestine. This was how awareness of a "Palestinian identity" was born. The Muslims clung onto this identity as a means of securing a territory that they had always inhabited but that the British were now offering to the Jews through the Balfour Declaration.

Once World War Two ended and the international consciousness had now been spurred on by the horrors committed in the Holocaust, the United Nations proclaimed the creation of the State of Israel on May 14, 1948. Six Arab nations immediately committed themselves to the destruction of this fledgling state and thus the War for the Independence of Israel was started.

Once that war ended, 650,000 Muslims had abandoned their homes in the territory where the fight had taken place. The Israelis did not allow them to return and did not compensate them for the loss of their property. The Arab nations also refused to assimilate the refugees. To this effect, David E. Long stated that:

"They (the Arabs) maintained that it was Israel's responsibility either to allow the refugees to return or to compensate them, whichever the Palestinians preferred. Out of this impasse the Arab refugee problem was born, and the bitterness engendered by it has been a major impetus for Palestinian terrorism." (10)

After the War of Independence, Israel greatly expanded its territories beyond the U.N. partition lines. What remained of Arab Palestine came to be known as the Gaza Strip and the West Bank or Cisjordania, the latter being annexed to Transjordan by Amir Abdullah, thereby creating the Kingdom of Jordan. On the other hand, the Gaza Strip came to be managed, though not annexed, by Egypt.

CHAPTER VIII

The hatred and frustration of the Palestinians started to manifest in increasingly intense terrorist activities. In the beginning it was just individuals or small groups who came from Gaza or the area controlled by Jordan, that crossed the border to commit isolated acts of robbery, vandalism and murder. By 1950 the Palestinian terrorists started to organize themselves, some with the backing of Egyptian intelligence services, which made them even more dangerous. In the two following years these activities became increasingly frequent. Between 1951 and 1953, at least 460 Jews died in terrorist acts promoted by the Palestinians. Thus, the nightly explosions, the shootings and deaths became frequent events, as frequent as the retaliation of the Jews against the Palestinians.

In order to organize these reprisals, the Jews created a special commando known as "Unit 101", under the direction of Ariel Sharon. The objective of the unit was to take revenge for each and every attack by the Fedayeens, the name adopted by the Palestinian terrorists. A good part of these attacks came from the Gaza Strip controlled by the Egyptians, where close to 200,000 Palestinians were barely surviving in refugee camps, a fertile breeding ground for terrorists. From the Golan Heights, on the Syrian-Israeli border, the Palestinians also launched frequent attacks against Jewish kibbutzes.

King Abdullah of Jordan was murdered in 1951 by nationalist Palestinians, who never forgave him annexing Cisjordania. The hashemite throne was passed on to King Talal, who suffered from mental problems. One year later, in 1952, he abdicated in favour of his son Hussein.

Gamal Abdel Nasser nationalized the Suez Canal in 1956. British, French and Israelis attacked Egypt, the two former took Port Said, Ismailia and Cairo whereas the Jews advanced by the Sinai Peninsula and reached the banks of the Suez Canal. Only President Eisenhower's intervention saved Nasser. American pressure forced the attackers to withdraw. Thus Nasser took on the stature of a hero before the other Arab nations, inasmuch as he was able to impose his conditions on the agressor powers, although thanks only to the U.S. Egypt kept the Canal, which continued operating as efficiently as ever. The Palestinians in turn not only gained nothing but came to understand Egypt's military weakness, a country they had hoped would help them. The frustration of the Palestinians reached the limits of despair and led them to even riskier terrorist acts.

It was not until 1964 that the Palestinians attained a level of organization that would enable them to act in a systematic fashion. In effect, in January of that year, the creation of the Palestine Liberation Organization (Munathamat Tahrir Filistin, or PLO) was decided and created in a summit of Arab nations that met in Cairo. At the time, Gamal Abdel Nasser was striving to impose his Pan-Arabian ideas, which interested or worried the nations of the region more than the fate of some impoverished Palestinians, whose terrorist activities many times were the cause of frequent discomfort. To try and control these activities the PLO was created, whereby Palestinian military units were made up, trained and armed but above all supervised by the other Arab nations.

In 1967 the Jews took over the territories that had been the bases for the Fedayeens in the West Jordan bank, Jerusalem, the Golan Heights, the Gaza Strip and the Sinai Peninsula, up to the banks of the Suez Canal. The discouragement of the Palestinians was getting worse. They had already lost their trust in the capabilities of the remaining Arab nations to help them recover what they considered to be their territories and properties. They therefore tended to become even more radical.

In February 1969, Yasser Arafat was elected president of the PLO's Executive Committee, a position he holds to this date.

In practice, the PLO seemed to harbor two different entities: a political one that became the voice of the Palestinian people and another more violent one that sheltered many terrorist organizations, as for instance the al-Fatah ("conquest" in Arabic) founded by Arafat in Kuwait in 1957, the Palestinian Liberation Front, the Palestinian Front for Popular Fight, the Sa'iqa, etc.

Although the Six Day War had ended with a total victory for Israel, the hostilities never completely ceased. Frequent attacks were led by both sides, giving rise to mounting tensions between the U.S. and the USSR. The latter, in an effort to increase its participation in the Middle East, had initiated a policy of warfare supply and financial aid to the Arab countries. Now therefore, if the Kremlin was committed to the victory of the Arabs, the Americans were also committed to Israel's victory, inasmuch as they thought it to be a key element to avoid Soviet expansionism in the area. Not much imagination is needed to understand that there was a great risk that both superpowers could be led into a progressive escalation of the conflict and fall into an abyss where the risk of a possible nuclear war could be envisaged.

Fearful that this might happen, Washington and Moscow urged that a ceasefire be signed. This finally took place on August 7th, 1970.

The ceasefire became another source of frustration for the Palestinians. If the Arab nations gave up hostilities against Israel, how were they to recover their territories?

Consequently, the PLO decided to take its own course of terror. Thus, at the beginning of September, four commercial airplanes were kidnapped, keeping hundreds of passengers hostage for several days and finally freeing them but destroying the planes.

By 1970, these actions had become a veritable headache for King Hussein of Jordan. Inasmuch as the Jewish policy was still to avenge any attacks in their territory, Jordan was frequently the target of these retaliations, since the Fedayeens had practically become an autonomous power within that nation. The situation led King Hussein to confront the guerrillas.

In June 1970, the PLO carried out an aborted attempt against the king. Once again, on the 1st of September of the same year, Arafat's people attempted against King Hussein's life, attacking the automobile that was carrying him in Amman. By September 15th, a civil war had broken out in Jordan. On September 17th, Jordan army units attacked the Palestinian refugee camps towards the north of their capital, using war tanks, armored cars and all the force of their well-trained military force. The camps were massacred. Although the number of victims was never disclosed, it is estimated that that night alone about 7,500 Palestinians died and many others fled to Syria and Lebanon.

Syria reacted immediately. Hundreds of Syrian tanks were deployed to the frontier with Jordan. Nixon announced that, in the event that the troops of Syria, Iraq or any other nation of the Arab League were to attack King Hussein, the U.S. was willing to intervene in favour of Jordan. On September 18th, the White House received a note from the Kremlin, stating that they had no intentions whatsoever to meddle in Jordan and asked Washington to also abstain.

Between the 18th and 21st of September, 1970, over 300 Syrian tanks penetrated into Jordan, defeating the country's defenses and advancing towards Amman. Through Kissinger and William Rogers, Nixon launched a strong public warning: Syria must stop the invasion! Simultaneously, he ordered that the American naval presence be reinforced in the Mediterranean and put 20,000 soldiers in a state of alert.

In the meantime, Israel mobilized its forces to the Valley of Beit Shean, flanking the columns of Syrian tanks in a maneuver that would represent an evident threat for Damascus.

The American attitude probably put an end to the crisis. In his memoirs, Nixon stated that:

"In the end Jordan under Hussein's courageous leadership saved itself. By the morning of September 22, the Syrian tanks were once again heading back toward the border. Rabin called early in the afternoon to confirm that the tanks had left Jordan and that the rebel forces were in disarray. He adscribed Hussein's victory to the tough American position, the Israeli threat, and the superb fighting by Hussein's troops."(11)

The aforementioned events became the worst catastrophe for the Palestinians. They were baptized "Black September", a name adopted by one of their most fearful terrorist organizations.

Thus, the PLO's general headquarters had to be transferred from Jordan to Lebanon. Together with the leaders of al-Fatah, they started to plan new terrorist attempts. The left faction of the al-Fatah gave rise to the fearful Black September organization headed by Salah Khalif, whose actions would eclipse those of all the other Palestinian groups. They were responsible for the murder of eleven Israeli athletes in the 197 Munich Olympic games, as well as the death of American ambassador Clio Noel and his assistant Curtis Moore in Khartoum in March 1973.

On November 13, 1974, Yasser Arafat got the United Nations to recognize the PLO as the representative of the Palestinian people. Arafat was invited to the U.N., where he addressed a historical speech before the General Assembly. As part of his new strategy he announced a moratorium in his organization's terrorist activities.

The pacifist tactics announced by Arafat infuriate his second lieutenant, Abu Nidal (a pseudonym meaning "father of the struggle"), who thereby created a new group named the al-Fatah Revolutionary Council, which would come to be the most feared Palestinian terrorist organization. The hatred between Arafat and Nidal turned them into mortal enemies. Throughout the years, Nidal's organization has carried out numerous attempts against Arafat and has murdered at least a dozen PLO officials.

Meanwhile, since the PLO had been expelled from Jordan in 1970, its leaders had transferred to Lebanon, and had created a state within a state. Thousands of Palestinian refugees had settled in camps in that country. These camps constituted veritable guerrilla training camps, from which many terrorist attempts against Israel were launched.

In truth, Lebanon was an artificial nation, without historical frontiers, created from the remains of the Ottoman empire. It had practically all that was needed to attract the misfortunes it has gone through. In the first place, it was geographically located between Syria and Israel. To make matters worse, its population was divided between Maronite Christians and Muslims, who never ceased to be at odds. The Muslims in turn, were divided into sunnites and shiites and had their own wars to wage.

In an attempt to achieve a certain degree of stability, certain constitutional provisions in Lebanon have divided government posts among representatives of both religious groups. It was therefore arranged that the president had to be Christian and the prime minister a Muslim.

However, after the 1967 Six Day War, hundreds of thousands of Palestinians had taken refuge in Lebanon, from where they organized constant guerrilla attacks against Israel. The problem acquired tragic proportions when after the expulsion of the Palestinians from Jordan in 1970, dozens of thousands went to Lebanese territory and the PLO's general headquarters also relocated there.

In Lebanon, the Maronite Christian factions were opposed to the terrorist activities of the extremist wing of the PLO against Israel inasmuch as these brought about Jewish reprisals. The Muslims in turn saw in the PLO an ally in their ongoing fight against the Christians. Besides, the Palestinian refugees meant an increase in the Muslim population, thereby broadening their power base. The Muslims also received aid from the Syrian government. To make matters worse, an important part of the Muslim population was shiite, an additional element to be added to the reigning chaos, since they maintained an internal struggle against the sunnites, aspiring to a greater participation in the public affairs of the nation.

By 1975 the situation in Lebanon was so tense that a civil war finally broke out, desolating and destroying that nation up to the present day and spreading death and misery in a seemingly never-ending struggle. The sunnite and shiite Muslim factions and the Maronite Christians all claimed the right to control Lebanon. Syria went even further, by stating simply that Lebanon had no right to exist since it had been artificially created by France, its former colonial ruler. Syria's long-term aspirations were to transform Lebanon into a de facto colony.

Israel backed the Christians. The PLO fully endorsed the Muslims. Now therefore, to add to the confusion, Syria decided to intervene in pro of the Christians. In effect, the Syrian president Hafez al-Assad, a mortal enemy of Israel, was also an enemy of Arafat, the PLO leader. The Syrian president's strategy was to maintain a balance among the struggling groups in Lebanon and did not wish Arafat's power to be increased in that nation.

The situation therefore was becoming increasingly chaotic. Syria and Israel saw Lebanon as a threat, inasmuch as it was a potential base from which to organize an attack against these territories.

Finally, Syria invaded Lebanon in 1976, allegedly because of the need to reestablish a balance among the fighting factions. In the meantime, the Palestinian guerrilla attacks against Israel continued unabated.

A peace treaty known as the Camp David Agreement was signed in 1979 between Egypt and Israel, whereby Israel pledged to withdraw from the occupied territories in the Sinai and to give back to Egypt the oil fields developed in that area. A popular referendum in Egypt approved the peace treaty with Israel. Menachem Begin, Israel's Prime Minister, a former terrorist chief of the Irgun, and Egyptian President Anuar al-Sadat, responsible for unleashing the Yom Kippur war against Israel, agreed to exchange ambassadors. The agreement was fiercely criticized by other Arab nations, repudiating Egypt for having accepted Israel's right to exist. The Palestinians in turn pledged to destroy the Camp David Agreement by any means available. Anuar al-Sadat, murdered by Muslim fundamentalists in October 1981, would pay with his own life for signing the agreement.

By the year 1981, the situation in Lebanon was getting worse. In June and July of that year, the Israeli government launched aerial attacks against the PLO guerrilla camps, from where rockets and artillery had been shot against north Israel.

The Americans, in the meantime, were attempting to restore peace by all means. Ambassador Philip Habib put forth all his efforts put these were in vain. Although the parties signed a ceasefire, this was immediately violated. It finally became evident that Israel was preparing a large-scale invasion of Lebanon. To this effect, Ronald Reagan in his memoirs declared that:

"... I emphasized my personal commitment and that of the United States to the support of Israel. I supported its right to defend itself against attack, but appealed for Israel not to go on the offensive unless it was the victim of a provocation of such magnitude that the world would easily understand its right to retaliate.

Israel's response was, in effect: Mind your own business. It is up to Israel alone to decide what it must do to ensure its survival."(12)

In June 1982, Palestinian Fedayeens assassinated the Israeli ambassador to London. The attempt was in fact executed by Abu Nidal's group. However, Israel used this as an excuse and on June 6th, Israeli forces invaded Lebanon purportedly to eliminate the PLO guerrilla. According to Menachem Begin, the Israeli invasion was supposed to penetrate only 24,8 miles into Lebanese territory in order to reach the Palestinian camps that sheltered the terrorists. Ariel Sharon, Israel's Defense Minister thought otherwise. In a matter of hours, his forces had Beirut under siege.

The armies of Syria and Israel entered into combat although they both wanted to destroy the PLO forces that had been trapped in Beirut's western side. The battle became a sort of war "of all against all". In a few hours, the Israeli aviation force had shot down more than seventy Syrian planes. Meanwhile, in Beirut, the PLO was fighting for survival and unwittingly helped the interests of its circumstantial enemies, the Syrians. The Lebanese government in turn watched powerless the curse that had befallen its country.

Finally, a U.N. multinational force with U.S., French and Italian troops, in an effort to restablish peace and backed symbolically by the Lebanese president, pledged to expel the members of the PLO from Beirut and disperse them into several nations, such as Algeria, North Yemen and Tunez. From that time onwards, the PLO headquarters was established in this latter nation. The U.N. thus considered that to be the means to contribute to restoring peace in Lebanon.

Bashir Gemayel, the young president of Lebanon, offered its country to the U.S. as a strategic point in the Middle East. For him, the presence of an American military base in Lebanon would serve to pacify the region as well as being the only possibility for the Israeli and Syrian forces (the latter called Arab Dissuasive Forces) to abandon his country forever.

On September 14th, 1982, Gemayel was murdered by a Palestinian group. This led to the immediate return of the Israeli army which attacked and massacred close to seven hundred Palestinian refugees in the Sabra and Shatila camps.

In view of the fact that the Syrian and Israeli armies never completely withdrew, a second group of U.N. multinational forces with U.S., French and British troops was organized with the purpose of attempting to put an end to the civil war among the Maronite Christian and Muslim factions.

On April 18th, 1983, an attempt was made against the U.S. Embassy. In effect, a suicidal guerrilla attack by a small explosive-laden truck crashed against the entrance gates of the embassy. This explosion destroyed the eight-story building, killing seventeen Americans and an even greater number of

Lebanese citizens. Amazingly, the ambassador was rescued uninjured from the rubble of the eighth floor.

On October 23rd, 1983 another more drastic attempt was made by an apparently Muslim guerrilla to a building housing multinational force troops. Over 241 American and 40 French soldiers died in the explosion.

In the following days, a commission chaired by Admiral Robert L. Long was set up, with the purpose of investigating the reasons for the aforementioned tragedy. Finally, on December 23rd, 1983, the commission concluded its investigation recommending the Defense Secretary to adopt the disciplinary and administrative steps considered appropriate against the commanders of the Navy Amphibian Units and Disembarkation batallion for not having taken the necessary security measures to avoid the catastrophic loss of lives. However, President Reagan considered that those men had already suffered quite enough and ordered

"...(that they) ought not to be punished for not comprehending fully the nature of terrorism."(13)

The tension in Beirut mounted during the following days. The American soldiers of the multinational force sent to the zone to restore peace unwittingly confronted the Arab Dissuasive Forces sent by Syria, whose presence also in theory was to restore a balance in the acting trends in Lebanon in order to avoid a civil war. The objective of both was to annihilate the guerrilla; however, they ended up fighting one another. This was to be expected, since in the end, Syria's forces continued to respond to USSR interests which did not see with pleasure the presence of American troops in Lebanon.

President Reagan finally sent out an order to the American soldiers that if the Syrian forces shot against American troops, they should be faced with a "vigorous and prompt response". The day after imparting these instructions, on the second of December of 1983, the Syrians launched surface-to-air missiles against American reconnaissance planes. Furious, the Americans ordered that the 28 bombers from the Kennedy and Independence aircraft carriers attack Syria's missile-launching pads. On December 14th, the war vessel New Jersey shot its 16-inch cannons against Syrian targets, five minutes after the latter had shot at American reconnaisance planes.

In sum, the situation which had befallen on Lebanon had gone beyond any analyst's predictions. That old saying that "the friends of my friends are my friends; the friends of my enemies are my enemies and the enemies of my enemies are my friends" had ceased to be. In view of the fast-changing relations among friends and enemies in Lebanon, the situation could be summed up in one phrase: The whole world was the enemy of the whole world.

The truth is that the complex motives in the minds of the Palestinian guerrillas and the strategies of the rulers of the Arab nations surpassed any Western world practical, logical, structured and orderly capacity of comprehension.

In any event, after one of the most frustrating peace missions, the U.S. decided to withdraw from Lebanon in January 1984. The Lebanese government was now presided by Amin Pierre Gemayel, a Christian and brother of the assassinated Bashir Gemayel, and the prime minister was Rashid Karami, a Muslim. However, the violence in Lebanon had no limits. On June 11, 1987, Karami was killed by a bomb that exploded in the helicopter he was travelling in.

No-one understands how the long-suffering population of Lebanon has been able to survive the dramatic years of senseless bloodshed.

In fact, during the war between the Arab-Occidental Alliance and Iraq, the Palestinian refugees in Lebanon had relaunched their attacks against Israel in an evident attempt to drag that nation into the war and with the hope of thus breaking the Arab front.

The PLO is still an active organization under the direction of Yasser Arafat, who can be defined as a strategist of survival. In effect, after having overcome all manner of mishaps and attempts, surrounded by one of the most violent and resentful human groups, Arafat continues to be the representative of the Palestinian people. Alternately the object of admiration and hatred of many leaders, Arafat was able to overcome the Jordan crisis, in which his forces were decimated. From there, his headquarters were transferred to Beirut, and was the object of a simultaneous attack by the Maronite Christian forces, the Jews and the Syrians. Once again he moved to Tunez, where he has had to face the resentment of a great part of his followers that are opposed to his tactics. Some of his enemies are Abu Nidal, a former lieutenant and one of the most fearful terrorist leaders, Ariel Sharon, who was to become Israel's Minister of Defense, a hero of the Yom Kippur war and the author of the invasion on Lebanon, Hafez al-Assad, the Syrian president, who attempted by all means to eliminate him physically and also from the head of the PLO, as well as many other men of importance who have sworn to his death. Arafat and the Palestine cause continue however very much alive. As he stated in a U.N. speech, Arafat could mean peace or war. He has alternately resorted to both. He has recognized Israel as a nation but has never stopped making all efforts to destroy it. He has made a thousand promises and has broken them all.

Arafat reappeared in the international political scenario as an ally of Saddam Hussein. He was the carrier of Saddam's demands and threats to the al-Sabah family of Kuwait. He probably is the person who has done most to convince the

Palestinian people that Saddam Hussein represents their greatest hope.

Undoubtedly the Palestinians have resorted to violence, carried away by the frustration of having lost their land, their homes and their properties. There is also no doubt that the Palestinians inhabiting Israel or the occupied territories have been the subject of the most unjust discrimination. Those who sought refuge in other countries are now victims of a diaspora, much like the Jewish people had been for many centuries.

In the midst of the scenario of ancestral violence that has so far been described, it seems difficult to conceive a possible agreement between the Jews and the Palestinians that would bring about a permanent state of peace in this agitated region. The deep hatred entrenched throughout many generations will take long to disappear. The positions adopted by both groups are opposed due to the simple fact that both have solid grounds for claiming the same territories. Peaceful cohabitation does not seem feasible; therefore force must be exerted in order to defend what they consider to be their rights.

The creation of the State of Israel gave back the Jews the homeland from which they had been expelled by the Romans in biblical times. These people are willing to shed their last drop of blood to defend their nation, a land of arid soil ingeniously transformed into a fertile garden that increasingly resembles the "land of milk and honey" promised by God to Moses during the 40-year stay in the desert. "Next year in Israel", a prayer repeated in the heart of every Jew for over two thousand years, was finally answered on May 14, 1948, when the UN proclaimed the creation of the State of Israel and the Diaspora came to an end.

In the absence of the Jews those territories had been successively populated by other inhabitants. Eighteen centuries have undoubtedly given solid grounds for other populations to claim rights over this land. These are inhabitants who pray daily in the direction of Mecca and whose lives, laws and customs are based on the teachings of the Koran. For these people, Jerusalem, as well as Mecca and Medina, are sacred cities. Thus, the end of the Jewish Diaspora gave way to a new diaspora for many Palestinians. Violence was a sort of holy war backed by millions of Arabs living close to the despised Jewish enclave, painfully entrenched in the heart of Islam.

Until recently, Israel seemed to have a well-defined position that was set in stone. In Menachem Begin's words,

"Millenia ago, there was a Jewish kingdom of Judea and Samaria where our kings knelt to God, where our prophets brought forth a vision of eternal peace, where we developed a rich civilization which we took with us in our hearts and in our minds on our long global trek for over eighteen centuries and with it we came back home.

King Abdullah (of Jordan) by invasion conquered parts of Judea and Samaria in 1948 and in a war of most legitimate self defense in 1967 after having been attacked by King Hussein we liberated with God's help that portion of our homeland. Judea and Samaria will never again be the West Bank of Hashemite Kingdom of Jordan which was created by British colonialism..."(14)

1993: Rabin and Arafat

Iraq's invasion of Kuwait brought about profound changes in the entire Middle East region. Once the conflict ended, the U.S. seemed even more determined to seek a solution to the Palestinian problem. Yasser Arafat, now cloaked in the peace effort, once again emerged as an infallible presence and offered to gain the backing of the Arabs in exchange for Palestinian autonomy. Endless negotiations ensued in all the capitals of the Arab world as well as in Washington, Moscow, London and Paris.

Arafat was aware that he had to proceed slowly and carefully. Israel could not be expected to give way all at once. A new U.S. government, with Bill Clinton as president, favoured his intentions. Warren Christopher, the newly appointed Secretary of State, dedicated most of his efforts to drafting an agreement whereby all parties would make partial concessions in what had been until then unmovable positions. Christopher tirelessly met with the Jewish leaders, Syria's Haffez al-Assad, Jordan's King Hussein, Egypt's Hosni Mubarak and the leaders of Saudi Arabia, Kuwait and other countries. His itinerary did not however include Iran, inasmuch as he was aware that that nation was opposed to any peace accord with the Jews.

Finally, on September 13, 1993, Yitzhak Rabin, Israel's Prime Minister and Yassir Arafat, the PLO leader, backed by President Clinton, signed a declaration of principles in the White House gardens, whereby the Jewish nation pledged to grant the Palestinians autonomy in the Gaza Strip, Jericho and the West Bank. Endless ongoing negotiations are under way to analyze the scope of autonomy that could extend to the rest of Cisjordania and to study the withdrawal of Israeli troops from areas mostly populated by Palestinians. These agreements do not however include the eastern part of Jerusalem and the Jewish settlements.

Pursuant to the aforementioned agreements, Israel will not hand over sovereignty over these territories for now. It has simply granted autonomy to the Palestinians to control aspects such as education, health care, social welfare, taxes, tourism, internal security, etc.

It was likewise agreed that the Palestinians would elect an autonomous council to manage the areas handed over. Regarding this latter point, strong discrepancies have arisen between the negotiating parties. Whereas the Palestinians demand a legislative council of over one hundred members with full legislative powers - a sort of Parliament - Israel adamantly refuses on the grounds that an institution of that nature could constitute an element of sovereignty. This country has therefore proposed that the Palestinians elect an executive council instead, with far less members.

As was to be expected, this process of negotiations has been accompanied by deep discrepancies and all manner of confrontations, with the subsequent loss of human lives. According to Betslem, the Israeli pro-human rights center, less than one year after the signing of the Declaration of Principles whereby the Jewish nation had pledged to grant autonomy to the Palestinians, Israeli soldiers have killed 199 Palestinian nationals in the occupied territories and have tortured an even greater number. During that period of time, Israeli civilians, mostly settlers in the occupied territories, have killed 45 Palestinians, 29 of which died during the February 25, 1994 Hebron massacre.

Arab nationalists in turn have murdered 21 civilians and 8 Israeli soldiers in the occupied territories. 36 Jews were also murdered in various acts of violence carried out by Palestinians in these territories.

Yitzhak Rabin has recognized Syrian sovereignty in a region even more controversial than the Gaza Strip and Jericho and even came to propose a 3-year "marginal withdrawal" from the Golan Heights, during which time the Syrian government could prove its willingness to restore peace in that region. In Rabin's opinion, once that period expires, Israel and Syria could negotiate over the territory. This proposal, as was to be expected, met with strong opposition by the representatives of the Likud right-wing party, declaring that "we shall never leave the Golan" and the thirteen thousand Jewish settlers in that area.

According to the Likud, there are vital survival reasons for not returning the Golan Heights that were seized from Syria during the 1967 Six-Day War under any circumstances. This is a mountainous region towering over the plains that are home to two-thirds of the Israeli population. From these heights, the Syrians could bomb every city, every town and every kibbutz.

Rabin's proposal however, though unacceptable to the Likud, provoked the immediate interruption of negotiations with Syria. In order to restart the peace talks, Damascus has asked that Israel withdraw totally and immediately from the Golan Heights. Lebanon in turn has reiterated that it is not willing to negotiate with Israel until such time as a peace agreement between Syria and this nation is signed.

In sum, by October 1994, the situation in the Golan Heights is as follows: Israel has proposed a three-year marginal withdrawal, after which the terms and scope of a full withdrawal could be negotiated with Syria. This country in turn has stated its willingness to negotiate with the U.S. but not with the Jews and has put as a condition the full and immediate withdrawal of Israel. Tel Aviv maintains that it shall not pursue its intentions of leaving the Golan Heights until such time as Syria establishes diplomatic ties with the Jewish state and a peace agreement is signed. Lebanon in turn refuses to negotiate with Israel until an agreement with Syria is reached.

For many Jews, the agreements signed with Arafat and, furthermore, any negotiation that could possibly envisage the return of the Golan Heights, are a threat to the existence itself of the State of Israel. Arafat is perceived as the head of a terrorist organization who has sworn to destroy Israel and the pacifistic position he has currently adopted is merely a façade to take over the territories subject to negotiation. Some parties are convinced that once the PLO has taken a firm grip over these territories, they shall simply be used as a base to rekindle the deadly war backed by the remaining Arab nations, declared many years ago against Israel.

The position adopted by Islamic fundamentalist groups such as Hamas or the armed pro-Iranian Hezbollah Islamic resistance faction, are no less radical. They consider that Arafat has betrayed the Palestinian cause, inasmuch as he should never have accepted simple autonomy over the territories when the Arabs are pushing for full sovereignty. Hamas, Hezbollah and other extremist groups have sworn to continue employing terrorist tactics and launching attacks against the Israelis until the government of Tel Aviv withdraws completely from southern Lebanon. In reprisal, Israeli artillery continue to carry out frequent shoot-outs against the towns of Jabal, Abou, Rkab and Mlikh located in Lebanon, the seat of the Palestinian guerrilla factions.

Negotiations between Israel and the PLO have been frequently interrupted as a result of violent actions fostered by Islamic fundamentalist groups and also by the aggressive stance adopted by the Tel Aviv authorities in response to said actions.

Yitzhak Rabin has constantly issued warnings to Yassir Arafat, the PLO leader, to repress and disarm these groups. Arafat however, aware of his own unstable position, has refused to do anything in this regard, fearful that any attempt to do so might trigger a civil war among the Palestinians.

In spite of all these hindrances, the international community has strived to encourage the efforts of both leaders in a region that has been the source of uninterrupted violence and destabilization in the entire Middle East.

In this regard, on October 15, 1994, Rabin, Arafat and Shimon Peres - Israel's Minister of Foreign Affairs - were jointly awarded the Nobel Peace Prize for their efforts towards achieving peace in the region. This decision brought about many disputes among the members of the committee in charge of choosing the winners. Kaare Kristiansen, a member of said committee, resigned in protest due to the fact that the maximum recognition to world peace would be granted to one of the planet's most notorious terrorists as well as to the leaders of one of the most violent states on the face of the earth.

The Simon Weisenthal Center, world-famous for its relentless persecution of Nazi criminals, protested the naming of Arafat as recipient of the Nobel Peace Prize. Rabbi Marvin Hier, spokesperson for the organization, stated that "the prize should be the culmination of a lifetime dedicated to the peace cause. While it is true that Arafat in the last two years has significantly contributed to the peace process, most of his life has been dedicated to international terrorist activities".

At the same time, the Iranian president Ali Akbar Hashemi Rafsanjani ardently declared: "I believe that granting the peace prize to Rabin is a joke, insofar as a person who has caused over four million people to become refugees has been awarded the Nobel Prize."

It seemed strange to many that the American Secretary of State did not share the award. The peace negotiations between Israel and the Palestinians did not originate fundamentally from the willingness of both parties, but rather from the tenacious efforts and pressure exerted by the U.S. and Warren Christopher in particular.

A few days before the award was granted, Hamas kidnapped Nachshon Waxman, an Israeli soldier and threatened to kill him unless the government of Tel Aviv released two hundred Palestinian prisoners. This action once again interrupted the peace talks. On the same day that the winners of the Nobel Peace Prize were announced in Sweden, a commando of the Israeli security forces carried out an operation to free the kidnapped soldier. The kidnappers killed the soldier before being shot down by the Israeli commando, both sides having suffered several casualties.

From Damascus, Hamas immediately issued a press release announcing that it shall continue its struggle against any peace accord between Israel and the PLO. It warned that Waxman's kidnapp "shall not be the last operation". The death of the soldier was attributed by Hamas to "a vile and despicable action brought about by Rabin's arrogance inasmuch as the movement was willing to free the prisoner if the Israeli government had fulfilled their petitions".

The final outcome of the peace negotiations between Israel, the Palestinians, Syria, Lebanon and Jordan, seems difficult to predict. The success of the conversations shall depend in great measure on the capacity of Rabin and Arafat to convince their respective peoples. The Nobel Prize shall doubtless contribute to strengthen the positions of both leaders.

The international community should pray for a happy ending to the peace process that is under way. In the words of Shimon Peres himself, "peace has not yet been attained. The road has been paved and we have begun to put out the fires of unfathomable hatred and violence that have unjustifiably cost the lives of many people to whom we owe our existence and our future."

However, it is considered by many that in view of the countless obstacles in the way of the peace process, it seems difficult that this can be achieved on a permanent basis. Those who believe this are convinced that this is only an interval in the midst of violent times. Externally imposed artificial solutions and the well-intentioned pressures of the White House will be hard pressed to solve the real problems affecting the inhabitants of that region seemingly condemned to unavoidable violence.

The Israeli-Jordanian Peace Agreement

On October 17th, 1994, Yitzhak Rabin and King Hussein of Jordan -a descendant of Mohammed- announced that an agreement had been reached to enter into a peace agreement between the two neighbouring nations, thereby ending a belligerent situation that had existed since the creation of the Jewish state in 1948. This agreement, whereby Israel gives back territories in exchange for peace, includes several basic aspects, among which the following could be highlighted:

-Israel shall return most of the territory claimed by Jordania and Amman shall accept other land in substitution for that being exploited by the Israelis.

-Both nations shall equally distribute the scarce fresh water reserves in the territories included in the peace negotiations. The joint construction of two dams in the Yarmuk and Jordan rivers has also been agreed upon.

-Diplomatic ties between both nations shall be established and ambassadors shall be exchanged.

-Jordan pledges not to participate in any alliance against Israel nor to allow its territory to be used for attacks against the Jewish state.

The U.S. in turn has announced that it shall write off a billion-dollar debt with Jordan, in the interest of promoting peace in the region.

Unfortunately not all parties have accepted the peace agreement. The Hamas movement protested on October 18, 1994, and a bomb exploded in the center of Tel Aviv, with the consequent loss in civilian lives. That same day, the Islamic integrationist movement, with 16 seats from a total of 80 in the Jordanian Parliament, has announced that it shall oppose "by all means available" the peace treaty between the hashemite kingdom and Israel.

Arafat in turn has also had a fiery reaction to this agreement, which in his opinion undermines the rights of the Palestinians to Jerusalem. "This is a shameless transgression" stated Arafat "to the Declaration of Principles signed between Israel and the PLO and the letters exchanged between both parties regarding Jerusalem and the Muslim and Christian sanctuaries". This leader also declared that Israel's promise to grant a special role to Jordan for the administration of the holy places has been entered into ahead of the final negotiations that were to take place in 1996 between the PLO and Israel.

Thus, King Hussein of Jordan and Arafat, mortal enemies since the events known as "Black September", having taken a united front with Saddam Hussein when Iraq invaded Kuwait in 1990, are once again face to face as a result of the peace treaty signed between Tel Aviv and Amman.

Syria has also had a negative reaction. President Haffez al-Assad considers that his country is being put in a tight spot inasmuch as Israel has already entered into peace agreements with two of that country's most important neighbours: Jordan and Egypt. However, Syria still has the backing of Lebanon, a nation that has ratified that it shall never sign a peace treaty with Tel Aviv without Syria's prior agreement.

In the meantime, in spite of the peace talks that have been carried out between the governments of the region, the Islamic fundamentalist groups continue to remain firm in their opposal to these negotiations.

There is no doubt that these territories that saw the birth of Jesus Christ, that were ruled with Solomon's wisdom, that have witnessed the perseverance of Moses and the obedience of Abraham, these lands which were the birthplace of virtuous prophets honoured by Christians, Jews and Muslims, all of whom venerate Jerusalem, and the homeland of saintly men that have shone on the face of the earth, deserve a better destiny. This fate, however, is sowed with the seeds of discord and antagonism, resentment and vengeance. This peace so yearned for shall have to overcome a wide abyss before it can take root in this part of the world. Let us hope that God will enlighten the leaders of that region considered by many to be holy, so that they may have the strength to overcome the deadly walls of thorns that men have built up to feed their hatred.

Artificial Countries and Frontiers

Most of the territories in the Middle East had been controlled by the Ottoman empire for many centuries. The United Kingdom was not displeased by this situation, since the Turks were a barrier between the Russians and British interests in Asia. Nevertheless, during World War One, the Ottomans pledged an alliance with the Germans.

Under those circumstances, the Arabs saw the opportunity to free themselves from Ottoman domination. Sharif Hussein of Mecca was contacted by the British since they considered him to be the maximum representative of the Arab nationalists. Hussein thus signed an agreement with Sir Henry MacMahon by means of which the Arabs pledged to rise up against the Ottoman empire meanwhile the British agreed to back Arab independence once the war had ended.

For a non-Muslim mind, it is not easy to understand the magnitude of the commitment taken on by Hussein. To this regard, from the religious point of view let us mention that the Ottoman sultan was also the Islamic Caliph and therefore was considered to be the maximum religious authority for sunnite Muslims. The sultan of Turkey, being the Caliph, declared a Holy War ("Jihad") in November 1914, calling all the Muslims of the world to fight against England, France and Russia.

However, Shariff Hussein, anxious to free himself from Turkish domination that in practice was almost nominal, and wishing to have a kingdom that he hoped would encompass the greater part of the Middle East, rebelled against the authority of his religious leader and in 1916 signed an agreement known as the "Hussein-MacMahon Correspondence".

Evidently, the British did not feel very committed to that agreement, since before six months had expired the Sykes-Picot Agreement was signed, by means of which, once the war had ended, the Arab territories would be divided into areas of influence. Thus, Syria and Lebanon would be in the French area whereas Iraq and Transjordan would be dominated by the British. Palestine, in turn, a name taken from biblical times, was not part of any territorial entity existing at the time, so it would fall under British rule. In November 1917, by means of the Balfour Declaration, part of those territories were offered to create a homeland for the Jewish people. Other Arab territories left from the remains of the Ottoman empire were offered to Italy, by means of the 1917 St. Jean de Maurienne Agreement. In sum, the commitments entered into were so plentiful that it would be too long to detail all of them.

Once the First World War ended in 1918, the victorious powers in Europe found that it was impossible to fulfill all the agreements and give out all the territories that had been offered. Lloyd George and Clemenceau, the British and French heads of government therefore dedicated endless and tense negotiations to solving the problems. David Fromkin in his book "A Peace to End all Peace" stated that:

"It was an era in which Middle Eastern countries and frontiers were fabricated in Europe. Iraq and what we now call Jordan, for example, were British inventions, lines drawn on an empty map by British politicians after the First World War; while the boundaries of Saudi Arabia, Kuwait, and Iraq were established by a British civil servant in 1922, and the frontiers between Moslems and Christians were drawn by France in Syria-Lebanon and by Russia on the borders of Armenia and Soviet Azerbaijan."(15)

In 1919 Great Britain had extended its influence over the entire Middle East region. Egypt was declared a British protectorate and likewise Kuwait. The Persian Gulf emirates were passed on to the British. Even Persia was also included under the British sphere of influence, as an informal protectorate.

To decide the future of the present-day territories of Saudi Arabia, Iraq and Kuwait, a conference was held in 1922 which concluded with the signing of the Al-Uquayr Treaty that defined the frontiers in rather an arbitrary fashion, sometimes by drawing a simple straight line in the maps and without taking into account any ethnic or geographical considerations whatsoever. In 1923, one year later, the Kuwait-Iraq frontiers were marked off.

As a result of the aforementioned agreements, a "neutral zone" was created between Iraq, Saudi Arabia and Kuwait. Iraq's frontiers that isolate it from the sea were also set, being its only outlet to the Persian Gulf through a narrow body of water called Shatt al-Arab, formed by the confluence of the Euphrates and Tigris rivers.

Syria and Lebanon were in turn left under French authority. After lengthy diplomatic negotiations, the Mosul area was finally granted to Iraq, in spite of the insistence by the French that the same should belong to Syria.

In summary, the European powers believed that they could change the map of the Islamic world without bearing in mind the bases themselves of its historical and political existence. This created a veritable geographical chaos. Frontiers were set and names were given to countries, but inasmuch as oftentimes these were artificial, no true stable nationalities were established.

In the following years, the states drawn on Middle East maps achieved independence one by one. However the problems arising from the artificial situation continue to gravitate over their rarefied political realities, thereby contributing to foster the unending and recurrent violent episodes that characterize the region.

The agreements whereby European powers created states and defined frontiers in the Middle East were aimed at solving problems existing in the Western world, leaving aside the problems this would cause in the affected region. To this effect, Christine Moss Helms asserted that:

"At least twelve states have appeared as newly created political entities in the Arabian Peninsula since World War I;

almost without exception, subsequent acceptance of their borders by native inhabitants was accompanied by turmoil. Some areas were so contested that boundaries remained totally undefined, while neutral zones between Iraq and Saudi Arabia and Kuwait and Saudi Arabia evolved as the only workable solution to intractable political problems. One study has estimated that there have been at least twenty-two active boundary disputes in the region since 1900 and no fewer than twenty-one instances in which redress was sought by military means. International boundaries have ostensibly been settled only to be brought once again to the negotiating table."(16)

It is not feasible therefore that in the foreseeable future the problems created by the lack of foresight of the Europeans after World War I may be overcome. Decisions taken at the time shall continue to be the source of violence for many decades to come. The Middle East is thus condemned to continue indefinitely the same course of endemic violence which seems to be predestined since the origins itself of the history of mankind.

The Kurds: The Forgotten People

In their eagerness to create countries, the Europeans left out a population inhabiting the frontiers of Turkey, Iran, Iraq and Syria, a region called Kurdistan and homeland to the Kurds.

At present there are over 17 million Kurds with their own ethnic, cultural, religious and linguistic identity.

From the ethnic viewpoint, they are Indo-European, the same as Iran's population. They therefore have no ethnic relationship with the Arabs. From the religious standpoint, they are sunnite Muslims which differentiates them from Iran's people. Linguistically speaking the Kurds have four dialects, different among them but with the same common root. The Kurdish dialects are Indo-European in origin and belong to the same linguistic family as Persian. It is worthwhile mentioning in this regard that there is no relation between the

Kurds or the Arabs or between the Kurdish tongue and Turkish. Also, Turkish and Arabic belong to two totally different linguistic families.

The Kurds currently represent about 18% of the population in Turkey, 16% in Iran, 23% in Iraq and 11% in Syria. About 14,000 Kurds also live in the former USSR.

(Add here map of the Kurdish people)

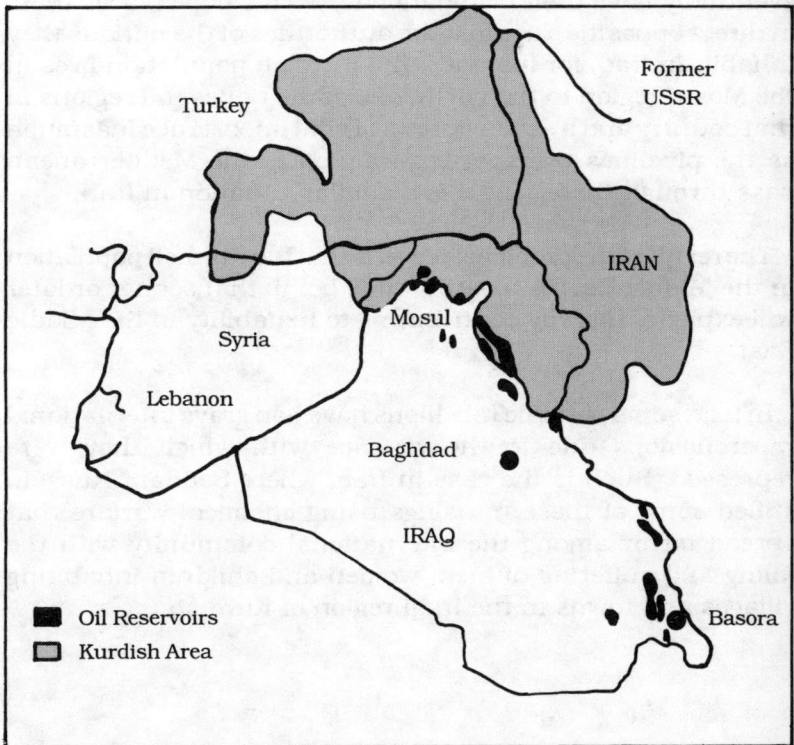

The Kurdish People

They are basically shepherds which is probably the reason why they were forgotten when the European powers started to draw countries in the empty Middle East maps. For that same reason, the Kurdish population has never been attracted to the political causes of the countries they inhabit. They have never stated a great interest in Syria's or Iraq's expansionary ambitions. During the Iran-Iraq war, all they wished was to remain neutral. Inasmuch as they are not Arabs, they never took any notice of the ambitious Pan-Arabian goals of some of the countries in the region.

In conclusion, the only aspiration of the Kurds has been to eventually have their own nationality. This hope places them in direct opposition against the authorities of the nations they inhabit. In Iraq, for instance, the Kurdish population lives in the Mosul region to the north, one of the richest oil regions in that country and a strategic area of vital importance inasmuch as the pipelines transporting Iraqi oil to the Mediterranean pass through there. There is a similar situation in Iran.

The result of the problems posed is that the Kurdish population in the Middle East is a sort of time bomb that sooner or later will explode, thereby contributing to instability in the Middle East.

In fact, some periodic rebellions have had grave international repercussions due to the violence with which they were repressed. Such is the case in Iraq, where Saddam Hussein stifled some of these uprisings using chemical warfare that spread terror among the international community with the kiling and suffering of men, women and children inhabiting villages and towns in the Iraqi region of Kurdistan.

Notes

1.-Ronald Reagan. AN AMERICAN LIFE. page 407.

2.-H.A. R. Gibb. MOHAMMEDANISM. AN HISTORICAL SURVEY. page 81.

3.-David Lamb. THE ARABS. JOURNEY BEYOND THE MIRAGE. page 6.

4.-Sir John Glubb. A SHORT HISTORY OF THE ARAB PEOPLES. page 40.

5.-Quoted by Emmanuel Sivan. RADICAL ISLAM. MEDIEVAL THEOLOGY AND MODERN POLITICS. Page 20.

6.-David Fromkin. A PEACE TO END ALL PEACE. Page 297.

7.-David C. Martin and John Walcott. BEST LAID PLANS: THE INSIDE STORY OF AMERICA'S WAR AGAINST TERRORISM. Page 325.

8.-Paul Johnson. MODERN TIMES. page 420.

9.-Paul Johnson. IBIDEM. page 491.

10.-David E. Long. THE ANATOMY OF TERRORISM. page 33.

11.-Richard Nixon. THE MEMOIRS OF RICHARD NIXON (Touchstone). page 485.

12.-Ronald Reagan. OP. CIT. page 419.

13.-Caspar W. Weinberger. FIGHTING FOR PEACE. page 165.

14.-Quoted by Ronald Reagaon. OP. CIT. page 433.

15.-David Fromkin. OP. CIT. page 17.

16.-Christine Moss Helms. IRAQ. EASTERN FLANK OF THE ARAB WORLD. page 44.

OIL MARKET PERSPECTIVES

Perspectives for the World Oil Market

An increase in world energy requirements would be linked to a set of variables, one of which worth mentioning is the economic performance in the industrialized and developing nations. Other factors affecting the demand for energy would be advances in technology, production costs and the market price of various energy sources, as well as environmental protection measures, etc.

By late 1993, world oil demand was close to 67 million barrels per day. Bearing in mind the foregoing, it is estimated that growth in demand could be about 1 to 2 percent per year. Thus, depending on the actual scenarios that would take place, demand for crude oil could be calculated at around 76 to 83 million barrels per day by the year 2003.

From the long-term perspective, and based on estimates by the World Energy Council, it is expected that world energy demand shall double by the year 2020. Taking into consideration that oil is slowly losing ground to other sources available in the energy market, it could conservatively be expected that world oil consumption shall be in excess of 100 million barrels per day by the aforementioned date.

As regards world supply, the oil production of non-OPEC nations is expected to moderately decline, inasmuch as in many cases, forseeable market prices would not justify investments in the generation of new barrels.. Besides, the duration in theory of the reserves (calculated by means of dividing proved oil reserves by world production figures), puts in evidence the existence of a limited amount of reserves. In this regard it would be interesting to analyze some specific cases:

THE U.S.: By early 1993, that nation's proved oil reserves were 26,250 million barrels. Production was 7.2 million barrels per day and consumption was in excess of 16 million b/d. The duration in theory of U.S. crude proved reserves could barely last 9.9 years. A fall in American oil production is expected in the next few years, while the recovery experienced in that nation's economy will translate into the need for the increasing importation of oil.

THE UNITED KINGDOM: By early 1993, the UK's proved reserves were 4,144 million barrels, whereas production had reached 1.8 million b/d. The theoretical duration of reserves is thus barely 6.4 years.

THE EEC: Jointly, the EEC members have available by early 1993 a volume of 6,412 million barrels of proved oil reserves. Daily production was set at 2.2 million b/d and consumption of oil products by those nations is in excess of 11.5 million b/d. The theoretical duration of the community's oil reserves is 8 years.

Canada: With proved reserves of 6,104 million barrels and a daily production of 1.6 million b/d by early 1993, the duration in theory of Canada's crude reserves is estimated at 10.6 years.

THE FORMER SOVIET BLOC: By early 1993, the nations formerly comprising the USSR had joint proved crude oil reserves of 57 billion barrels. Production at that time reached 9.2 million barrels per day. The duration in theory of reserves was therefore 17 years. It is worthwhile mentioning on the other hand that since 1987 there has been a substantial decrease in the daily production of the former-USSR countries, down from a production of 12.5 million b/d. It is expected that this downward trend shall continue during the decade, due to the lack of maintenance and overproduction in many oil fields.

Heavy investments shall be required to solve the problems that have accumulated and this is not foreseeable in the near future taking into account the panorama of political uncertainty prevailing in those countries.

The case of nations such as Japan, Korea, Taiwan, Singapore, etc. is even more serious. Being great consumers of energy and lacking oil reserves, they are faced with the need to import practically all of their growing oil consumption demands.

In sum, towards the end of this decade a progressive decline in the production of most of the non-OPEC oil-producing nations is to be expected, particularly in the United States and former Soviet bloc countries. This reduction may be partially compensated by production increases in countries such as Colombia, China, Mexico and Vietnam.

By the beginning of the Twenty-first century a recovery in Russia's production could take place. However this shall not be enough to cover the decline in production in the North Sea fields, the United States and some other nations that are currently meeting their own energy demands with domestic production.

As is evident from the examination of the aforementioned data, the majority of the industrialized nations present a strong deficit in their energy requirements. In coming years, a substantial increase in the energy consumption of the Third World is also expected to occur. This all leads to the conclusion that sooner or later, the world shall once again be faced with a shortage in oil supplies.

To this effect, Dr. Subroto, the former Secretary General of OPEC, stated by 1989 that:

"It is known that reserves of OPEC member nations are ample, the largest in the world, close to 84% of the total proved reserves - some 910,000 million barrels - (not including centralized economy countries). Reserves in the non-OPEC nations at the current production rates would last about 19 years, whereas those of OPEC could last over 100 years."(2)

Now therefore, only six of its thirteen members will be in a condition to substantially increase their levels of production. These six countries, by reason of the volume of their proved reserves of hydrocarbons, representing over 91% of OPEC's total proved reserves, are the following:

<table>
<tr><td>Saudi Arabia</td><td>Iran</td></tr>
<tr><td>Iraq</td><td>Kuwait</td></tr>
<tr><td>Arab Emirates</td><td>Venezuela</td></tr>
</table>

Upon analyzing the prospects for the world oil markets, it is likewise important to take into account aspects relating to production costs. The data supplied as follows can illustrate the point:

Production Costs per Country

a) Countries with production costs below US$ 2 per barrel:

-Saudi Arabia
-Kuwait
-Arab Emirates

b) Countries with production costs between US$ 2 and US$ 3.50 per barrel:

-Venezuela
-Iran
-Iraq

c) Countries with production costs between US$ 3.50 and US$ 7.00 per barrel:

-The former USSR (CEI)
-Libya
-Nigeria
-Gabon
-Ecuador

d) Countries with production costs between US$ 7.00 and US$ 9.00 per barrel:

-Algeria
-Mexico
-US (West Coast)
-Indonesia
-China
-Argentina

e) Countries with production costs between US$ 9.00 and US$ 12.00 per barrel:

-United Kingdom
-Norway
-US (Alaska)
-Colombia

f) Countries with production costs in excess of US$ 12.00 per barrel:

-European Economic Community
-Zaire

The Case for Venezuela

Of the six OPEC nations in a position to take on a sustained growth in its production capacity, Saudi Arabia, Kuwait, Arab Emirates, Iran, Iraq and Venezuela, this latter country stands out since it is the only one not located in the conflictive Persian Gulf region and because it has traditionally been the Western World industrialized nations' most reliable source of oil.

Of the nations mentioned, Venezuela is the only one not directly or indirectly involved in any war conflict that threatens not only world peace but also the reliability of energy supplies.

It is worthwhile mentioning that Venezuela has kept an ongoing struggle to increase the benefits derived from oil. The country's aspirations have always revolved around economic conditions, and achievements in this regard have always been made through negotiations with international oil companies. Venezuela has never put its oil at the service of a political cause, except in the case of World War II, when the country increased its oil production to contribute to the Allied Forces' war efforts. Different is the history of the Middle East, where secular conflicts have many times transformed the oil of the region into a political sword.

As shown in the previous chapter, the truth is that due to a set of religious, political, ethnic circumstances and other reasons as well, some of which have been succintly stated in this book, the Middle East is unfortunately condemned to continue being an area of endemic violence, subject to frequent outbursts of conflicts as has happened in the past.

These conflicts have posed serious threats for the reliability of world energy supplies in the following occasions: 1956, the nationalization of the Suez Canal; 1967, the Six Day War and the subsequent closing of the Suez Canal during eight years; 1970, the displacement of oil markets due to Qaddafi's revolution (though Libya is not located in the Persian Gulf, it perhaps was the first nation to transform its oil into "a sword at the service of Islam" and has no qualms about publicly endorsing terrorism); 1973 due to the Yom Kippur or Ramadan War (the name varies depending from the standpoint, whether Jewish or Arabic) with the subsequent oil embargo against the Western nations; 1979 with the fall of the Shah of Iran and the Islamic fundamentalist revolution led by Ayatollah Khomeini; 1982 due to the Iran-Iraq war which not only lasted eight years but also threatened to interrupt oil traffic in the Persian Gulf and to close the Strait of Hormuz, through which most of the Middle East oil is transported to the international markets; and finally, 1990, with Iraq's invasion of Kuwait.

It is difficult to believe that in the forseeable future the Middle East region may find a permanent peace. One way to achieve this objective would be to install powerful military bases in the region. This choice has of course two main setbacks: the first is that if the cost of this military operation were to be distributed among the barrels of oil produced in the area, the cost per barrel would probably reach astronomical proportions, that one way or another would end up by cancelling profits to the Americans. The second, more powerful setback is the push this would give to a quick expansion of Islamic fundamentalism in the region that would generate irrepressible forces that would finally overthrow all the conservative monarchies of the Gulf.

In contrast, developed and developing nations can resort to the predictable and stable alternative to meet their growing energy needs, represented by Venezuela, a nation strategically located in the Western hemisphere, historically qualified as a reliable and trustworthy supplier, geographically located in an optimum point due to its proximity to the markets, politically incorporated to the group of democratic nations whose stability is a guarantee required by the consumer nations and which, culturally-speaking, is part of the Western Christian civilization.

In this regard, Venezuelan hydrocarbons have all the fundamental conditions of an energy source. Given the enormous dependence of energy world-wide, there are three basic qualities that should be met: abundant, economical and a reliable supply.

Let us for one moment stop and examine the foregoing. The generalized usage of a source of energy evidently requires large investments in facilities and all manner of equipment to enable the production of this source according to conventional production methods. Evidently nobody would be willing to carry forward these investments if an abundance of the source in question did not exist.

On the other hand, in view of the influence of the cost of energy on the manufacture of any product, for a specific energy agent to be used it must be economical. When we say economical we are talking in relative terms. In other words, it must be economical in comparison to the cost of any alternate source of energy.

But besides, closely connected to the foregoing, an energy agent must have a reliable supply. This is indispensable. The damage for developed and developing nations of interrupting the source of energy would be so great that the world cannot run the risk of depending on an unreliable source of energy.

The reliability of the Venezuelan oil supply has been amply proved. During each of the crises that have been analyzed in the course of this book, Venezuela's oil has substantially contributed to solving energy shortage problems. The fact that

Venezuelan oil is economical vis-a-vis other energy sources is demonstrated by its vigorous presence in the international markets where it has successfully competed. Let us thus analyze the abundance requisite.

We shall begin by referring to our oil reserves. In this regard, it is worthwhile clarifying that there are different types of reserves: in the first place, the "proved" resources which are those located in a more precise manner by exploration drilling programs in known reservoirs. Then there are the "probable" reserves, those found in little-explored fields or which could possibly be extracted from known fields if extraction procedures were improved. Finally, there are the "possible" reserves, the estimation of which is based on the extrapolation of discoveries already made, or by analogy with the geographical conditions in favorable zones.

Venezuela's Ministry of Energy and Mines conservatively estimates our "proved" reserves in the amount of 65 billion barrels, approximately 6.7% of the entire world's proved reserves and about 9% of those of OPEC. The duration in theory of these proved reserves would be 75 years.

The Ministry of Energy and Mines makes no reference in its official statistics however, to the "probable" reserves. To this effect, the national oil industry has been guiding its exploration efforts towards increasing the higher-value oil reserves, i.e., the light, medium and condensed crudes. These efforts have been particularly concentrated in marking off the great hydrocarbon reservoirs located to the north of Monagas State, an area considered to be one of the world's most important oil regions.

In fact, many technicians in the industry believe that those fields hold reserves that are as important as those located in Lake Maracaibo. Based on current discoveries and the interpretation of data that may be applicable to the area as a whole, it is estimated that this new oil province of Monagas State reserves could hold some 12 billion barrels of oil. In a relatively short time frame, the drilling of numerous wells required to demarcate the dimensions and characteristics of these reservoirs will be completed and these reserves will be officially incorporated into our proved oil reserves. Based on these estimates, some experts predict that these reserves are approximately as large as those located in the North Sea and Alaska together.

The Monagas state area where these discoveries are taking place presents an evident advantage cost-wise. This is a region where oil production has been carried out for many years. The wells up to now had been exploited at shallower depths where the oil was heavier. However, this previous exploration provided the region with a basic infrastructure that can now be used to full advantage without having to resort to additional costs.

The new discoveries in the North Andean flank to the southeast of the Lake Maracaibo basin, as well as the Guarumen geographical area located between the states of Portuguesa, Cojedes and Guárico are also being studied with the same optimism.

In sum, throughout our oil history beginning with Zumaque Well No. 1 in 1914, Venezuela has developed hydrocarbon reserves located at relatively shallow depths producing mainly heavy crudes. Deeper wells reaching the Cretaceous formation are being drilled by modern methods, showing that there is an enormous potential that has practically remained untouched. Perhaps the greatest advantage is the quality of the crudes in these new discoveries. Thus, the papers presented in the Vth Congress of Geophysics held in Caracas in October 1990 made reference to the technological challenge posed to Venezuela by the "virgin" reservoirs of hydrocarbons located 20,000 feet deep.

If, together with the "probable" and "possible" reserves, we were to include those located in the aforementioned regions and in others with promising prospects, we would arrive at a conservative figure estimated at around 40 billion barrels of light and medium crudes, apart from the proved reserves that have already been mentioned.

However, we have not yet mentioned the reserves of a hydrocarbon that due to its low-polluting characteristics, is considered to be one of mankind's future energy sources: natural gas. In this regard, Venezuela also has abundant amounts, with proved reserve volumes of over 25 billion equivalent-barrels of oil. These reserves that in 1992 were about 3,651,332 million cubic meters, place Venezuela in the eighth place worldwide.

Lastly, we shall mention the largest oil field in the entire world: the Orinoco Oil Belt. To give an idea of its size, suffice it to say that the entire world's proved oil reserves are estimated at 999 billion barrels. The Orinoco Belt alone is estimated to hold over 1.3 trillion (1.3×10^{12}) barrels of oil in situ, most of which is extra heavy oil. The reserves existing in the Belt could in theory support a production of over 7 million barrels per day for over 100 years.

It is estimated that by 1992 the proved reserves in the Orinoco Oil Belt exceeded the 270 billion barrel-mark (3). Said reserves, which include only those that can be exploited by current procedures, have been conservatively estimated. As the explotation continues in the region and development techniques are updated, the proved reserve figures shall substantially increase, as well as the percentage of recovery of the giant volume of hydrocarbons that lie in the Belt. Most of this crude however is not of the conventional type and is therefore not sold as oil, nor does it compete with the so-called conventional hydrocarbons, nor shall it be included in OPEC's eventual quotas.

The oil in the Belt is the raw material for manufacturing Orimulsion ^{tm}, a fuel that can replace coal as a base load for power plants. It is a new, highly economical product, the production of which is based on a practically limitless supply of this raw material. Its commercialization at an international level has begun with great success under the label "liquid coal". It is worthwhile mentioning however that, precisely because it is a product that competes with coal, its price is necessarily much lower than that of other hydrocarbons, therefore its profit margins are lower. This is why it is produced under a different branch of our hydrocarbon industry and possible profits shall depend on attaining high production volumes. Medium-term plans contemplate the development of a production of 500 thousand barrels of Orimulsion per day, which is an efficient alternative, especially in the electricity-generating market.

Apart from the brilliant future for orimulsion, there are other noble ways to exploit the vast hydrocarbon reserves found in the Orinoco Belt. Technologies are available for the production of upgraded crudes using the extra-heavy oil found in that area.

In this regard, since World War II, Hitler's Germany already had the capability to produce synthetic fuel by means of hydrogenation processes which used coal as its raw material. Thanks to advances in technology, those processes, as well as others can now be used in a cost-efficient manner to take advantage of the extra heavy crudes found in almost unlimited quantities in Venezuela in the Orinoco Belt.

To sum up, Venezuela's energy potential is as follows:

65 billion barrels of proved oil reserves
50 billion barrels of probable light and medium oil reserves
25 billion equivalent-barrels of oil in proved natural gas reserves
1.3 trillion barrels of hydrocarbons in the Orinoco Belt, of which 270 billion barrels can be considered already proved.

If we add the abundant coal reserves and the gigantic hydroelectric-generating capacity of the Caroní river and the Andes, we could safely conclude that Venezuela is probably one of the countries with the greatest energy-producing potential in the entire world.

Now therefore, this should lead us to an evident conclusion. We gain nothing by having this enormous potential if at the same time we do not have the resources to develop them. In this regard, several considerations could be proposed.

First: Given the geopolitical situation in the Middle East, it would seem evident that the U.S. will try to gain some profit from the enormous war effort incurred in confronting Saddam Hussein.

For the reasons analyzed in the course of this book, we consider that this possibility shall necessarily imply enormous military expenditure to maintain stability in the region, whereby the U.S. and the industrialized nations will possibly have to resort to alternate sources of energy or to sources that supplement in a greater degree their oil supply requirements. In this regard, Venezuela is an optimum alternative.

Second: To take advantage of its huge hydrocarbons reserves it is only natural that Venezuela should promote a upstream downstream integration process. This integration implies sustained growth and investement for which an opening policy is crucial.

Third: The combination of the two previous points seems to point to Venezuela's evident convenience in opening its doors to foreign capital so that, in partnership with (public and private) national capital, a vigorous expansion policy in our oil activities be carried out.

In effect, even though Venezuela seems to constitute an optimum choice to contribute in a relevant manner to the growing world energy demands, this could only become true if the investments required were to be carried out to develop its potential.

Even in the case that Venezuela could carry out by itself these investments by means of foreign financing, there would be a risk that developments in other places could give rise to an eventual excess of production, in which case oil prices would go down and once again a foreign debt would be incurred, a situation that the country has already gone through in recent years.

The possibility of a partnership with foreign capital to develop our oil wealth would contribute not only the added technological benefits but above all the possibility of guaranteeing stable foreign markets for our hydrocarbons. This is perhaps the most relevant point that should be taken into account when studying an eventual change in the course of our oil policy.

Finally, it would be worthwhile to mention that one of the goals of all the governments of Venezuela has been to decrease dependency on oil and to attempt to diversify our economy insofar as possible. In this regard, if we concentrate a high percentage of public investment precisely in the oil sector, we would be achieving the reverse. That is why we consider that foreign investment in this sector could represent a valuable contribution for the complete development of the hydrocarbon industry. In this manner, not only would funds be freed that could be invested in other sectors, but the state profits would contribute an abundant source of additional resources by means of which the diversification of the economy could be promoted.

It is about time that we base our future, not on the perpetual remembrance of the worst disgraces of the past but rather in the mature study of the best prospects before us. Let us leave behind the ancient complexes and accept that if modern Venezuela has been capable of controlling almost 7 percent of the United States' domestic gas market, thanks to investments carried out in that country, we could also hold negotiations with other transnational companies in order to determine conditions that would be advantageous for all parties involved.

It is about time that we take full advantage of Venezuela's natural resources, to earn for our nation the position guaranteed by its energy and human potential in the concert of developed nations. Previously we were at a disadvantage since we lacked the preparation to deal under equal terms with transnational companies. Nowadays, however, the situation has changed. PDVSA is at present transnational and is one of the world's largest oil companies.

The Middle East war has opened an opportunity for Venezuela, a "window" as John W. Kingdon would call it, when referring to the precise moment when an object should be launched into space, but that in this case could apply to the proper "political window" to launch Venezuela on the road to prosperity and development.

Opening up the Venezuelan Oil Industry

Since 1958, when democracy was instituted in Venezuela, this country had announced that no oil concessions would be granted to foreign companies. The goal at the time was to nationalize the hydrocarbon industry. This objective was timely achieved after an impeccable negotiation process carried out in 1975 with the foreign companies. Thus, on January 1st, 1976, the oil industry passed into the hands of the Venezuelan State.

In subsequent years, Petróleos de Venezuela S.A. (PDVSA) has had an extraordinary performance and has become one of the world's leading oil companies. It is not only in charge of developing the hydrocarbon sector but also handles the country's petrochemical and coal-mining activities. Its scope is not limited to the national territory. In effect, PDVSA has made important investments abroad, in line with its plans aimed at conquering international markets.

Thus, in the refining sector, apart from the domestic refineries with a joint installed capacity of 1.2 million b/d, PDVSA also has interests abroad that increase its refining installed capacity to a figure in excess of 2 million barrels per day.

In the U.S., PDVSA owns 100 percent of CITGO, adding close to 600 thousand barrels per day of crude oil to its refining installed capacity, apart from the 12,500-plus service stations that provide Venezuelan fuel to the final consumers. Thanks to partnerships with other local companies such as UNOVEN Co. and Lyondell/Citgo, Venezuela has access to other facilities with an added refining capacity of some 420 thousand barrels per day.

In Europe, PDVSA's activities with various partnerships with Neste, VEBA Öel, Ruhr Öel and Nymäs Petroleum, which operate in Germany, Belgium, Great Britain and Sweden, guarantee the placement of Venezuelan crudes in large refineries with an installed capacity of around 760 thousand b/d.

In order to meet the requirements of these large refinery complexes, PDVSA is purchasing close to 700 thousand barrels per day from other oil-producing nations. It would be logical to assume that the country's interests would best be served if these volumes of oil were to be produced domestically. As a logical result of this, the opening up of our country's hydrocarbon sector to foreign capital is once again being proposed.

In fact, for the first time since 1958 - with the sole exception of some service contracts granted in 1970 but which were never carried out - Venezuela is undertaking a process that will enable national and foreign private capital to become involved in the development of activities in the oil industry.

This process of opening up was initiated in 1993, when National Congress approved a new partnership with foreign capital which was given the name Strategic Partnership Contracts. The first three contracts that have been approved are the following:

-The Cristobal Colón Project, with Lagoven (a subsidiary of PDVSA), Shell, Exxon and Mitsubishi as partners, aimed at exploiting the vast offshore natural gas reserves in the northeastern region of Venezuela. It is estimated that the full development of this project will require investments in the order of $10 billion.

-The Strategic Partnership Contracts between Maraven (a subsidiary of PDVSA) and Conoco on the one hand and

Maraven-Total-Itochu-Marubeni on the other hand for the production and improvement of the extra heavy crudes found in the Orinoco Belt. Both projects shall require investments of around $6 billion.

In the same avenue of opening up opportunities for participation by national and foreign private capital, bidding processes were held in 1993 to award contracts for the operation of inactive fields. By 1994, these contracts had added some 30 thousand barrels of oil per day to the domestic production.

From 1994 onwards, an additional scheme to attract foreign capital to the development of our hydrocarbon industry is being set up in Venezuela, called the Profit Sharing Agreements. By means of these negotiations, the opening up of the Venezuelan oil sector to foreign investments shall undoubtedly become one of the more relevant changes being produced in the oil industry worldwide.

It is estimated that Venezuela's oil production with this internationally-renown scheme, shall be increased by some 500 thousand barrels per day by the beginning of the next decade.

Total investments for the development of new areas is estimated at around $10 billion. It is expected that with the first contracts, some 23 billion barrels of additional light and medium crude reserves shall be found, as well as some 10 trillion cubic feet of natural gas.

A final very important comment is related to PDVSA. Anyone coming to Venezuela to discuss contracts or projects related to oil and gas, will no encounter simply a country with a hydrocarbon rich soil. It will enter into dealings with PDVSA, a national company that has evolved into a world-class corporation, which speaks the language, masters the technology, knows the business and has a strong position in the markets with important equity in the U.S. and Europe. This certainly should be an encouraging factor for our potential partners.

Notes

1.-MINISTRY OF ENERGY AND MINES. Petroleum and other Statistical Data. 1989. page 192.

2.-Dr. S. E. Subroto, OPEC Secretary General. Speech pronounced on the occasion of the 11th Conference of the International Associaton of Energy Economy. Caracas, 26-28 June, 1989.

3.-Andrés Sosa Pietri, President of Petróleos de Venezuela S.A., "PDVSA: 15 years later", speech pronounced on the occasion of the XVth anniversary of the company. August 30th, 1990. Documents 90, No. 2, page 5.

CONCLUSIONS

I

The crisis unleashed by Iraq's invasion of Kuwait cannot be seen as an isolated phenomenon. It is in truth one more chapter in the unending series of violent outbursts periodically affecting one of the planet's most unstable regions. The solution for each of these recurrent conflicts seems to sow the seed for a new confrontation. This has happened in the past and it seems as if it shall continue in the future.

The reasons for the endemic warring characterizing the inhabitants of the Middle East are abundant. Many of these go back to the origins of history itself, being this area as it were, the birthplace of civilization. It is also the meeting point between East and West, a region of complex geopolitical problems that have evolved throughout history.

Still in our days the clash of three cultures continues in the Middle East: Judaism, Christianity and Islamism. The enriching contributions of each to universal civilization seem to become transformed into a frenzy of destructive fanaticism when the members of these cultures are forced to live together in a confined geographical space. The result is that some displace the others, whereby modern-day diasporas are generated - as is the current case of the Palestinian people - or otherwise giving rise to endless civil wars such as in Lebanon.

To make matters worse, the mistakes committed by the triumphant powers after the First World War which put an end to a wisely established order in the Ottoman empire whereby the population had been organized in religious communities with a mutual respect of their rights, was added to the ancestral reasons for hatred. By creating artificial countries and frontiers, the European powers seem to have definitely marked these territories with a tragic sign and have condemned them to be perpetual victims of a dissociating force that drives them to fight one against the other.

It is ironic that opposite trends coexist in the region, which, must unite in order to subsist. Unfortunately, the Pan-Arabian illusion contrasts with the reality of some frontiers, in many cases artificial at that, reference points within which the leaders of each nation can exert their authority. Which leader is willing to sacrifice his power or his cause in pro of a desired yet utopian Pan-Arabian unity that will force them to submit to the authority of an adversary ? Formulas of this nature were attempted in the past by Nasser, but not even his messianic leadership and his almost magical influence over the Arab masses could keep together for long the proclaimed United Arab Republic, a circumstantial union between Egypt and Syria.

II

In addition, nature gave many of the Middle East nations the most coveted wealth of our times: oil.

Oil, like all other energy sources, must meet three main requisites: it must be economical, abundant and there must be a reliable supply.

If, to the cost of the barrel of oil produced in the Middle East, we were to add the military cost of keeping the lines flowing from the Persian Gulf, as well as an illusory relative political stability in the area, we would have to conclude that this is the most expensive petroleum in the world. This affirmation is even truer in the case of American consumers who have to pay with their taxes the cost of their country taking on the role of "universal police" in that region.

The 1990 conflict between Iraq and Kuwait has extended the problem to other consumer nations. Thus, for instance, who else but the Japanese citizen shall end up paying the $9 billion offered by his government to cover the military expenses of the last Gulf conflict ? Will the same not apply to contributions by the Germans ? Let us state the example of these two countries because, though they did not send troops to combat, they however contributed money to the expense of the war. In the case of other nations such as England, France, Italy, etc. the situation is even more dramatic, inasmuch as they have to add the risk of losing the lives of the soldiers they sent, apart from the monetary contribution.

We thereby see that the allegedly low Persian Gulf hydrocarbon costs are but a myth.

On the other hand, it is a fact that oil reserves in the Middle East and in the Gulf states in particular are abundant. However it is also true that supply is far from being reliable. Proof of this are the various crises that have been mentioned in this book.

Furthermore, at one time or another, some Islamic oil states have used their wealth as a powerful political weapon, as a result of the traumas undergone in the past which is part of a geopolitical reality that cannot be escaped. An entire philosophy has also been developed to justify their actions in this regard.

A fundamental aspect of their interests is the common fight against the State of Israel. Peace negotiations being currently advanced among that nation, the Palestinians and their Arab neighbours have opened a glimmer of hope in that regard. The success of these negotiations, however, seems strewn with obstacles.

We have analyzed in previous pages the deep religious implications unleashed in the entire Middle East region by Islamic fundamentalism. The Muslim religious leaders almost without exception consider that an intolerable contamination with Western ideas has taken place and that this is a serious threat for Islam. Fundamentalist ideas have therefore come to be an enemy a thousand times more dangerous for the Western world than the temporary problem of a crisis generated by Saddam Hussein.

III

To take up the case of oil once again, if we suppose that world demand is to grow at a moderate but constant rate of 1 to 2 percent per year, it seems evident that soon there could be another period of energy shortage. To cover this simple increase in demand, the short-term development of a bountiful potential of additional production will be indispensable.

Currently, 84 percent of oil proved reserves in the world (excluding former socialist countries) are concentrated in OPEC countries. 91 percent in turn lie in the subsoil of the following nations: Saudi Arabia, Iran, Iraq, Kuwait, Arab Emirates and Venezuela.

Venezuela stands out among the aforementioned states inasmuch as it is the only country not located in the conflictive Persian Gulf region and because it has traditionally been a most reliable supplier to industrialized nations.

CONCLUSIONS

The volume of proved and probable oil reserves in Venezuela is so substantial that we can safely say that this is one of the countries in the world with the largest energy potential. Added to which there are abundant natural gas reserves and the phenomenal possibilities of the Orinoco Oil Belt, the hydrocarbon reservoir which the greatest volume in situ known in the entire planet.

The development of Venezuela's oil potential likewise evidently requires great investments. The following considerations are therefore put forward:

First: that Venezuela by itself does not have the sufficient resources to carry out these investments.

Second: that if one of the main objectives of the country's policies is to diversify the economy to decrease our dependency on such an unstable sector as oil, it would be a contradiction to dedicate such a high percentage of our resources to invest them precisely in the hydrocarbon sector.

Third: that the possible contribution by foreign capital would not only serve to hedge the risks but would also guarantee a more stable participation of Venezuelan oil in foreign markets. Sharing the risk with foreign partners that would defend our hydrocarbons in their respective markets seems to make sense.

Fourth: that if PDVSA can carry out investments in other nations to take advantage of the possibilities offered in other markets, also other nations should be in capacity to make investments in the Venezuelan oil industry, leaving behind positions of Third World complexes that should have been forgotten long ago.

IV

In view of the foregoing, it seems evident that Venezuela is in a position to become a valid alternative as a relevant contributor to the growing world oil demands. For this to happen, however, foreign investment must be given access not only to refining or petrochemical plants projects but also in the exploration and exploitation phases that are truly the only phases where an increased production can be attained.

Lastly, the industrialized nations must also take a decision of vital importance. They could choose to increase their oil dependence on the Gulf nations or they could try to increase by percentage their oil supplies from Venezuela.

With regard to the Gulf nations, these have never hid their intentions to use their oil as a political weapon. An increased American military presence in the Middle East, that would in turn help to intensify the exploitation of the area's oil wealth, would probably end up by unleashing the forces of Islamic fundamentalism, Western world's fiercest enemy.

Venezuela is strategically located in the Western hemisphere, has historically shown itself to be a reliable and trustworthy supplier, is geographically located in an optimum point close to the markets, is politically incorporated to the group of democratic nations and is culturally speaking a part of Western Christian civilization.

BIBLIOGRAPHY

ALLIDAY, FRED. **The Iranian Revolution in International Affairs**, monograph part of the paper titled "Oil and Security in the Arabian Gulf", London, Croom Helm Ltd, 1983.

AMBROSE, Stephen E. **Eisenhower: Soldier and President**, New York, Simon & Schuster, 1990.

ANDERSON, Jack with BOYD, James. **Oil, The Real Story Behind The World Energy Crisis**, London, Sidgwick and Jackson Ltd., 1984.

ANDERSON, Jack. **Middle East, Oil Dealers**, Buenos Aires, Ediciones La Flor, SRL, 1974.

ANGELI A., Marco. **The International Economic Order and Oil Prices**, Caracas, IFEDEC, 1988.

ARON, Raymond. **The Imperial Republic**, Buenos Aires, EMECE, 1973.

BETANCOURT, Rómulo. **Venezuela, Politics and Oil**, Caracas, Monte Avila Editors, 1986.

BLACK, Edgar. **Churchill**, Barcelona, Gandesa Biographies, Grijalbo, 1963.

BURKE, Edmund and LAPIDUS, Ira M. **Islam, Politics, and Social Movements**, University of California Press, 1988.

CADRI (Committee Against Repression and for Democratic Rights in Iraq). **Saddam's Iraq**, London, Zed Books Ltd., 1990.

DELAMAIDE, Darrel. **The Debt Shock, the entire history of the World's Credit Crisis**, Barcelona, Planet Editorial S.A., 1985.

EMERSON, Steven. **The American House of Saud**, New York, Franklin Watts, 1985.

ENGLER, Robert. **The Politics of Oil, Private Power & Democratic Directions**, Chicago, Phoenix Books, The University of Chicago Press, 1967.

EVANS, Douglas. **Occidental Energy Politics**, Buenos Aires, Troquel Editorial S.A., 19809.

FARID, Abdel Majid. **Oil and Security in the Arabian Gulf**, London, Croom Helm Ltd. 1983.

FROMKLIN, David. **A Peace to End all Peace**, New York, Avon Books, 1974.

GARATE, Martín. **NUMERO** magazine, Caracas, June 10th, 1990.

GEORGE, Antonius, **The Arab Awakening**, New York, Capricorn Books, 1965.

GIBB, H.A.R. **Mohammedanism**, New York, Mentor Books, 1955.

GLUBB, Sir John. **A Short Story of the Arab People**, New York, Stein and Day Publishers, 1970.

THE SECOND WORLD WAR GREAT CHRONICLES, Volumes I, II and III, Mexico, Reader's Digest, 1967.

GRENON, Michel. **The World Energy Crisis**, Madrid, Alianza Editorial, 1974.

HALLWOOD, Paul and SINCLAIR, Stuart. **An interpretation of the economic relations between OPEC and non-oil** producing developing nations during the '70s, OPEC Magazine No. 53, 1981.

HARB, Mohammed. **Oil War: The Secret Minutes of the Arab Oil Ministers Meeting**, Cairo, General Printing Company, 1974.

HARTSHORN, J.E. **Politics and World Oil Economics: An Account of the International Oil Industry in its Political Environment**, New York, 1962.

HEIKAL, Mohamed H. **The Road to Ramadan**, New York, Quadrangle Books, 1975.

HIRO, Dilip. **Chronicle of the Gulf War**, Merip Reports Nos. 126/127, July/September 1984.

JOHNSON, Paul. **Modern Times**, Caracas, Javier Vergara Editors S.A., co-edition with Alfadil Editions, 1988.

KENNEDY, John F. **The Strategy of Power**, New York, Harper & Row, 1960.

KISSINGER, Henry. **My Memoirs**, Buenos Aires, Atlantida Editorial S.A., 1979.

KISSINGER, Henry. **Years of Upheaval**, Boston, Little, Brown & Co., 1982.

KLEBANOFF, Shoshana. **Oil for Europe: American Foreign Policy and Middle East Oil**, unpublished paper, Claremont Graduate School, 1973.

KNOWLES, Ruth S. **America's Oil Famine: Its Cause and Cure**, Oklahoma, University of Oklahoma Press, Norman, 1980.

KUBBAH, Abdul Amir. **OPEC, Past and Present**, Vienna, 1974.

LAMB, David. **The Arabs, Journeys Beyond the Mirage**, New York, Vintage Books, 1988.

LAQUEUER, Walter. **Confrontation: The Middle East and World Politics**, New York, Quadrangle Books, 1974.

LONG, David E. **The Anatomy of Terrorism**, New York, The Free Press, 1990.

MARTIN, David C. and WALCOTT, John. **Best Laid Plans: The Inside Story of America's War Against Terrorism**, New York, Harper & Row, 1988.

MILLER, Judith and MYLROIE, Laurie. **Saddam Hussein and the Crisis in the Gulf**, New York, Times Books, 1990.

Ministry of Energy and Mines, **Oil and other Statistical Data**, Caracas, 1975-1989.

Ministry of Foreign Affairs, Republic of Venezuela. **Carracciolo Parra Pérez, Chancellor of Venezuela**, Caracas, Foreign Policy Library Foundation, 1989.

MOSS HELMS, Christine. **Iraq, Eastern Flank of the Arab World**, Washington, The Brookings Institution, 1984.

NASSER, Gamal Abdel. **The Philosophy of the Revolution**, Cairo, Ministry of National Guidance, 1954.

NIXON, Richard. **The Memoirs of Richard Nixon**, New York, Simon & Schuster Inc., Touchstone, 1990.

ODELL, Peter R. **Oil and World Power**, New York, Penguin Books, 1979.

OTAIBA, Mana Saeed al. **OPEC and the Petroleum Industry**, New York, John Wiley & Sons, 1975.

REAGAN, Ronald. **An American Life, The Autobiography**, New York, Simon & Schuster, 1990.

ROSSI GUERRERO, Felix. **Diary of an Oil Diplomat**, Caracas, Institute for International Studies of the Ministry of Foreign Affairs, 1987.

SAMPSON, Anthony. **The Seven Sisters**, Barcelona, Grijalbo, 1986.

SANCHEZ GUERRERO, Gustavo. **The Nationalization of Oil and its Economic Consequences**, Caracas, Monte Avila Editors, 1990.

SHARON, Ariel. **Warrior, an Autobiography**, New York, Simon & Schuster Inc., Touchstone Books, 1989.

SHIRER, William L. **Rise and Fall of the Third Reich**, Barcelona, Luis de Caralt, 1962.

SIVAN, Emmanuel. **Radical Islam, Medieval Theology and Modern Politics**, Yale University, 1985.

SOWAYEGH, Abdulaziz al. **Arab Petro-Politics**, London, Croom Helm Ltd., 1984.

SPEER, Albert. **Memoirs**, Barcelona, Circle of Readers, 1970.

STOCKING, George W. **Middle East Oil: A Study in Political and Economic Controversy**, Nashville, Tenn., Vanderbilt University Press, 1970.

SUCCARI, Owais R. **International Petroleum Market: Policy Confrontations of the Common Market and the Arab Countries**, Louvain, Université Catholique de Louvain, 1968.

TORO HARDY, Alfredo. **The Venezuelan Challenge: How to Influence American Policy Decisions**, Institute for Latin American Higher Studies, University Simón Bolívar, 1988.

TRUMAN, Harry S. **Memoirs**, New York, Doubleday, 1955.

USLAR PIETRI, Arturo. **Venezuelans and Oil**, Caracas, Banco de Venezuela, 1990.

VALLENILLA, Luis. **Rise, Decline and Future of the Venezuelan Oil**, Caracas, Monte Avila Editors, 1990.

VIVAS GALLARDO, Freddy. **Venezuela-U.S.A.: Decisive Crossroads**, Caracas, Central University of Venezuela, Faculty of Legal and Political Sciences, unpublished paper.

WEINBERGER, Caspar W. **Fighting for Peace, Seven Critical Years in the Pentagon**, New York, 1990.

YERGIN, Daniel and HILLDEBRAND, Martin. **Global Insecurity, Beyond Energy Future**, New York, Penguin Books, 1983.

ZANONI, José Rafael. **The Price of Oil, its determining factors and fixing by OPEC**, Caracas, Central University of Venezuela, School of Economic and Social Sciences, 1981.

ESTE LIBRO SE TERMINO DE IMPRIMIR EN
LOS TALLERES DE EDITORIAL TEXTO
AV. EL CORTIJO, QTA. MARISA, Nº 4
LOS ROSALES - CARACAS - VENEZUELA